HASE CHROMIUM BRASS & COPPER ES

HROMIUM IS BEST OVER BRASS OR COPPER

HASE CHROMIUM BRASS & COPPER SPECIALTIES

HROMIUM IS BES BRASS OR COPPER

CHASE

HASE CHROMIUM BRASS & COPPER SPECIALTIES

HROMIUM IS BEST OVER BRASS OR COPPER

HASE CHROMIUM BRASS & COPPER SPECIALTIES

1930s Lighting
Deco & Traditional by Chase

Text by DONALD-BRIAN JOHNSON
Photography & Design by LESLIE PIÑA

Research Associate: BARBARA WARD ENDTER
Cross-Reference Index: GARY M. PIPER
Price Guide: JOHN & DONNA THORPE
Photography Associate: RAMÓN PIÑA
Additional Photography: DALE ENDTER
JACQUELINE JONES-RIDGE

Schiffer Publishing Ltd®
4880 Lower Valley Road, Atglen, PA 19310 USA

Dedication

For Marilyn and Nancy, and for Erin, who lights up everyone's life.

The centaur, trademark of the Chase Brass & Copper Co., embellished with sunbeams for the 1934 Lighting Fixtures catalog.

Front: A selection of Chase favorites by noted designers. *From left:* #17048, the "CONSTELLATION LAMP" by Walter Von Nessen; #27010, Lurelle Guild's "CONSOLE LAMP"; #01001, the "GLOW LAMP" by Ruth Gerth. *Courtesy of John and Donna Thorpe*

Back: From the 1934 Chase Lighting Division catalogs, Everett Henry's illustration of a Classic Modern interior.

Library of Congress Catalog Card Number: 00-100983

Type set in Benguiat Bd BT/ZapfHumnst BT

ISBN: 0-7643-1137-9
Printed in China
1 2 3 4

Published by Schiffer Publishing Ltd.
4880 Lower Valley Road
Atglen, PA 19310
Phone: (610) 593-1777; Fax: (610) 593-2002
E-mail: Schifferbk@aol.com
Please visit our web site catalog at **www.schifferbooks.com**
We are always looking for people to write books on new and related subjects. If you have an idea for a book, please contact us at the above address.

This book may be purchased from the publisher.
Include $3.95 for shipping.
Please try your bookstore first.
You may write for a free catalog.

In Europe, Schiffer books are distributed by:
Bushwood Books
6 Marksbury Ave.
Kew Gardens
Surrey TW9 4JF England
Phone: 44 (0)208 392-8585; Fax: 44 (0)208 392-9876
E-mail: Bushwd@aol.com
Free postage in the UK. Europe: air mail at cost.

Contents

Acknowledgments 4
Introduction 6

Chapter 1: "Lighting Up Chase: A Brief History" 7
Chapter 2: "Leading Lights: The Chase Designers" 14
Chapter 3: "Blazing A New Path: Through-Design At Chase" 31
Chapter 4: "Bright Ideas: Marketing Chase Lighting" 45
Chapter 5: "The Chase Lamps Gallery" 59
Chapter 6: "The 1934 Chase Lamps Brochure" 93
Chapter 7: "Carrying A Torch: Chase Battery Lights" 108
Chapter 8: "The Chase Lighting Fixtures Showroom" 116
Chapter 9: "The 1934 Chase Lighting Fixtures Brochures" 131
Chapter 10: "The 1937 Chase Lighting Fixtures Catalog" 159
Chapter 11: "Shutting Off The Lights: The End of Chase Lighting" 190

Endnotes 191
Bibliography 192
Chase Lighting Cross-Reference Index & Price Guide 195

Acknowledgments

Our sincere appreciation to the many members of the Chase Collectors Society, who have graciously shared their knowledge, collections, and hospitality with us. Your generosity has made our series of Chase books possible! Once again, special thanks for notable contributions to ace researcher Barbara Ward Endter, whose zest for locating elusive information is limitless, and to Gary M. Piper and John and Donna Thorpe, for their invaluable reference and price guides, as well as their Chase expertise.

In addition, we wish to thank: Mrs. Rodney Chase; Dale Endter; Charles M. Johnson, Sr. and Patricia P. Johnson; Jacqueline Jones-Ridge and Harry Ridge; Chuck Kaplan; Danny Kaplan; Chris Kennedy, DESIGNbase; Stephen and Joanne Klender; Hank Kuhlmann; Olga Laylon and the late Harry Laylon; Peter Linden; Eric Menard; John Myhre; Paula Ockner; Mr. and Mrs. John G. O'Neill, Jr.; H. James Pierce; Ramón Piña; Carla Ruihley, Secretary to the President, Chase Brass & Copper Co., Inc.; Tom Simpson; Tetsumasa Suda; Barry L. Van Hook; Chuck and Kim Zuccarini, and, of course, Peter Schiffer, Jennifer Lindbeck, Anne Davidsen, and the staff at Schiffer Publishing.

This page: "THE ELBA," #E 323, an Empire-themed fixture by Lurelle Guild. *Courtesy of John and Donna Thorpe*

Facing page: Bring on the battery tester: a collection of Chase battery lights. *Front:* Three examples of "THE PILGRIM CANDLELIGHT," #11255. *Center:* "CANDLELIGHT," #11150, 5-1/2" h. *Back:* #16004 "SCONCE LIGHT," 7-7/8" h. *Courtesy of John and Donna Thorpe*

Introduction

"We have tried not to make novelty knick-knacks, but sturdy honest designs of good materials that will last from generation to generation, because their taste is not a matter of fashion, but rather the choice of the best of every generation."

F.S. Chase, President
Chase Brass & Copper Co., 1934

In his Foreword to the 1934 Lamps catalog, Mr. Chase neatly summed up the goals of the newly-formed Chase Lighting division: delivering goods of quality, and giving customers their money's worth. The company's no-nonsense commitment to its own high standards was one reason Chase lamps and fixtures easily outsold all competitors, and remained favorites with the public from the early 1930s until the outbreak of World War II. Equally important, however, was the innovative approach Chase took to home lighting. Under the leadership of its chief lighting designer Lurelle Guild, Chase premiered the concept of "through-designed" lighting. No longer was there a need to rely on what the catalogs called "ugly, out-of-date lighting, with ornate overembellishments of no particular period." Thanks to Chase, consumers could now light an entire room Empire-style . . .or add a Georgian flavor. . .or embrace the primitive with Early American. The adventurous could opt for Classic Modern, (particularly popular during the Deco era), a "halfway point between present day furnishings and those more extreme ones which may come in future years."[1] Whatever the choice, there was good news for Depression buyers: thanks to Chase, they would find that choice affordable.

1930s Lighting: Deco & Traditional by Chase traces the development of the Chase Lighting division, the designers who made it possible, and the radiant assortment of lamps and lighting fixtures that resulted from their efforts. It's designed as a companion piece to our earlier book *Chase Complete*, which chronicles the Chase Specialty division, and its vast output of metal giftware. Although a number of lamps were marketed in the Specialty catalogs, the sheer volume of Chase lighting products demanded a book devoted solely to this topic. Those seeking an in-depth study of other aspects of Chase history are directed to the earlier work, as well as to our catalog compilations, *The Chase Catalogs: 1934 & 1935* and the forthcoming *Chase: The Beginning and End of an Era*.

Provided in this book are descriptions and photos of every known Chase lamp and battery light produced by the company during the existence of the Lighting and Specialty divisions (overall from 1930-1942). Also included is every lighting fixture produced by Chase through 1937. While some new fixtures continued to join the line through 1941, later additions were either basic variations on already-existent designs, or utilitarian pieces with no defining stylistic elements. To avoid repetition, they are not included here.

A glowing galaxy of Chase lamps! *Front row, from left:* #6176 "SUTTON," 14" h.; #17048 "CONSTELLATION," 8-1/2" h.; #01001 "GLOW LAMP," 8-1/4" h.; #27010 "THE CONSOLE LAMP," 17" h. *Back:* # M 500 "THE ARCADIA," 18-1/2" h.; #6323 "ACADEMY," 15-3/4" h. *Photo by Jacqueline Jones-Ridge. "THE ARCADIA" courtesy of John Myhre. All other lamps courtesy of Gary M. Piper*

Although comprising just a microdot in the nearly 125-year history of the Chase Brass & Copper Co., the heyday of Chase Lighting was a boon for collectors of 1930s lighting. Today, these lamps and fixtures stand as vivid examples of the Age of Industrial Design in full flower. We continue to appreciate both the ingenuity that went into their creation and the timeless appeal of their stylings. The prediction of F.S. Chase—that his company's lamps and fixtures would be "the choice of the best of every generation"—has proven true.

Donald-Brian Johnson
Leslie Piña
November, 1999

"We are sure that our customers, as they look at these lamps, will appreciate the careful work that has gone into their manufacture, and feel that the results have fully justified the production of such products for the American public."

F.S. Chase, 1934

Chapter 1
Lighting Up Chase: A Brief History

"Chase Companies, Inc., is entering the electric lighting fixture business. For the past three years, according to Rodney Chase, assistant secretary, the company has been studying every angle of the industry, and has carried on an extensive personal survey of all important dealers. From these, the company has evolved definite plans regarding the line and its distribution. The coming Chase line is newly designed in every part by professional designers, and will sell at moderate prices."

Metal Industry
May, 1934

But let's go back to the beginning. Before the Chase Lighting division came the Chase Specialty division. And long before that came the Chase Brass & Copper Co. itself, home of over "33,000 brass articles, 33,000 manufacturing problems. . .and 33,000 solutions!"[1]

At Dawning

The Chase Brass & Copper Co. was born in 1876, as the "Waterbury Manufacturing Company" of Waterbury, Connecticut. Originally a manufacturer of brass industrial components—everything from bathtub stoppers to birdcage springs—Chase early on saw the advantage of branching out into whatever other venues might prove practical (and profitable). As F.S. Chase recalled, in his Introduction to the 1934 Chase Lighting Fixtures catalog, lighting products were high on that list:

> When I first came to work at the Manufacturing Plant of the Chase Companies in 1889, there was no such thing as electric fixtures. Edison had invented the electric light in 1879, but the commercial manufacture of electric bulbs and sockets was still in the experimental stage. There were 30 or more different designs of electrical sockets, each with its designer's claims for particular advantages of locking or screwing the bulb into its socket, and all of us despaired of ever getting one standardized design that would make possible the commercial manufacture and use.
>
> But even in those days, 50 years ago, we were in the lighting business, for candlesticks, oil lamps, and gas jets were the lighting fixtures of that day, and we were making them. A few years later we were making, very quickly, electrical sockets and electrical fixture parts.

The key word here is, of course, "parts." Chase made the parts, and those parts were then sold to manufacturers and assemblers, who put them together and sold the completed products under their own company names. Despite the occasional novelty produced by Chase in its entirety (such as the "CANDLELIGHT," #11150, patented in 1914), the company served primarily as a jobber: turning out the components that others would transform into a finished product.

In 1925, Chase purchased its previous customer, The American Brass & Copper Co., a New York corporation engaged in the warehousing and merchandising of brass products. Among those products were electrical fixtures, at last giving Chase the opportunity to sell something completely assembled, rather than piece-by-piece. However, it was not until the 1929 stock market crash, and the onset of the American Depression, that the company began to seriously explore the idea of a full-scale consumer division. As traditional sources of revenue dried up, new sources merited consideration; one of the most practical proved to be the manufacture of consumer giftware. Chase had the facilities, it had the skilled craftsmen, and it certainly had the requisite raw materials. Who needed a middleman? Instead of simply providing component parts, Chase would now provide the finished product as well.

Seeing the Light

"You'll enjoy entertaining with these lovely things—enjoy buying them for yourself or your friends. They're so smartly designed, so constantly useful in dozens of ways, and—best of all—so inexpensive."

Chase Specialties advertisement, 1935

Depression buyers wanted the look of luxury at a price they could afford. Thanks to its use of relatively inexpensive raw materials, this was a demand Chase could meet. The Specialty division, established in 1930, provided a steady stream of brass, copper, and chromium giftware items—from smoker's articles to drinking accessories. An emerging breed known as "industrial designers," inspired by the challenge of making the functional attractive, brought their talents to Chase, Revere, Manning-Bowman, and similar manufacturers. Visionaries such as Lurelle Guild, Walter Von Nessen, and Harry Laylon saw the possibilities inherent in metal design, and made the most of it. The new

Chase giftware line offered a wide variety of sleek and streamlined pieces at highly competitive prices—and consumers were immediately hooked.

With Specialty sales booming, Chase continued to expand. Thanks to the popularity of a limited selection of lamps offered in the earliest catalogs, adding a separate Lighting division was a logical progression. In this, as F.S. Chase noted, the company stood apart from its competitors:

> Upon examination, we found that while there were many excellent lamps of china, pottery and glass, there were very few lamps on the market of brass, copper, and chromium plated brass. Such lamps as we did find were made in small quantities, and their prices seemed very high to us. Our judgment was that people would welcome a line of lamps which would be moderate in price, designed to harmonize with different periods of decoration, and which would use brass, copper, and chromium plated brass in a new way. We have produced such lamps.[2]

Guiding Light

Actually, Lurelle Guild produced them. As detailed in Chapter 2, Chase was fortunate enough to capture the interest of a designer so prolific that he was known to churn out nearly one thousand designs a year. While other Chase designers made significant contributions to the line, it was Lurelle Guild who, in 1934, came up with the over 70 lamps and nearly 175 fixtures that formed the backbone of the Chase Lighting division during its entire existence. Guild also designed the ideal setting in which to display them: the "Classic Modern" Lamps Gallery and multiperiod Fixtures alcoves of New York City's Chase Tower, which opened its doors in 1934:

> The new line of electric lighting fixtures produced by the Chase Brass & Copper Co. was shown to a throng of several hundred architects and decorators at a private view in Chase Tower, 10 E. 40th St., New York, on May 15th. Chief interest of the day lay in the new fixtures. These occupy the entire 48th floor, which Mr. Guild designed in eighteen rooms, each room being decorated and furnished in its own period. The present line represents another advance in the industry of an extent which is generally admitted to be revolutionary.
>
> *The Gift and Art Shop*, June, 1934

Guild also pioneered the concept of "through-design" in home lighting: lamps as well as lighting fixtures following a central theme, such as "Colonial" or "Early English." It was a canny choice. While the goal may have been to eliminate the lighting hodgepodge common in many homes of the time, the result was to prompt more sales. If, for instance, a complete selection of lamps, as well as fixtures, was available in the "Federal" style, what homemaker would be content without a matched set? Guild proudly reflected on this achievement in "The Designer Speaks," his Introduction to the 1934 Fixtures catalog:

> This is the first time that so complete a line of lighting fixtures has been offered that encompasses all of the periods and is fresh in inspiration and studied in design. Years of experience, since the very beginning of the electrical fixture, is the background which the Chase Companies bring to this new line, marking an outstanding and progressive step in the development of good lighting.

Lamps and More Lamps

> *"Your customers get quality and a combination of good workmanship and reasonable prices when you sell them Chase Lighting Fixtures. We have combined the best in modern design with modern scientific lighting."*
>
> Chase Lighting Fixtures catalog, 1937

The next explosive increase in lighting product can be seen in the 1937 Fixtures catalog. Up until then, the Chase lighting line remained primarily the Guild line, with only occasional new additions, such as Helen Bishop Dennis' "DRUM" nightlight, #01010, of 1935. However, the 1937 catalog listed over 100 new fixtures, none credited to specific designers. Some were variants of already existing fixtures (such as #1193, a "ONE-LIGHT BRACKET" closely related to "THE JUPITER," #M 521, which it replaced). Most of the additions stressed practicality, led by the "EVEN-GLOW" series, which featured "scientifically designed" open-top bowls, intended to provide pleasing, soft, glareless light.

While the thematic divisions of 1934 were still in evidence—Georgian, Empire, and the rest, including a short-lived new category, "Neo-Classic"—the presentation was more down-to-earth. Even the numerous Guild holdovers from 1934 were shorn of their colorful titles, with such fanciful monikers as "THE ZEUS" and "THE ELYSEE" transformed to the more mundane (but easier to comprehend) "SIX-LIGHT CEILING FIXTURE #540" and "BEAM LIGHT #343."

A souvenir postcard depicting "The Chase Building, Grand Street, Waterbury, Conn.," early headquarters of the Chase Brass & Copper Co.

Increasing the Wattage with S & J

> *"For many years Chase has designed, and made in its own factory, the lamps sold by Steele & Johnson. Now this lamp line has been consolidated with the Chase line of Specialties, and both are now made and sold by the Chase Brass & Copper Co."*
>
> Chase Specialties catalog, 1939

Founded as the "Steele and Johnson Button Company" in 1858, S & J was another of Waterbury's manufacturers of brass goods. Purchased by Chase in 1935, Steele and Johnson continued to market goods under its own banner for several years. A New York City showroom opened in 1935 at 200 Fifth Avenue (former location of the Chase showroom), and a 1936 Steele and Johnson catalog offered what *The Gift And Art Buyer* described as "lamps and gifts presented in an attractive manner." However, on January 1, 1938, Chase took over all sales of Steele & Johnson lamps. The reason, according to the next year's Chase Specialties catalog, was increased ease of operation:

> This means that our customers have the advantage of being able to buy both lines from one concern; it means one salesman to see instead of two, only one order to make out, one invoice to pay, one shipment to receive.

The consolidation of the Steele & Johnson line (or at least the most attractive parts of it), into the Chase Specialty line meant a final major infusion of new inventory for Chase Lighting. First appearing in the 1939 Chase Specialties catalog were over 60 lamps previously marketed by Steele & Johnson, most (but not all) identifiable by a "6000" series inventory number. Many of the Steele & Johnson items were standard-issue "household" lamps—modestly attractive enough to complement a decor without dominating (or dictating) it. Urn-like shapes such as the "BEDFORD," "REGENT," and "WINTON" held sway. Also popular were lamps with focus on a central column, among them the "AMBASSADOR" and "SUTTON." More imaginative designs included the "COMMANDER," with an etched design on its metal column, and the "KIDDIE LAMP," a perfect complement to all those Chase "DRUMS" and "COLONELS" that had come before. Nine of the Steele and Johnson lamps made 1939-only appearances, including the "SENTINEL," #6171, and the "PRISCILLA," #6131, whose names (though not designs) were identical to previously released Chase lamps. As the 1939 catalog indicated, the end result was "a line large enough and varied enough in style and price for you to select all your table lamps from one source."

Fading Light

The history of the Chase Lighting division was a brief, but brilliant one. With the onset of World War II, the company turned its attentions toward war production, and the lights went out, never to be relit. While it lasted though, Chase Lighting shone brightly; the creative spark of its talented designers ignited a lighting legacy that still dazzles today.

> "It is quite needless to state that all the beauty of these lamps would have been futile if not backed by that sturdy construction, skillful craftsmanship, and broad vision which the Chase Brass & Copper Co. has instilled in the line. While at no time would they allow any construction detail, however minute, to be overlooked, they succeeded through months of careful study and exhaustive effort in producing this line in a scale of prices that will make lamp history."
>
> Lurelle Guild
> Chase Lamps catalog, 1934

Above: Frederick S. Chase assumed the presidency of Chase Brass & Copper Co., in 1918. During his tenure, the Specialty and Lighting divisions of Chase were established, and achieved prominence.

Right: Awarded October 13, 1914, to Adolph Recker, this early patent was marketed by Chase as #11150, the battery-operated "CANDLE-LIGHT."

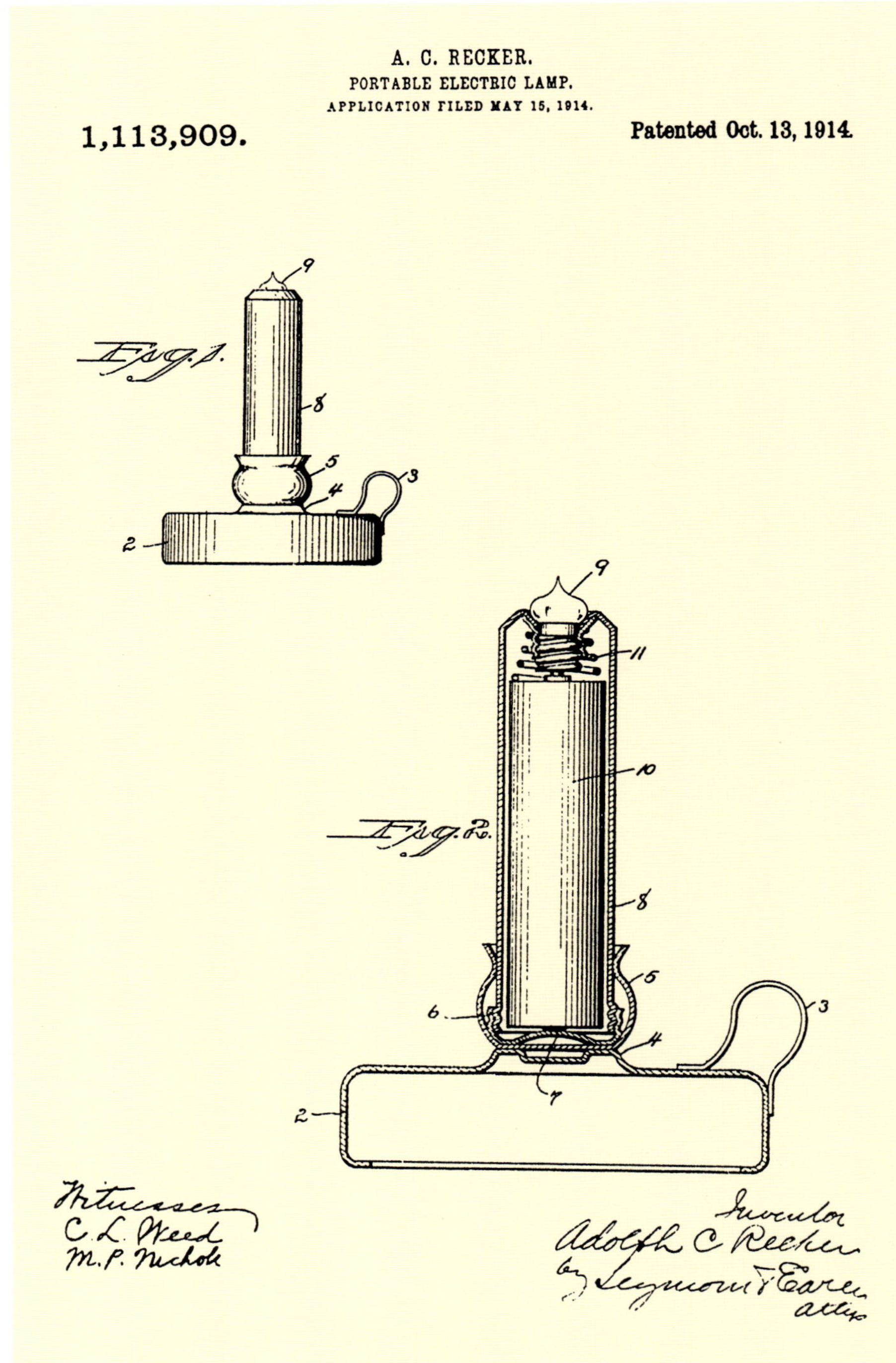

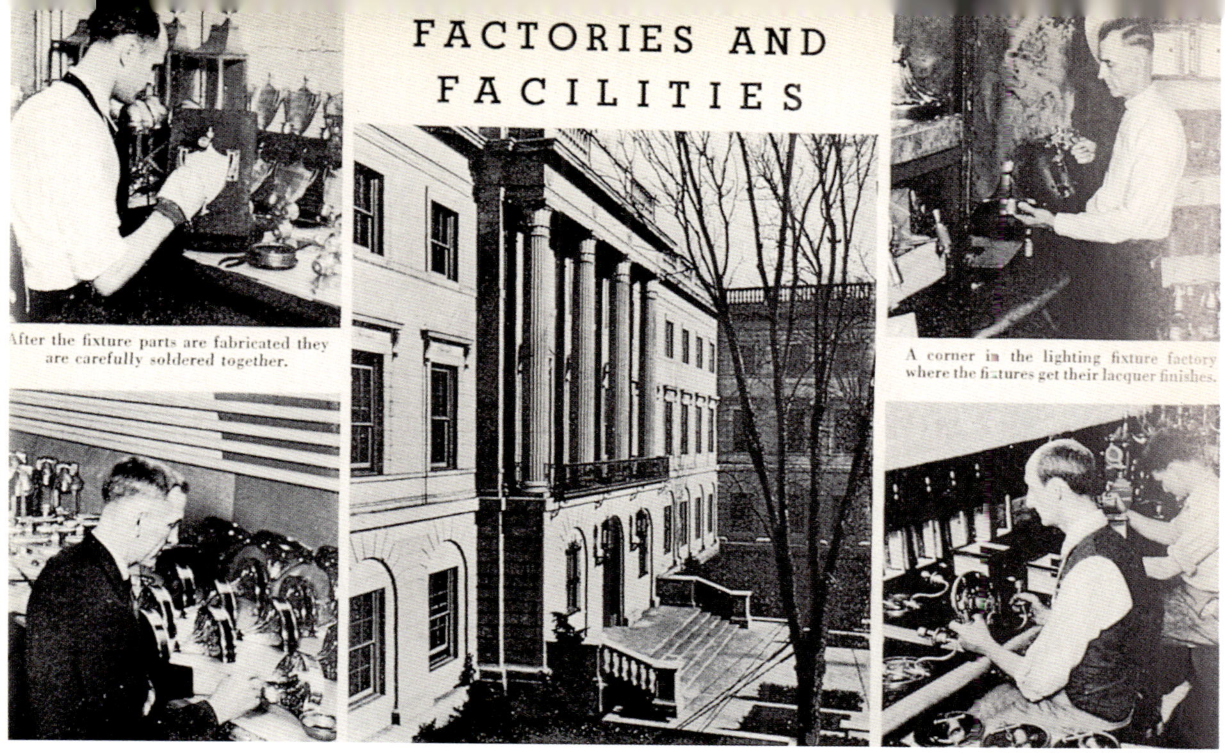

"Factories and Facilities." This excerpt from the 1934 Lighting Fixtures catalog depicts the main Chase building, and various steps in lighting fixture production.

From the same catalog, views of the various Chase mills and factories, circa 1934.

Top: Steele & Johnson logo.

Top center: Waterbury, Connecticut, headquarters of the Steele & Johnson Manufacturing Company. Following the company's mid-1930s acquisition by Chase, various Steele & Johnson lamps appeared in Chase catalogs. In 1938, the entire Steele & Johnson line moved under the Chase banner.

Right: 1934 *Waterbury Directory* advertisement for Steele & Johnson Mfg. Co. Among the numerous products listed: "Lamps and Gift Wares."

STEELE & JOHNSON MFG. CO.

Benjamin L. Coe, Pres.
Benjamin S. Coe, Sec., Treas. and Gen. Mgr.

Brass Goods from Sheet, Wire, Rod and Tubing

SHELLS, Drawn, Stamped and Spun. Stamped Shells up to 24 inches diameter. NUTS, Square and Hexagon. WASHERS, Flat, D Hole Spring. MACHINE SCREWS, Rolled Thread, Brass and Iron, Round, Flat and Special Head, Bibb, Cock and Holder Screws. CHAIN, Brass and Iron Jack, Plumbers', Safety and Ladder also Brass and Iron CHANDELIER CHAIN. BUTTONS, for Uniforms, ORNAMENTS and NOVELTIES. SUPPLIES for Lighting Fixtures, Electrical and Plumbers' trades. Automatic Screw Machine Products. Lamps and Gift Wares. Special goods made to order.

779 SOUTH MAIN STREET

N. Y. Office, 200 Fifth Ave. Chicago Office, 605 West Washington Blvd.

Left: Chase lamp #6198, the "CIRCLETTE" is shown at left with original shade. The identical lamp at right is marked "Steele & Johnson." 8-3/4" h. *Courtesy of John and Donna Thorpe*

Above: Another pair of look-alikes: the "SAYBROOK," #6035. The Steele and Johnson version is at right. The "SAYBROOK" was a dual-purpose lamp, adaptable for table or wall-mount use. A model with plastic diffusing reflector, #6304, was also available. 12" h. *Courtesy of John and Donna Thorpe*

Light on the Dark Spots in the American Home

by **Chase**

IF you are sitting in "somebody's" living room at this moment, glance at the lighting fixtures. Ten to one they look exactly as they shouldn't look—ornate, out-of-date, poorly designed. Even in homes that are otherwise modern and well decorated you will often see these unattractive "dark spots"—ugly, obsolete lighting fixtures that belong to a previous generation—and look it!

Richmond Ceiling Fixture. Finished entirely in Federal Brass. $25.00

Why haven't they been changed? Why do we modernize our homes; redecorate and refurnish our rooms but not refixture? For two very good reasons: *in the past*, lighting fixtures of good design have been hard to find and, if found, were quite expensive. We say "past" because only last year *the first complete line of authentically designed lighting fixtures at reasonable prices* was put on the market by Chase.

Jefferson Wall Bracket. One or two lights. Federal Brass finish with two lights, $12.50; one light, $10.00

Bennington Wall Bracket. Finished in satin chromium, antique brass or weathered brass. $10.50

Lenox Ceiling Fixture. Finished in satin chromium, antique brass or weathered brass. $17.50

You have only to look at Chase Lighting Fixtures to appreciate their good taste. Even in the small pictures on this page you can see they are beautiful. But you must see Chase Fixtures "in the flesh" to know how utterly different they are from lighting fixtures of the past. No gingerbread. No ornate trimmings or decorations. Instead, authentic designs from each period of architecture so that whatever the style of your home you can now have fixtures in it that really belong!

Independence Wall Bracket. Finished entirely in Empire Brass. $12.00

Talleyrand Wall Bracket. Finished in Empire brass with gunmetal mirror. $12.50

Brighton Wall Bracket. Finished in pleasing tones of black and gold. $8.50

Framingham Wall Bracket. Finished in satin chromium, antique brass, weathered brass, or ivory and gold. $3.25

Included in the Chase line are genuinely designed Early English fixtures. Quaint Early American sconces, lanterns and ceiling fixtures. Graceful Georgian fixtures for stately Colonial homes. Beautiful Federal fixtures. For homes done in the Empire manner, authentic Empire fixtures. And, for modern interiors—smart, new Classic Modern designs.

Augusta Ceiling Fixture. Simple, attractive design. Polished chromium, $3.25. Antique brass finish. $2.75

Newport Wall Bracket. Polished chromium finish. Also made with convenience outlet. $1.70

Jupiter Wall Bracket. Chromium back plate, with frosted glass shade decorated with chromium band. $5.50

Dolphin Wall Bracket. Chromium finish with frosted glass. $7.50

Nantucket Lantern. Black finish, $8.25; Colonial brass or antique copper finish, $9.00

And never have fine fixtures cost *so* little! Beautiful brackets by Chase start at $1.65. Handsome ceiling fixtures from $2.10. Lovely lanterns of brass or copper for as little as $7.50.

(Above, left). Hartford Lantern. Finished in Colonial brass, antique copper, or black. $15.00

(Above, right). Haddon Hall Wall Lantern. Finished in either black, $17.50; or half-polished iron, $18.50

Saybrook Lantern. Finished in Colonial brass or black. Bracket type in brass, $15.50; in black, $14.00. The chain hanger type in brass, $12.50; in black, $11.00

Of course you want to know more about Chase Lighting Fixtures than we can possibly tell you here. So send the convenient coupon below. It will bring you a beautiful *free* booklet showing *all* Chase Fixtures, prices, and where to see them.

CHASE

*Chase Brass & Copper Co., Incorporated**
Dept. A-1, Lighting Fixture Division
Waterbury, Conn.

You may send me your FREE illustrated booklet showing all *Chase Fixtures and name of dealer nearest me.*

Name..

Address..

City.......................... *State*..........

* Subsidiary of Kennecott Coppe. Corporation

Top left: Among the Chase lamps and fixtures most popular with today's American Art Deco collectors are those in the Classic Modern style, designed by Lurelle Guild. Shown are four Classic Modern selections from the 1934 Fixtures catalog, "well designed for the position they will occupy in the modern room." Here, # M 526, "THE MINERVA," "using light itself for its decorative as well as its utilitarian value." 17" h.

Top center: "THE ROMA," # M 527, featuring laurel leaves silhouetted against the light source. 8-1/2" h. x 8-1/2" d.

Bottom left: # M 640 "THE CYPRUS." The star-shapes have been left clear on the frosted glass exterior. 11" d.

Bottom center: # M 543, "THE SYBIL," "illustrative of the way in which Classic Modern design can achieve pure beauty without sacrificing the principles of scientific illumination." 24" overall length, 14" d.

Above: "You have only to look at Chase Lighting Fixtures to appreciate their good taste." The promotional push for the Chase Lighting Division was in full swing by the time of this November 1935 ad in *The American Home.*

Chapter 2
"Leading Lights: The Chase Designers"

Prolific industrial designer Lurelle Guild, whose extensive line of lamps and lighting fixtures was introduced by Chase in 1934.

"Only a good designer and a sympathetic manufacturer working together could produce the splendid and diverse patterns that comprise Chase lighting fixtures and lamps. Behind the designs lies the romance of tradition, and something of that romance and awareness of tradition will pass over to those who select them for their home. They are calculated, in the finest sense, to stimulate a justifiable pride of ownership."

Richardson Wright, Editor
House & Garden, July, 1934

Mr. Wright's comments were typical of many that poured forth in 1934. New York City's Chase Tower had just opened, with its magnificent display of Chase lamps and fixtures. Elegant new catalogs from the Chase Lighting division heralded an extensive inventory for both product lines. Chase was on the brink of renewed public acclaim—and the cornerstone of it all was designer Lurelle Guild.

Enlightening America

An art graduate of Syracuse University, Guild began his professional career as a magazine illustrator and writer, with his work appearing in such publications as *McCall's* and *Woman's Home Companion*. Interior design work for the magazines prompted him to look for ways of bringing his ideas to concrete life. As a March, 1935 article in *Modern Plastics* noted:

> In 1926, the urge to create things as well as illustrate them became so strong that Guild entered the field of industrial designing, where he has given original line and form to thousands of objects, increasing their beauty and utility, and therefore their sales as well.

From his first humble project—designing tombstones—Guild moved quickly upward. His design projects ran the gamut from refrigerators to roller skates, with clients as diverse as Montgomery Ward and Wear Ever Aluminum Co. In each case, the goal was to provide efficient operation and attractive appearance at a cost acceptable to both manufacturer and consumer. "Beauty alone," stated Guild, "does not sell."[1]

Guild was a master of redesign, researching each project thoroughly before making any revisions. His Wearever teakettle is a good example. Before Guild, teakettles usually had hinged handles, which dropped down to the side when not in use. The disadvantage, of course, was that the handles then became extremely warm, often charring from contact with the hot metal. For Wearever, Guild designed a rigid, plastic handle, which never became hot, and was comfortably placed for use. The manufacturer found that the new kettles required larger cartons, and asked for a revision. Guild countered by taking the problem to the consumer. An old and a new kettle, similarly priced, were displayed in the housewares department of a New York department store. 236 women were asked which kettle they would prefer; 232 chose the new design. It went into production, and was a major success. With results like that, Guild could confidently boast that he'd "never designed a product that was a commercial failure, and never lost a client.[2]

Lighting the way at Chase

Guild's successful track record was a major reason Chase showed no hesitation in entrusting the design plan of the entire Lighting division to his care. In coming up with new products, both company and designer were a comfortable match, focused on quality as well as on the bottom line. Cognizant of the prestige attached to attracting a major design name to their firm, Chase capitalized on its coup. Guild was also given the opportunity to design a variety of items for the Chase Specialty division, and Chase Tower, which opened in 1934, featured Guild-designed lamps and fixtures in Guild-designed settings. F. S. Chase, introducing the 1934 Lamps catalog, took justifiable pride in the company's Guild connection:

> Our designer, Mr. Guild, has made for us products that we think will appeal generally to people throughout the country. We have followed his designs very carefully, and we have produced them so exactly that architects, decorators, and others on whose taste we rely tell us that they are remarkably well done.

Laser-Like Precision

With every assignment he undertook, Guild researched the challenges thoroughly (in fact, exhaustively). Churning out nearly one thousand designs annually, he often prepared four finished drawings of each product, as well as an object model. As his comments in the 1934 Fixtures catalog indicate, Chase received the full Guild treatment:

> In designing this line, I have tried to translate for you all those things which heretofore have not been available. Indefatigable research has brought forth new forms as well as unusual conceptions of the better known motives in the decorative field: whether it be the eagle on the Federal sconce, molded from an early historic carving, hitherto undiscovered, or the sophisticated swag of a Classic Modern wall light. Nothing has been left unstudied to obtain consummate excellence in mass and detail, but in retaining this character of loveliness, faultless construction, ease of installation and practicability have remained pre-eminent in our minds, and have not at any time been sacrificed for effect.

"Consummate excellence," the lasting legacy of Lurelle Guild, and the more than 70 lamps and 170 fixtures he contributed to Chase.

NEWS

Facing page: In addition to his lighting designs, Guild also created numerous items for the Chase Specialty division. *Clockwise from left:* #90038 "PRETZELMAN;" #27014 "COLONEL'S LADY LIGHT;" #27001 "INDIVIDUAL CANAPE PLATES;" #27027 "NEWSPAPER RACK;" #90047 "LIQUEUR CUPS;" #28017 "JIGGER AND SWIZZLER SET." *Courtesy of John and Donna Thorpe*

This page:
Top left: Guild's February 6, 1934 patent for the "COLONEL'S LADY LIGHT."

Top center: Here's her partner: #27013 "COLONEL LIGHT." According to the 1934 Chase catalog, "the militant 'Colonel' will delight the child who is fortunate enough to own it." The Cossack hat shade could be tilted, to avert light from sleeping eyes. 9-3/8" h. *Courtesy of Danny Kaplan*

Top right: Patent for the "COLONEL LIGHT," also granted February 6, 1934.

Bottom left: A less whimsical Guild patent design for Chase, of a "CEILING TYPE LIGHTING FIXTURE."

Bottom center and right: "The Designer Speaks," Lurelle Guild's Introduction to the 1934 Chase Lighting Fixtures catalog, outlining the concepts that inspired his designs. Various Guild sketches decorate the copy, including, at top left, one of the artist himself!

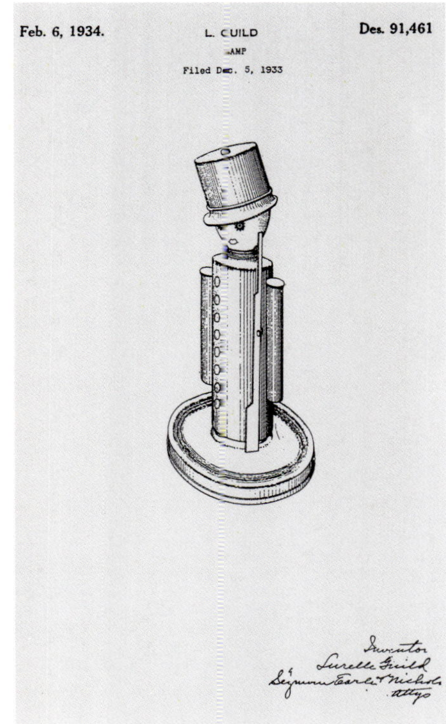

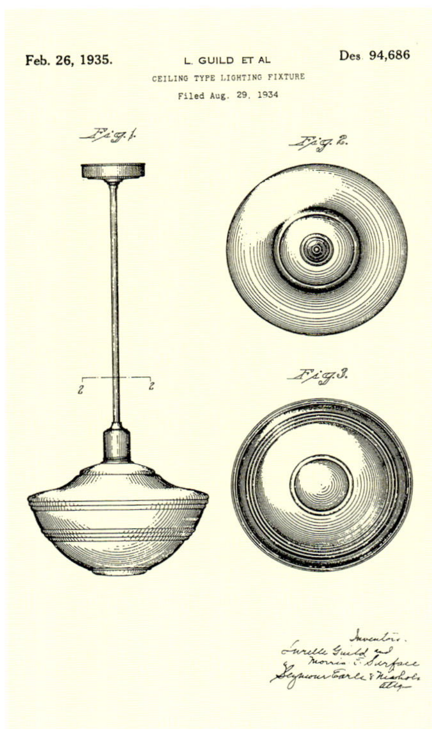

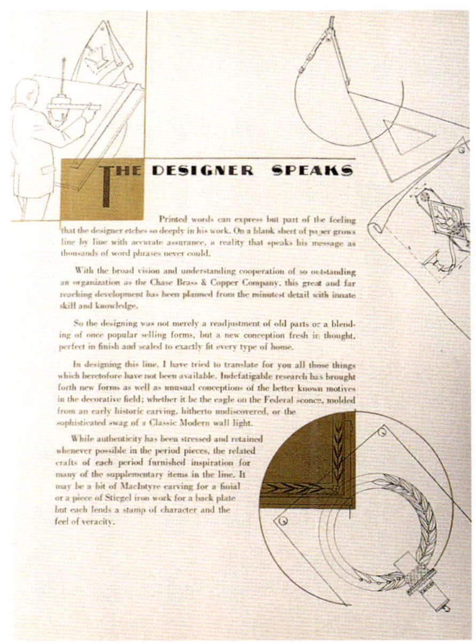

THE DESIGNER SPEAKS

Printed words can express but part of the feeling that the designer etches so deeply in his work. On a blank sheet of paper grows line by line with accurate assurance, a reality that speaks his message as thousands of word phrases never could.

With the broad vision and understanding cooperation of so outstanding an organization as the Chase Brass & Copper Company, this great and far reaching development has been planned from the minutest detail with innate skill and knowledge.

So the designing was not merely a readjustment of old parts or a blending of once popular selling forms, but a new conception fresh in thought, perfect in finish and sealed to exactly fit every type of home.

In designing this line, I have tried to translate for you all those things which heretofore have not been available. Indefatigable research has brought forth new forms as well as unusual conceptions of the better known motives in the decorative field; whether it be the eagle on the Federal sconce, molded from an early historic carving, hitherto undiscovered, or the sophisticated swag of a Classic Modern wall light.

While authenticity has been stressed and retained whenever possible in the period pieces, the related crafts of each period furnished inspiration for many of the supplementary items in the line. It may be a bit of MacIntyre carving for a finial or a piece of Stiegel iron work for a back plate but each lends a stamp of character and the feel of veracity.

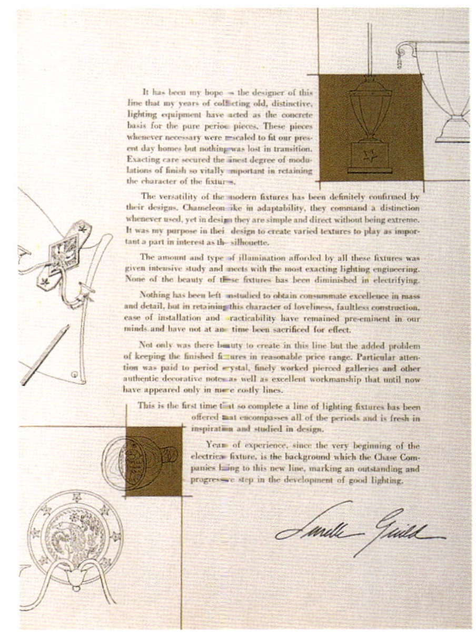

It has been my hope as the designer of this line that my years of collecting old, distinctive, lighting equipment have acted as the concrete basis for the pure period pieces. These pieces whenever necessary were rescaled to fit our present day homes but nothing was lost in transition. Exacting care secured the finest degree of modulations of finish so vitally important in retaining the character of the fixtures.

The versatility of the modern fixtures has been definitely confirmed by their designs. Chameleon-like in adaptability, they command a distinction whenever used, yet in design they are simple and direct without being extreme. It was my purpose in their design to create varied textures to play as important a part in interest as the silhouette.

The amount and type of illumination afforded by all these fixtures was given intensive study and meets with the most exacting lighting engineering. None of the beauty of these fixtures has been diminished in electrifying.

Nothing has been left unstudied to obtain consummate excellence in mass and detail, but in retaining this character of loveliness, faultless construction, ease of installation and practicability have remained pre-eminent in our minds and have not at any time been sacrificed for effect.

Not only was there beauty to create in this line but the added problem of keeping the finished fixtures in reasonable price range. Particular attention was paid to period crystal, finely worked pierced galleries and other authentic decorative notes as well as excellent workmanship that until now have appeared only in more costly lines.

This is the first time that so complete a line of lighting fixtures has been offered that encompasses all of the periods and is fresh in inspiration and studied in design.

Years of experience, since the very beginning of the electrical fixture, is the background which the Chase Companies bring to this new line, marking an outstanding and progressive step in the development of good lighting.

Lurelle Guild

Detail, Guild's sketch of # F 102 "THE SALEM EAGLE," a wall fixture in the "Federal" style. The central eagle design is a reproduction of a wood carving dating from 1790.

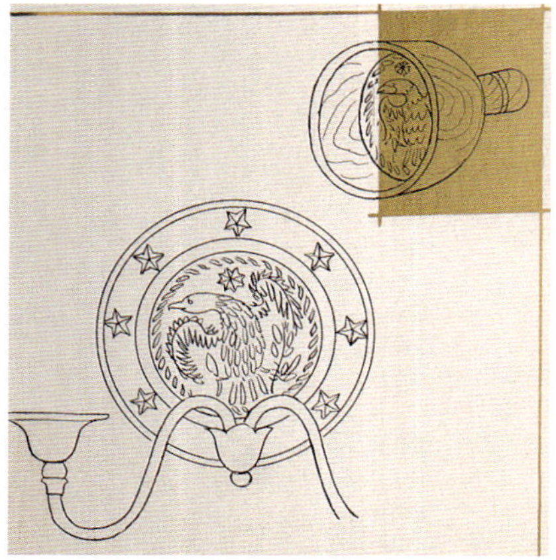

Beautifully lighting the hall of this charming Early American interior is the Chase Williamsburg Lantern, $18.50. In the living room: The Brookfield Ceiling Fixture, $37.50; The Connecticut Sconce $10.00. The four Chase Lamps, shown from left to right: The Admiral Lamp, $14.25, base only $12.00; The Mt. Vernon Lamp, $13.50; The Barnett Lamp, $12.00; and The Flying Cloud Lamp, $24.00, base only $15.00.

HOUSE & GARDEN *welcomes the* **FIRST ENSEMBLE** *of* **AUTHENTICALLY DESIGNED LIGHTING FIXTURES** *and* **LAMPS**

AT last, the long awaited improvement in lighting has come. For fifty years we have had electricity but in all these years no one has made fixtures and lamps of *truly authentic design at reasonable prices.*

If you've ever built a home; ever remodeled or redecorated, you know what a problem lighting fixtures have been. You either paid high prices for specially designed models or were forced to buy unattractive fixtures made of ordinary materials in bad taste.

No wonder "HOUSE & GARDEN" welcomes Chase Lighting—the first and most complete ensemble of authentically designed fixtures and lamps ever created—all beautifully styled by Lurelle Guild, eminent artist and designer, and finely executed in lasting, non-rusting brass by Chase.

Whatever the style or period of your home, refixturing now becomes easy and inexpensive for Chase Lighting includes charming sconces, brackets, lanterns, chandeliers, table and floor lamps of correct design and exquisite taste for every important period of decoration.

There are sturdy iron finished fixtures for brick and timber English homes. Quaint Early American and stately Federal fixtures and lamps for Colonial homes. And for Georgian, Empire, and Classic Modern homes, Chase Lighting includes every needed fixture and lamp. Priced so considerately, too! From one-third to one-half less than comparable fixtures ever cost before. Prices shown are for wired fixtures only—do not include small installation cost.

CHASE LIGHTING . . .

Detail, two different Guild renditions of # F 100 "THE MONROE," another "Federal" design. The flag and drum motif was "an exact tracing from a Continental coin."

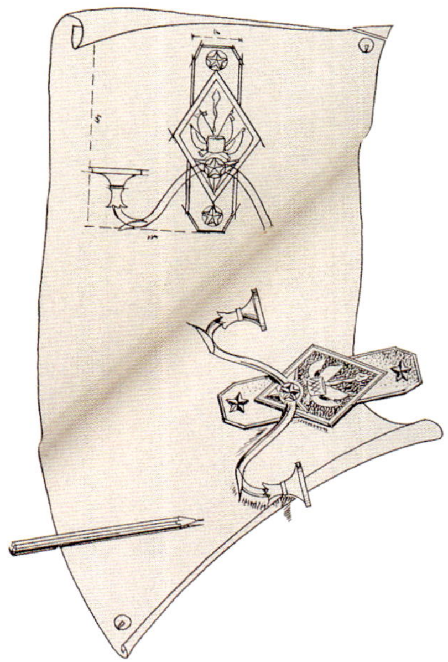

The design at left in this photo forms the base of the "Federal"-inspired lamp, "THE LIBERTY," # F 136. Precise utilization of the urn design at right is unknown, although similar shapes are used in various "Federal" and "Georgian" lamps and hanging fixtures by Guild. *1934 Lighting Fixtures catalog courtesy of John Myhre*

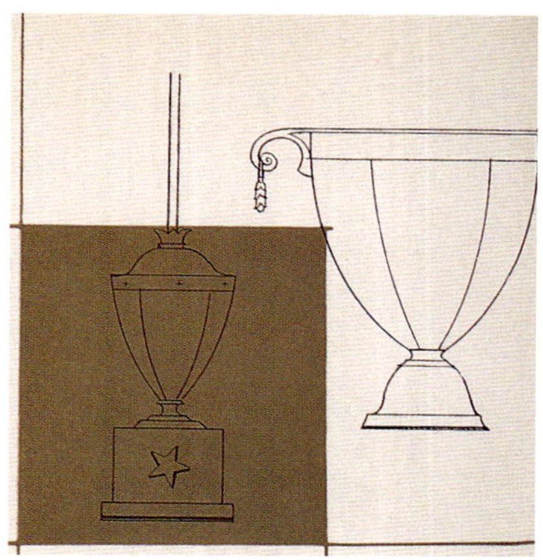

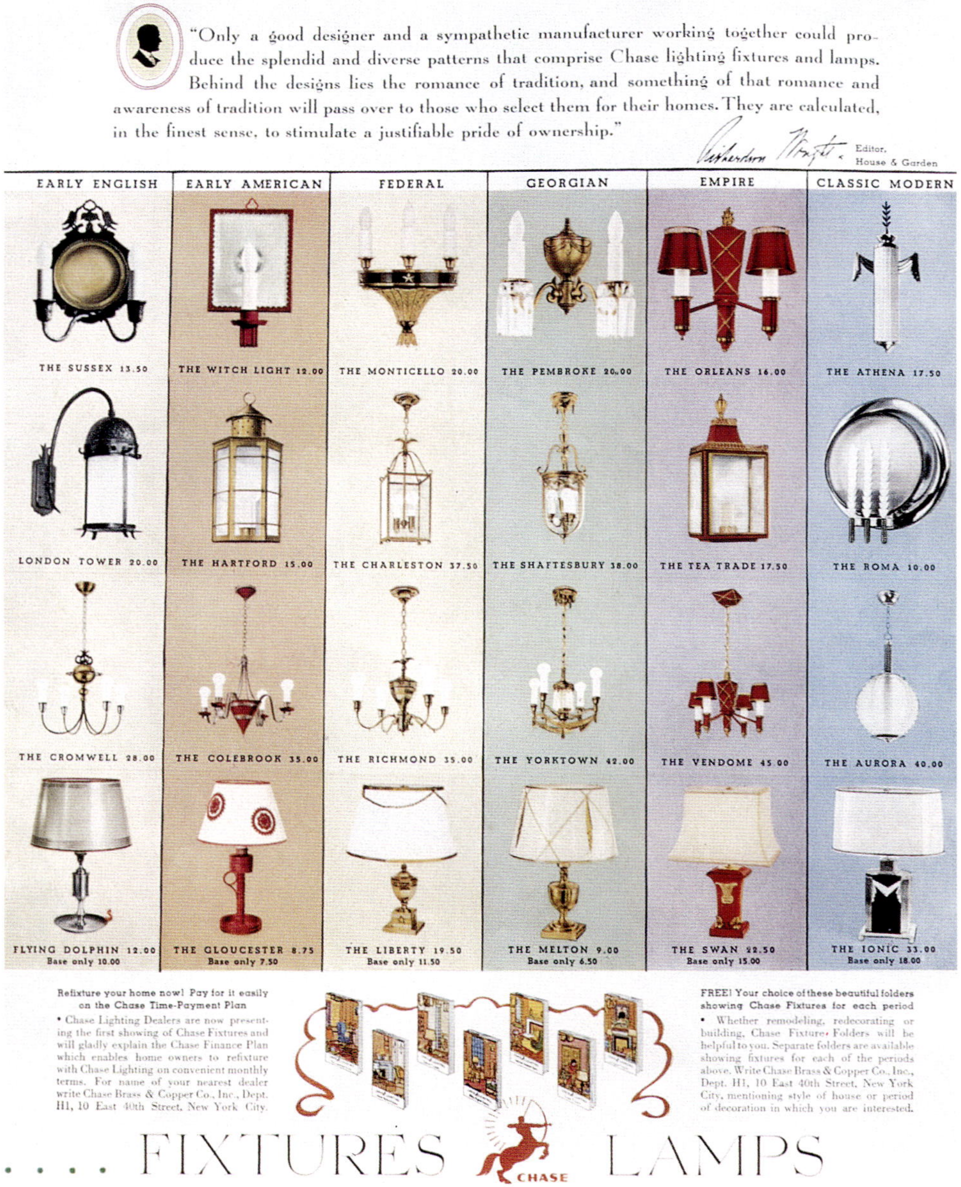

Facing page and above: Chase announced the new Guild-designed line of lamps and lighting fixtures, in a two-page ad appearing in the July 1934 issue of *House & Garden*. Highlights of the line were featured, along with Guild's illustration of an "Early American" interior. Kind (and presumably unbiased) words from *House & Garden's* editor were prominently displayed.

Staying with a good thing: the same ad appeared in the July 1934 issue of *House Beautiful*, with just a change in magazine title, and the editor's complimentary comments!

Top left: The first of a half-dozen of Guild's acclaimed Classic Modern fixture designs for 1934: # M 522, "THE ATHENA." The line of the frosted glass column is heightened with clear glass flutings. 23" h.

Top center: "THE ZEUS," # M 540. Empire decorations and Classic Modern styling blend in this hanging fixture. 45" overall height; 16-1/2" fixture height.

Top right: # M 533, "THE SEA HORSE." The foam-white appearance of the frosted glass cylinder "carries out the nautical spirit expressed in the sea-horse and the shell-shaped back plate." 11" h.

Bottom left: A modern adaptation of an Empire crystal chandelier, "THE PARIS," # M 541. "The prismatic effect of crystal is achieved by an ingenious alternation of clear and frosted glass." 12" h. x 18" w.

Bottom center: The polished chromium arrow of "THE DIANA," # M 520, bisects a laurel spray etched in burnished silver on the crystal frosted glass. 12" h.

Bottom right: "THE THOR," # M 525, distinguished by its combined use of a half-disc light and a circular back plate. 7-1/4" h., 4-1/2" projection.

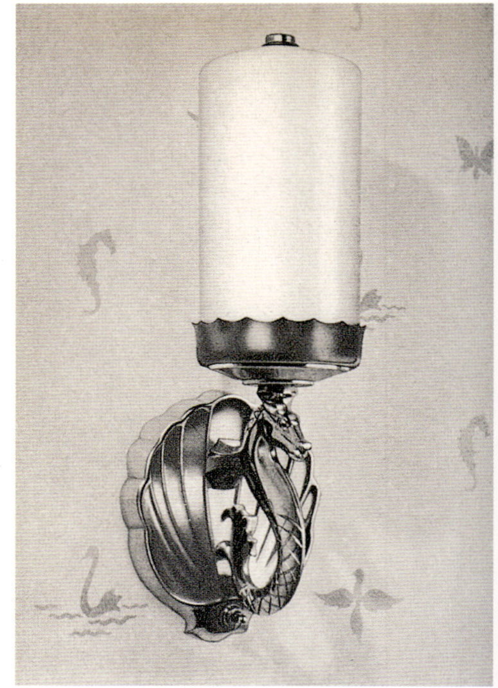
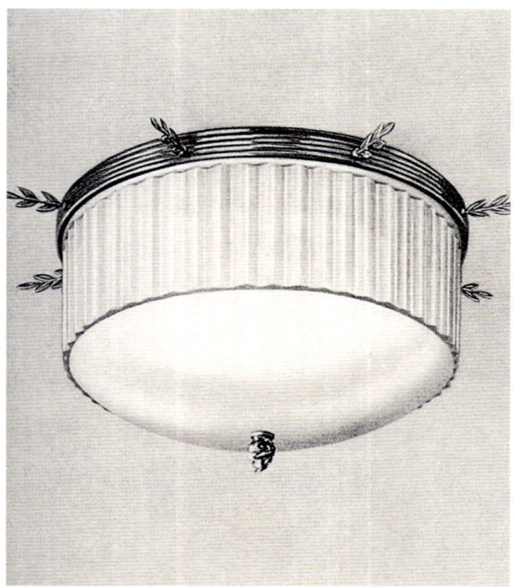

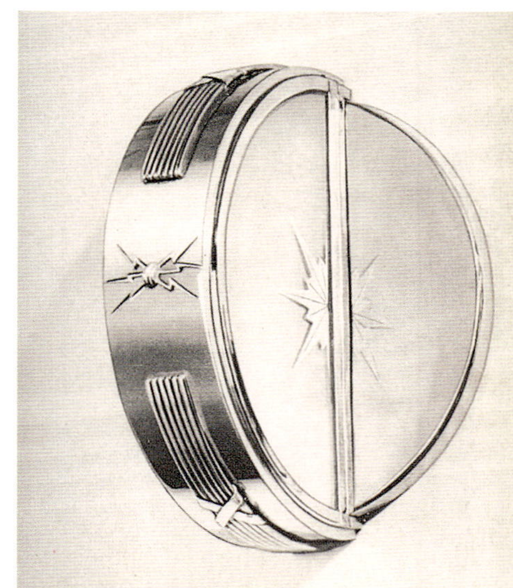

One view of the beautiful central gallery in Chase Tower. The alcoves on each side serve as individual showrooms for the various period fixtures, and each one is charmingly decorated in the style of the period represented.

Below, one of the many smartly styled alcoves in which Chase Lighting is displayed by periods. The furniture, decorations and curtains perfectly express the particular period represented and form a fitting background for the authentic designs of the fixtures on the walls and ceilings.

A CORDIAL WELCOME AWAITS YOU AT CHASE TOWER SHOWROOM

To all those interested in lighting, in fixtures and lamps, Chase extends a cordial invitation to visit Chase Tower at New York.

Occupying the entire 48th floor of one of New York's tallest buildings, the new fixture and lamp showroom is Classic Modern in decoration and contains some twenty rooms and alcoves devoted to the display of Chase Lighting.

Refreshing in its simplicity, the showroom is unique in that there are no rows of brackets along the walls or forests of ceiling fixtures hanging from above. Instead, the fixtures are segregated in various period rooms and alcoves off the main gallery where you may leisurely examine Chase fixtures and lamps in settings that are typical of each decorative period.

96

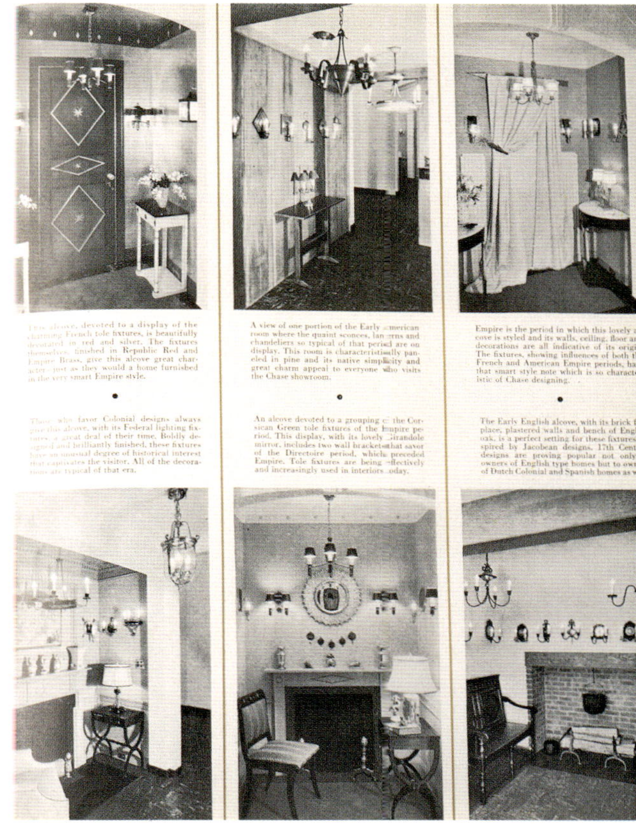

This alcove, devoted to a display of the charming French tole fixtures, is beautifully decorated in red and silver. The fixtures themselves, finished in Republic Red and Empire Brass, give this alcove great character—just as they would a home furnished in the very smart Empire style.

A view of one portion of the Early American room where the quaint sconces, lanterns and chandeliers so typical of that period are on display. This room is characteristically paneled in pine and its native simplicity and great charm appeal to everyone who visits the Chase showroom.

Empire is the period in which this lovely alcove is styled and its walls, ceiling, floor and decorations are all indicative of its origin. The fixtures, showing influences of both the French and American Empire periods, have that smart style note which is so characteristic of Chase designing.

Those who favor Colonial designs always give this alcove, with its Federal lighting fixtures, a great deal of their time. Boldly designed and brilliantly finished, these fixtures have an unusual degree of historical interest that captivates the visitor. All of the decorations are typical of that era.

An alcove devoted to a grouping of the Corsican Green tole fixtures of the Empire period. This display, with its lovely Girandole mirror, includes two wall brackets that savor of the Directoire period, which preceded Empire. Tole fixtures are being effectively and increasingly used in interiors today.

The Early English alcove, with its brick fireplace, plastered walls and bench of English oak, is a perfect setting for these fixtures inspired by Jacobean designs. 17th Century designs are proving popular not only to owners of English type homes but to owners of Dutch Colonial and Spanish homes as well.

Top left: Chase Tower at 10 East 40th Street, New York City. The top four floors comprised the Chase showrooms, with the entire 48th floor devoted to Guild's lamps and lighting fixtures.

Top center: On the 48th floor of Chase Tower, a "palatial, high-ceilinged corridor in the Classic Modern style, done in austere white." Eighteen doorways led to alcoves, each decorated in the style of a particular period, and featuring Guild-designed lamps and lighting fixtures appropriate to the era. The purpose, according to promotional releases, was to create a showroom free of "rows of brackets and forests of ceiling fixtures," with items displayed "just as they would be in a home."

Top right: Inside the alcoves. Shown are six of the small rooms outfitted by Guild to display his lamps and lighting fixtures to their best advantage.

Left: At the grand opening of Chase tower, May 15, 1934, etiquette maven Emily Post chats with Rodney Chase, Director of Public and Industrial Relations for the company, as Lurelle Guild, at right, awaits his turn.

Beyond Guild

While most in evidence, Lurelle Guild wasn't the only industrial designer lighting up Chase. Before, during, and after his tenure, other talents made their own unique contributions.

Some remain unknown. A Chase lamp or fixture is not credited to a specific designer unless a patent was filed, or the designer mentioned by name in advertisements, catalogs, or other company literature. The Index *of 1930s Lighting: Deco & Traditional by Chase* lists all currently known and verifiable design credits. Unattributed lights may be the work of designers who created other aspects of the line, or that of in-house Chase personnel whose contracts did not specify design credit. However, documentation supporting any final determination in such cases is, at present, lacking.

In several instances, a contribution to the lighting line was minimal. Among those making fleeting appearances in the Chase patent listings are Morris E. Surface, granted two 1936 patents for the mechanics of as-yet unidentified globed hanging fixtures; Richard W. Shoemaker, awarded a patent in 1938 for a fixture, also unidentified, with bowl and shade; and Edward F. Cleary, who received a 1939 patent for a shade used on Chase "Even-Glow" fixture #1547.

Prominent Lamp Lighters

Lamps by designers other than Guild were marketed by the Chase Specialty division. (The Gerths' "BALL LAMP," #A 11235/#01002 was also included in the 1934 Lamps catalog, as an "American Adaptation.")

"Designed for the American home of today that does not require period styles in its interior decoration," non-Guild Chase lamps were the work of some of the country's foremost industrial designers. Thumbnail sketches of each follow; more detailed profiles will be found in our companion book *Chase Complete*.

HELEN BISHOP DENNIS

Chase Director of Design in the early 1930s, Mrs. Dennis also contributed several of her own designs to the Specialty line, usually variations on a theme. Her playful fish figurine graced everything from candlesticks to ivy bowls, and her patented 1935 design for #01010, the "NOVELTY DRUM LAMP," was the first in a long parade of drum-inspired items by other Chase designers.

RUTH & WILLIAM GERTH

Although the Chase catalogs often mentioned "designs by Gerth and Gerth," Mrs. Gerth was the more visible partner. Prominent in the early years of the Chase Specialty division, the Gerths also contributed several attractive (and long-lived) lamp designs. Those credited include #01002/#A 11235 "BALL," and the ubiquitous "GLOW LAMP," #01001, created from a toilet float! Ruth Gerth was also the primary designer of Chase Tower's Specialty showroom.

HARRY LAYLON

Mr. Laylon's Chase career lasted longer—and resulted in more Specialty designs—than any other company designer. Nearly 100 giftware items are credited to Laylon, who joined Chase in 1933, and served as Director of Design from 1937 until 1940. In addition to contributing his own designs, and supervising the efforts of other Chase designers, Mr. Laylon created plans for "The Chase Shops," unique marketing centers for the company's product, set up in department stores nationwide. Equally adept at providing new concepts, or working within the boundaries of previously established Chase product themes, Harry Laylon's lamp designs include the jaunty "MASTHEAD LANTERN," #25008.

HOWARD REICHENBACH

Serving in a variety of positions at Chase, including Development Engineer and Product Engineer, Mr. Reichenbach also found time to contribute a number of staples to the Specialty line, including the "GAIETY" and "BLUE MOON" cocktail shakers. His "COMET" lamp design (#6151 metal shade, #6154 plastic shade) proved particularly popular, thanks to its adjustable half-circle bracket.

WALTER VON NESSEN

Of the Chase designers, Von Nessen had the greatest degree of experience in creating lamps and fixtures, prior to his tenure at Chase. New York's Nessen Studio, founded in 1927, was the source of many popular lamp designs, including Von Nessen's own swing-arm lamp.

Von Nessen was one of the earliest Chase Specialty designers, with ten of his pieces hitting the market in 1930, well before the first Specialty catalog was issued. His Chase lamps include #11240 "CONSOLE;" #17048 "CONSTELLATION;" #01015 "PLANET," and the aptly named #NS-597, "THE LAMP." The hallmark of Von Nessen's designs was functional elegance, with his work achieving recognition in several international exhibitions.

They keep on going . . . and going . . . and going

Several Chase patent-holders specialized in designs for non-wired, battery lamps. They include:

JOHN KING & RANDAL HALE

Only one Chase patent was issued to this design team. It was awarded in 1940 for the "Autoilluminant Writing Implement," better known as the "ILLUMINATED PENCIL," #9012, a variation on the flashlight. King was later Chase Specialty Sales manager; Hale, the company's development engineer, also coordinated shade purchases.

AUGUST MITCHELL

Chase flashlights were good sellers, and Mr. Mitchell designed both of them. The "BOMB FLASHLIGHT," #22001 first appeared in the 1933 catalog, and was part of the Specialty line until the division ended production in 1942. The "AIRALITE," also introduced in 1933, was featured through 1940.

ADOLPH RECKER

Mr. Recker held patents for two early Chase battery lamp designs. His first, for #11150, the "CANDELIGHT," was issued in 1914, well before the dawning of the Chase Lighting and Specialty divisions. In 1932, Mr. Recker was granted a patent for the "BINNACLE LIGHT" (#25001 battery, #25002 wired). The "BINNACLE" first appeared in the 1933 catalog, and continued through 1939, with variations ranging from plain frosted glass globes to illustrations depicting the 1933-34 World's Fair.

Making the Most of What You've Got

> *"Ruth Gerth, one of the more resourceful industrial designers, picked a copper toilet floater out of a dusty pile of them in a storage room at the Chase factory, squinted at it calculatingly, and out of her artistic imagination sprang a little glow lamp (#01001)."*
>
> *Design*. September, 1933

For a Chase designer, the ability to devise new and creative means of reusing existing inventory was a plus. Early designers raided the spare parts stock, often resulting in a best-selling brainstorm, such as Ruth Gerth's toilet-float "GLOW LAMP," or Lurelle Guild's "COLONEL" and "COLONEL'S LADY," cleverly constructed from metal tubing.

As the Specialty line output increased, so did the opportunity to cannibalize, and Chase lighting designers took full advantage. Bits and pieces of giftware items began showing up as unlikely components of various lamp offerings. The "MINERVA" vase, #03012 became, rightside up, the body of the "PARTHENON" lamp, #6138, and, upside down, that of the "REGENT," #6137. The "SALEM CANDLESTICK" base, #16008, sans finger ring, was the base of a host of Colonial-themed lamps such as the "BREWSTER," #6179. The bases of the "FARMERS' LANTERN" (#25006 battery #25007 wired), the "BINNACLE LIGHT" (#25001 battery, #25002 wired) and the "BOMB FLASHLIGHT," #22001, are identical. The "BACCHUS GOBLET," #90032, lent its base design to that of the "CONSTELLATION LAMP," #17048, with a "BACCHUS" base pair forming the body of the "CLIPPER" lamp, #6191. "BACCHUS" designer Ruth Gerth, no slouch herself when it came to creative ingenuity, would be proud.

Blending their individual talents under one banner, the Chase designers turned out a lamp inventory unmatched for its range and inventiveness. It was an illuminating achievement that, today, still casts its sunny beam.

> *"Printed words can express but part of the feeling that the designer etches so deeply in his work. On a blank sheet of paper grows line by line with accurate assurance, a reality that speaks his message as thousands of word phrases never could."*
>
> Lurelle Guild
> Chase Lighting Fixtures catalog, 1934

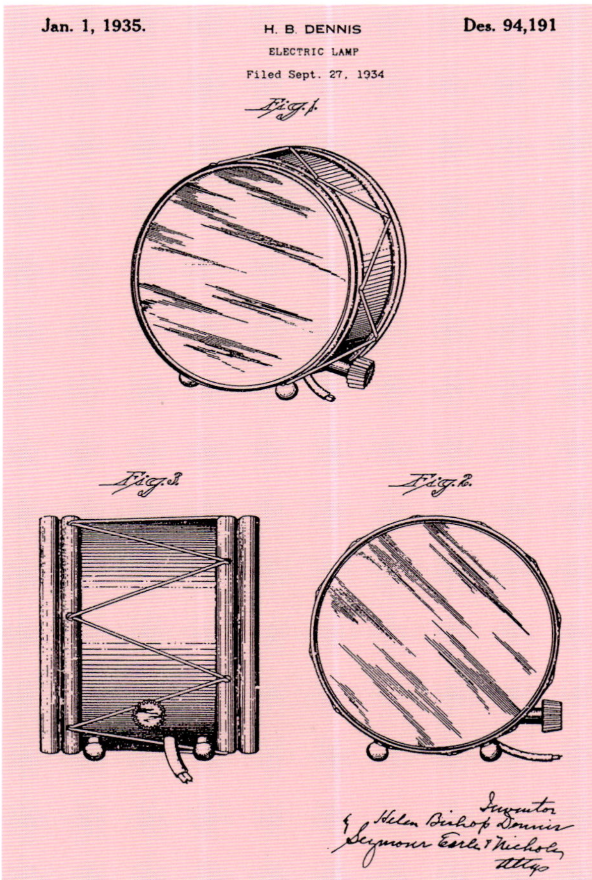

Top left: A design with longevity, Helen Bishop Dennis' military drum appeared in various permutations over the years. This, the "DRUM LAMP," #01010, made its debut in 1935. Soft diffused light came through the frosted glass "drum heads" of this novelty, designed for use as a night light. 3-1/4" deep. *Photo by Dale Endter. Courtesy of Barbara Endter*.

Bottom left: Helen Bishop Dennis' patent for the "DRUM LAMP," granted January 1, 1935.

Top right: A staple of the Chase lamp line, Ruth Gerth's "GLOW LAMP," #01001, appeared in every catalog from pre-1933 through 1941. The innovative Gerth used a toilet float from the Chase plumbing inventory for the lamp base. 8-1/4" h. *Courtesy of Danny Kaplan*

Bottom right: Among Harry Laylon's many designs for Chase was the "MASTHEAD LANTERN," #25008. Laylon joined Chase in 1933, serving as Director of Design from 1937-1940. The "MASTHEAD" was billed as ideal for "recreation room, bar, hallway, boy's room or porch." 8-5/8" h.

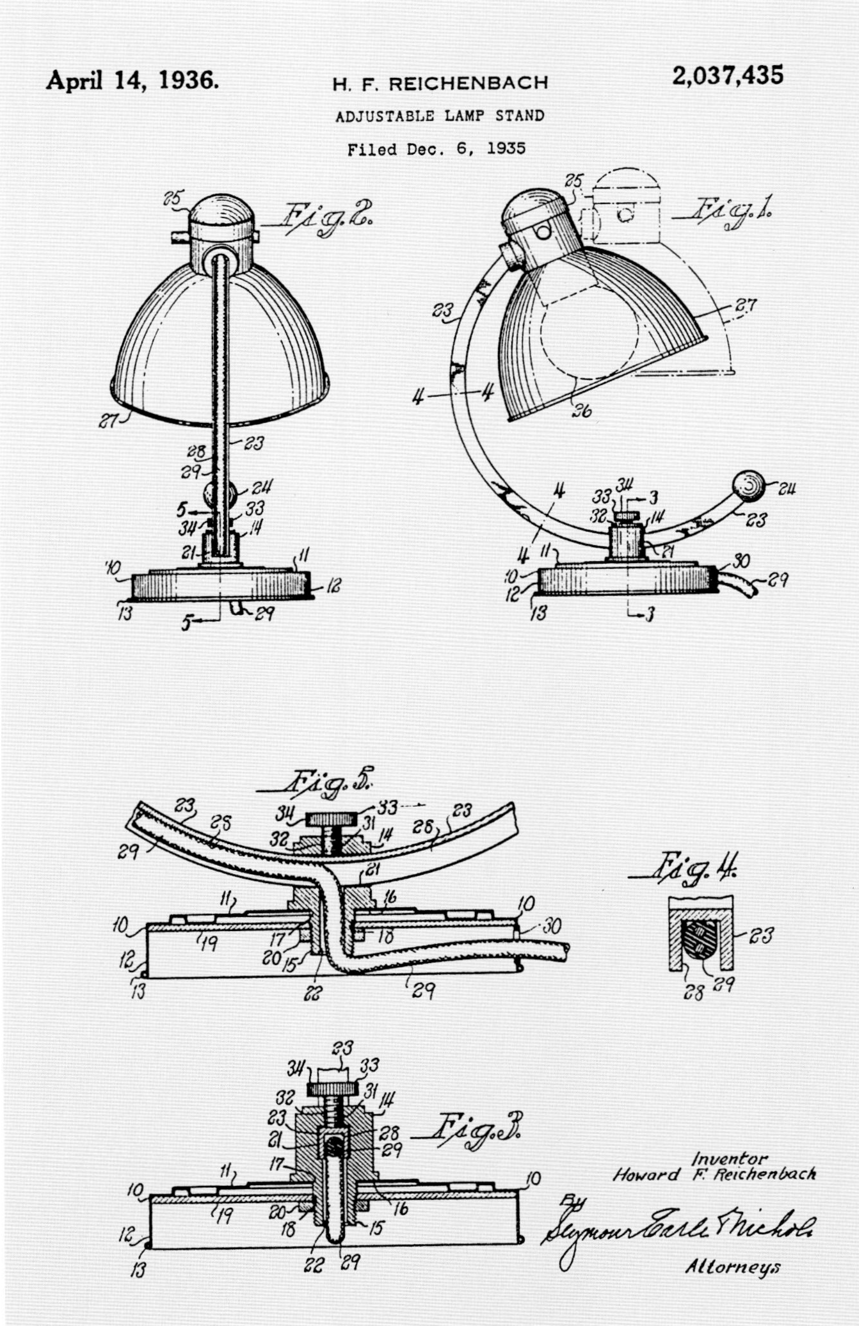

Above: Perhaps named in honor of its zooming tail, the "COMET," #6151, designed by Howard Reichenbach, appeared in the 1939 and 1940 Chase catalogs. A novel feature of this dual-purpose lamp was that the half-circle bracket could be moved, allowing the light to shine at any desired angle. 8-1/2" h. *Courtesy of Stephen and Joanne Klender*

Left: Patent for the "COMET," awarded to Reichenbach on April 14, 1936.

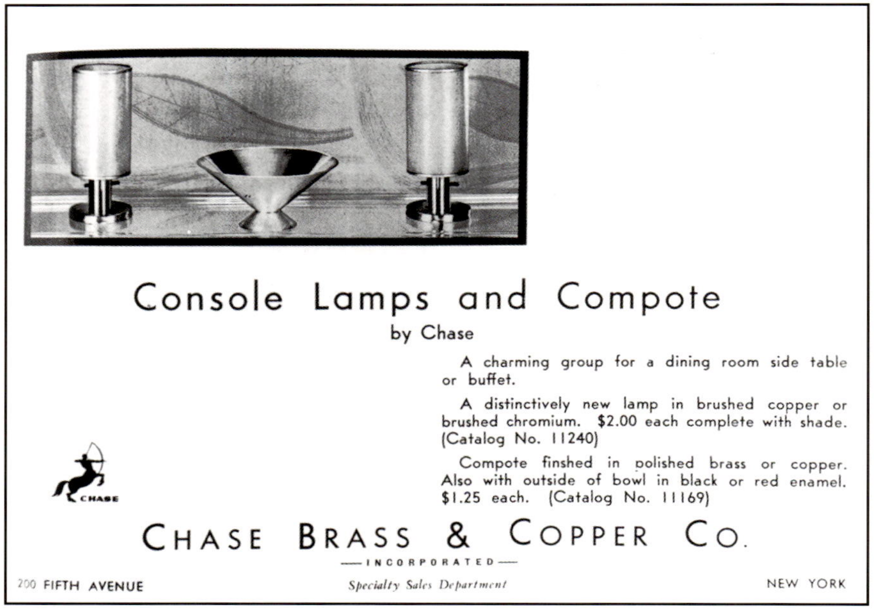

An early Chase design by Walter Von Nessen, #11240, the "CONSOLE LAMP," available in "brushed copper or brushed chromium." Also shown is Von Nessen's "COMPOTE UNUSUALE," #11169. This ad for both appeared in the May 1931 issue of *The Gift And Art Shop*.

Detail, "THE LAMP" stem.

Earliest of the Chase "curved stem" lamps is Von Nessen's "THE LAMP," #NS-597. *Photo courtesy of Gary M. Piper*

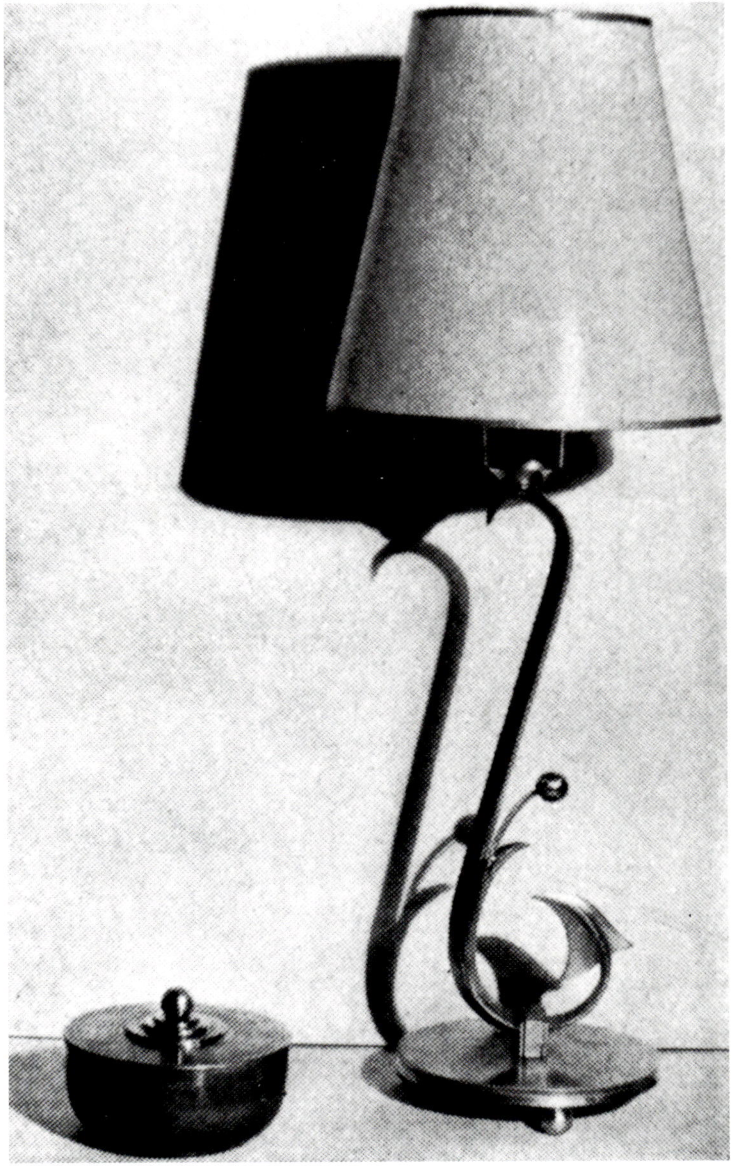

"THE LAMP" appeared in this September 1930 photo from *The Gift And Art Shop*. Also shown: Von Nessen's "CANDY JAR," #NS-316.

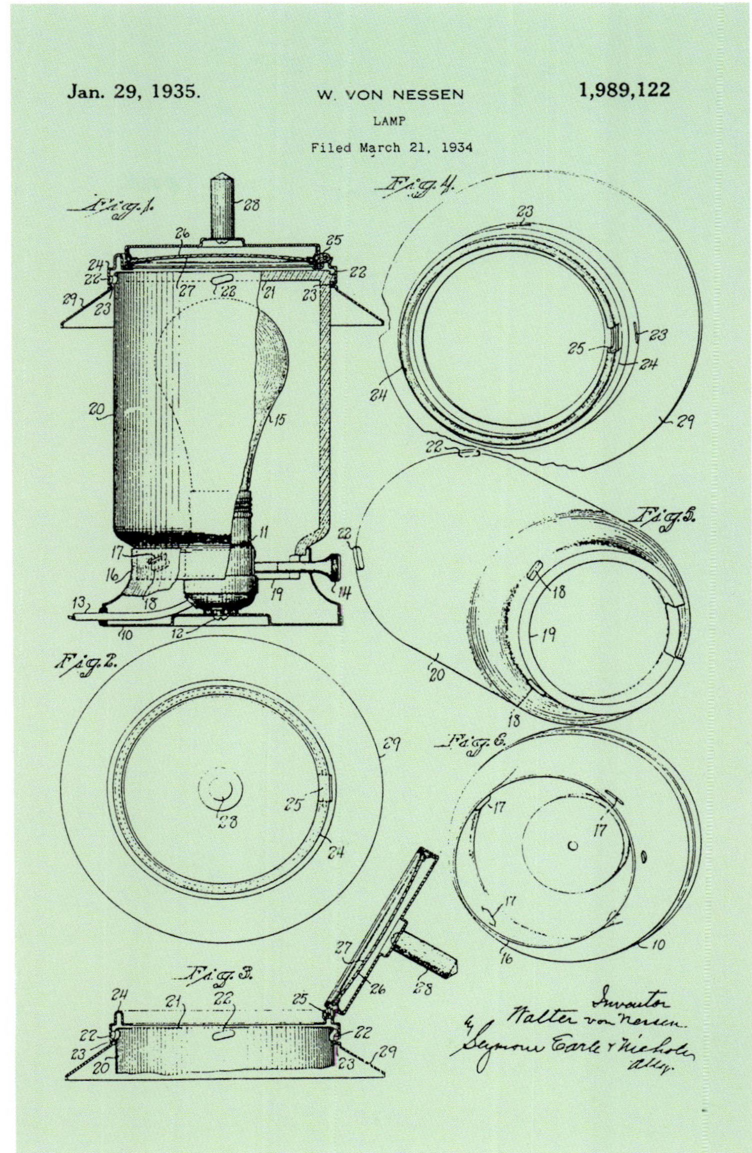

January 29, 1935 patent for an as-yet unidentified Von Nessen Chase lamp.

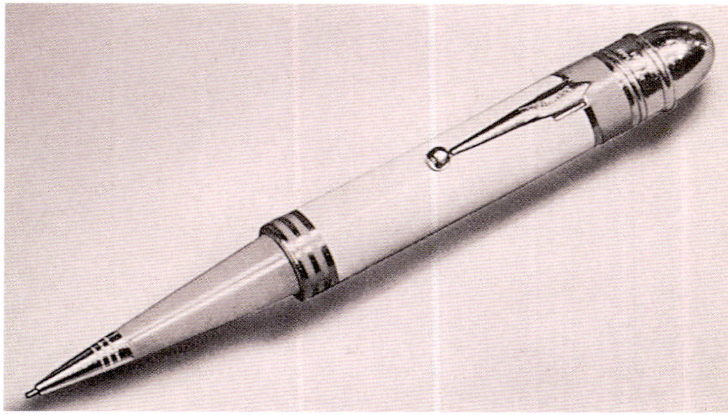

Top: "Invaluable for writing at night!" The "ILLUMINATED PENCIL," #9012, designed by John E. King and Randal L. Hale. 5-5/8" l.

Bottom: August Mitchell's "AIRALITE" flashlight, #22003, billed as "a smart and handy companion." 2" h. x 2-1/2" w.

Adolph Recker's "BINNACLE LIGHT" in its battery version, #25001. This spiffy nautical design was also available in a wired rendition, #25002. Special glass globes were produced for the 1933-24 Chicago World's Fair, the "Century of Progress International Exposition." 5-1/2" h. *Courtesy of Chuck and Kim Zuccarini.*

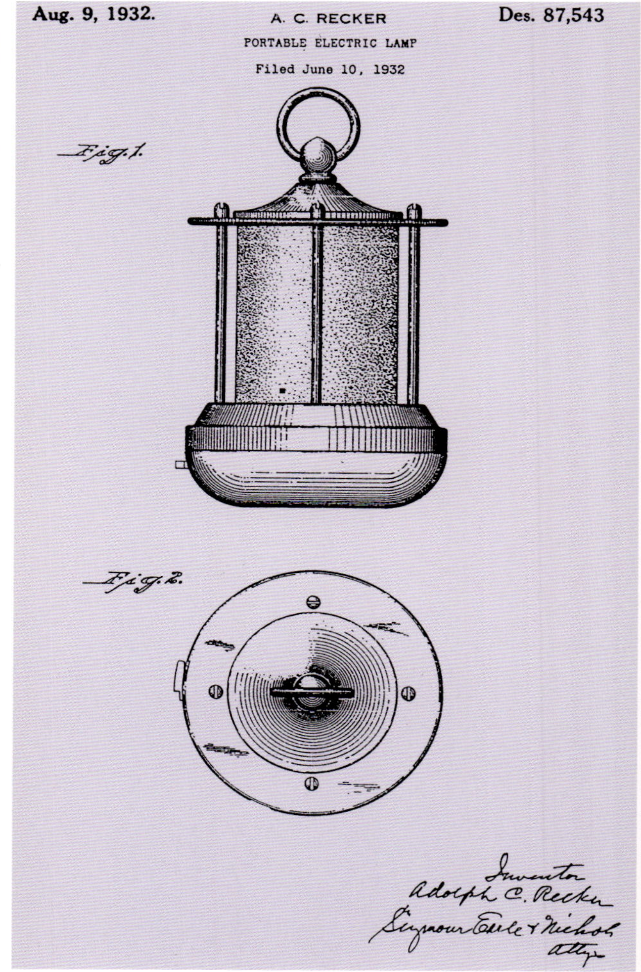

August 9, 1932 patent for the "BINNACLE LIGHT."

The "MINERVA VASE," #03012, in its original incarnation. *Courtesy of H. James Pierce*

The "MINERVA VASE" put to a different use. Down, it's the "REGENT," #6137, 18" h. Rightside up, it's the "PARTHENON," #6318, 18-1/4" h. *Courtesy of John and Donna Thorpe*

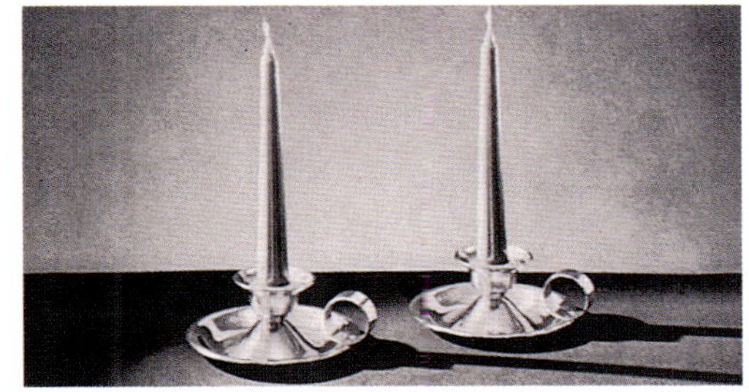

Top: A journey back to colonial days: #16008, "SALEM CANDLESTICKS," 2-1/4" h.

Bottom: The "SALEM," minus its finger ring, re-emerges as the base of the "BREWSTER," #6179.

Top left: The "BOMB FLASH-LIGHT," #22001: slip it over the wrist, hang it from a hook—or use it for a lamp base! 3-1/2" d. *Courtesy of Chuck and Kim Zuccarini*

Bottom left: The "BOMB" revisited, as the base of the "FARMERS' LANTERN" (#25006 battery, #25007 wired). 5-1/2" h. *Courtesy of John and Donna Thorpe*

Top right: "A grand glass to toast with!" Ruth Gerth's "BACCHUS GOBLET," #90032. 6" h.

Bottom right: Also a grand glass to make a lamp out of: Two "BACCHUS" bases lashed together with rope form the "CLIPPER," #6191. 15-1/4" h.

Chapter 3

"Blazing A New Path: Through-Design at Chase"

"Harmonious arrangement is the foundation for all good decorative schemes and one of the most important rules of successful interior decoration."

Lurelle Guild
Designed for Living

But what exactly was meant by "harmonious arrangement"? If you don't know the rules, you can't play the game—or purchase the product. For Chase, Lurelle Guild pioneered the concept of "through-designed" lighting. His lamps and fixtures focused on specific design periods, with the intent that the home decorator would purchase complete "sets" in whatever period best suited the existing decor (or captured the buyer's fancy). Available periods included: "Early English" (fixtures only); "Early American/Colonial;" "Federal;" "Georgian;" "Empire;" "Classic Modern;" and "American Adaptations." For the 1937 Fixtures catalog, a new category, "Neo Classic," was included, then quickly dropped the following year, with its remaining fixtures grouped under "Classic Modern."

But what of the design-impaired homeowner? If consumers were expected to "buy Federal," for instance, they needed to know exactly which specific design features that period encompassed. The Chase catalogs happily obliged, with informative essays covering the salient points of each style. The following excerpts from the 1934 and 1937 catalogs indicate how Chase made the buyer's life just a bit easier. They are as informative now (and as much fun to read), as they must have been then:

Early English

"The mode of living in the Jacobean period, as expressed by the spacious houses and stately furnishings of those historical days, reflects the life and manners of Early England as perfectly as our own modern homes reflect our life today. While Jacobean houses were of generous proportions and solidly constructed of brick, stone, and seasoned timbers, the rooms in these hospitable homes of 17th Century England were most livable. Walls were symmetrically paneled in rich oak—the beautifully ornamented plaster ceilings reflecting the warm glow of candle light from handsome wall brackets and splendid ceiling fixtures of gleaming brass, bronze, or polished iron.

"In keeping with the period, Chase has created a group of Early English Lighting Fixtures which are true to the traditions of 17th Century craftsmanship. In basic design they are faithful copies of Jacobean original forms, their purity being apparent in every fixture, from the sweep of candle arms to the careful modeling of top and bottom finials.

"Since the early English metalworkers created most frequently in iron, Chase presents its reproductions in half-polished iron and also in black iron. These finishes, of course, are applied to solid Chase brass which is the base metal of all Chase Lighting. Equally interesting in many Early English Fixtures is the combination of an English bronze finish with a wrought iron finish. This use of two metal finishes in combination is a refreshing theme which lends 'color' to Chase Early English Fixtures, giving them a rich and distinctive character often seen in armor, plateware, and other forms of the early metalworkers' art."

Left: A representative from the Chase "Early English" grouping: #J 721, "THE RISING SUN." The catalog description notes that 'the rollicking face of Old Sol gives this wall bracket a jovial personality. 11" h.
Courtesy of John and Donna Thorpe

Right: Detail, Old Sol's rollicking face.

Early American/Colonial

From 1937's "Early American and Colonial" selections, #1242, "FIVE-LIGHT CEILING FIXTURE." 36" overall length. *Courtesy of John and Donna Thorpe*

Above left: Another Early American design, "THE WITCH LIGHT SCONCE," # C 025. Bull's eye glass panes were originally used in the doorways of Puritan homes, and as used here give this sconce its name. The "WITCH LIGHT" was available in characteristic colonial colors: "barn red," "corn yellow," and "laurel green." 12" h.

Above center: Original Chase hang tag from the "WITCH LIGHT."

Above right: Tag reverse. *"WITCH LIGHT" photos courtesy of John and Donna Thorpe*

Left: The same thing in assorted sizes: three Chase lamps with a Colonial theme. #6192 "THE CHATHAM," 21-3/4" h.; #6179 "THE BREWSTER," 17-1/4" h.; #6168 "THE LENOX," 12" h.

"Beginning in 1620 with the settling of Plymouth by the Pilgrims, this period prevailed for over one hundred years, contributing quaint and native charm to the furniture, homes, lamps and lighting fixtures of our ancestors. The early settlers, fighting for every inch of soil, found little opportunity for creative craftsmanship. Limited by their crude tools and lack of materials, the furniture, fixtures, and hardware which they fashioned were necessarily simple in construction and of severe design. Later, when homes were somewhat established, the craftsmen started to produce in wood, metals, and glass, those priceless heritages which are ours today.

"In presenting a complete group of authentic Early American Lamps and Fixtures, Chase has hewed to the line of authentic reproduction-faithfully duplicating in every detail the native beauty of the sconces, lanterns, and chandeliers of pre-Revolutionary days. Included in the Chase Early American Fixtures group are an unusual number of lanterns—and rightly so, for lanterns were widely used by the early colonists. Particularly noticeable in several Chase Early American Fixtures is the use of color. Nearly all of the original sconces and ceiling fixtures were made of tin, and at a later date were painted—Barn Red, Corn Yellow, and Laurel Green being the favorite colors. Many superb effects are achieved in the use of the colors on Early American Fixtures—a decorative effect which Chase is first to create.

"Chase Early American Lamps offer today's homeowner a wide variety: the quaint 'BARNETT' lamp for a desk in the living room is also an ideal reading lamp—the 'GLOUCESTER,' reminiscent of whaling days—the 'MT. VERNON' lamp of more stately years. The Chase group of Early American Lamps is exceptionally well balanced, ranging from the more primitive candle lamps, authentically finished in tin or pewter, to lamps of later and more affluent days. Authentic lamps and fixtures for homes of the Colonial period will be warmly welcomed by both homeowners and decorator."

Federal

"Occasionally called 'Jeffersonian' and sometimes 'Late Colonial,' the Federal period occupied the years immediately following the American Revolution, continuing as late as 1830. It is generally accepted as the most elegant era that ever graced this country. Architecture and interior decoration reflected the vogue for classic simplicity which the Georgian designers, notably Adam, Hepplewhite, and Sheraton, were popularizing abroad. This style, as interpreted in America by Duncan Phyfe and other cabinet makers of the Federal era, produced a distinct American period of design which for sheer loveliness is the peer of any style ever produced.

"To the simplicity of pre-revolutionary interiors, the symbols of the Republic were soon added. Notable among them was the American eagle, emblematic of Washington's inauguration. Stars, equally symbolic of the young Republic, lent charm to the furnishings of the era.

"Bold and vibrant, in design and finish, Chase Federal Lamps and Fixtures authentically reflect the splendor and spirit of those days. In their precision and clean-cut crispness they will be welcomed as thoroughly companionable to the furnishings and decorations of the Federal era. Also welcome will be the wide range of shapes, styles, and finishes in this Federal group, among them circular, octagonal, and lyre-shaped brackets, the decorations including plaques, urns, stars, arrows, statuettes, and the American Eagle—all used in the most imaginative but thoroughly authentic manner.

The August 1934 *House Beautiful* urged readers to "picture these lovely Federal Fixtures and Lamps in your home." Illustrator Edward A. Wilson, "artist of note and authority on Colonial interiors," evidently did!

"The gracious dignity and simplicity of pure Federal design:" #F 101 "THE JEFFERSON." 9-1/2" h. *Courtesy of John and Donna Thorpe*

"In color, Chase Federal Lamps and Fixtures make available for the first time the striking decorative effects which have heretofore been limited to the most expensive custom-made items. In one exceptionally beautiful Federal bracket, Chase has combined dull silver with black; in another, Federal brass with dark blue glass. Two lamps, with their tinkling crystal prisms, are exquisite examples of Federal decoration. As decorations, each Lamp and Fixture lends color and charm to a room even when not illuminated."

Companion to "THE JEFFERSON," # F 120 "THE RICHMOND." 45" overall height; 12-1/2" h. fixture. *Courtesy of John and Donna Thorpe*

Inspired by a time when "iron men and wooden ships rode the waves," Federal lamp #F 134 "THE JOHN PAUL JONES" comes complete with a figure of the "Father of The American Navy, modeled exactly from contemporary engravings." The plaque depicts a famous sea battle, and the base is "draped with the garlands of glory." The Jones figurine reappeared in 1976, as a special statuette released in honor of the Chase Forging division's 100th anniversary. 21" h. *Courtesy of John and Donna Thorpe*

Georgian

"The Georgian period, often called the 'Age of Mahogany,' held sway throughout the 18th century. From 1714 on, three Georges in succession occupied the throne of England, and from them this period takes its name. In the field of furniture and decoration, the Georgian Period is unique. No period ever was popular so long, or had so many great designers contributing to it.

"The Georgian period in America was simply a transfer of the English style of the Georges to America, where it became popular after 1760. The styles and designs of Thomas Chippendale, the foremost designer of the middle Georgian Period, were as popular here as they were abroad, and Philadelphia, the center of cabinet making, produced exquisite copies of his designs. Chippendale's styles show the successive influence of French, Chinese, and Gothic forms. Homes that favored Chippendale furniture were filled with everything to enhance their elegance. The furniture was rich, with sumptuous carving and beautiful veneered surfaces.

"Suddenly, England turned from its ornate interiors, and in the late Georgian period a classic revival took place. This style was based on the ancient classic simplicity of Greece and Rome. It was inspired by the Brothers Adam, and they were followed by Hepplewhite and Sheraton.

"The entire Georgian period expressed a dignified, well-bred order of existence which is exquisitely reflected in the lovely designs of Chase Georgian Lamps and Lighting Fixtures. In their creation, Chase has favored the simpler Georgian designs as more fitting for present day interiors than the ornate combinations of gilt, silver, and glass, which characterized earlier Georgian design.

"In their superb finishes, Chase Georgian Lamps and Fixtures reflect the successive changes that came about at the hands of the various designers. While most of them follow the Georgian taste in the use of plain metal, or metal and glass, several of the wall brackets and lamps in this group are charming in Regent red, Adam green, or silver combined with Georgian brass. Color was used with exquisite taste by nearly all the Georgian designers for inlay and painted decoration, and Chase therefore applies color where appropriate.

"Chase Lamps and Fixtures are rich in the details that make Georgian interiors and design so pleasing. Authentically patterned after the original decorations of the famous craftsmen, Chase makes use of shells, urns, fretwork, flame finials, leaves and swag decoration, thus giving them a character and individuality that is distinctly 'in period.' One lamp is given great distinction by the use of genuine Wedgwood plaques which are inset in its base.

"Made of lasting Chase brass, these Lamps and Fixtures will endure for generations, and, because they originate from authentic forms, will always be 'in style.'"

Chase "Georgian" fixtures and lamps are featured in this ad from the September 1934 issue of *House Beautiful*. Consumers were informed that, thanks to Chase, they were no longer doomed to put up with "ugly, old-fashioned fixtures, simply because nice looking ones at reasonable prices were impossible to find." The illustration is by American artist Allen Saalburg.

Empire

"The French Empire and our own Federal period have much in common, in that both were expressive of a new-won liberty and independence. In America, Federal followed the birth of the young and victorious Federal government. In France, the Empire period, known at first as Directoire, was deliberately created as a new style of national art by no less a person than Napoleon. In America, the Empire period gradually supplanted the Federal period, and influenced furniture design and decoration in this country as late as 1850.

"The designers of the day adopted for their inspiration the classic forms of Greece and Ancient Rome, adding the patriotic and militaristic symbols expressive of the new French nation. Later, as Napoleon's military successes multiplied, the style, influenced by his desire to emulate the Caesars, became imperial and regal. Thus, French furniture and furnishings became richly decorated with the symbols of conquest. Shields, bundles of arrows, the Imperial Star, the Torch of Freedom, and the Victor's Wreath of Laurel adorned everything from mantelpieces to lighting fixtures and lamps.

"The variety of finishes provided in the Chase Empire group is characteristic of the decorative traditions of the period—ranging from chastely designed lamps and wall brackets, finished in Empire brass, to painted tole fixtures that exactly copy the painted chandeliers, wall lights, and lamps of that period. Chase offers the lovely tole designs in either Republic Red, Corsican Green, or Directoire White, with decorations of Empire gold. Other Chase Lamps, in Empire brass and black, complete a group that is exceedingly varied in its offering of distinctive period forms.

"Deserving especial mention are three of the many charming wall brackets in the Empire group. They are distinguished by the use of gun-metal mirrors framed by drapery swag or laurel leaf designs, and are cited as fine examples of the formal decorative effects achieved by the classic French school.

"As the Federal and Empire periods were rather closely related in spirit and character, quite a few Chase Federal Lamps and Fixtures are thoroughly correct for Empire interiors—examples being those which are characterized by the star, arrow, laurel leaf, or lyre decorations."

From *House Beautiful*'s October 1934 issue: an "Empire"-themed room, with Chase lamps and lighting fixtures available "for only $6.37 a month!" Depression-strapped consumers were invited to write for details on the "Chase Refixturing Partial Payment Plan."

Lurelle Guild's exquisite Empire fixture, "THE ELBA," # E 323. A "Victor's Wreath of Laurel" frames the circular gunmetal mirror. 11-3/4" h. *Courtesy of John and Donna Thorpe*

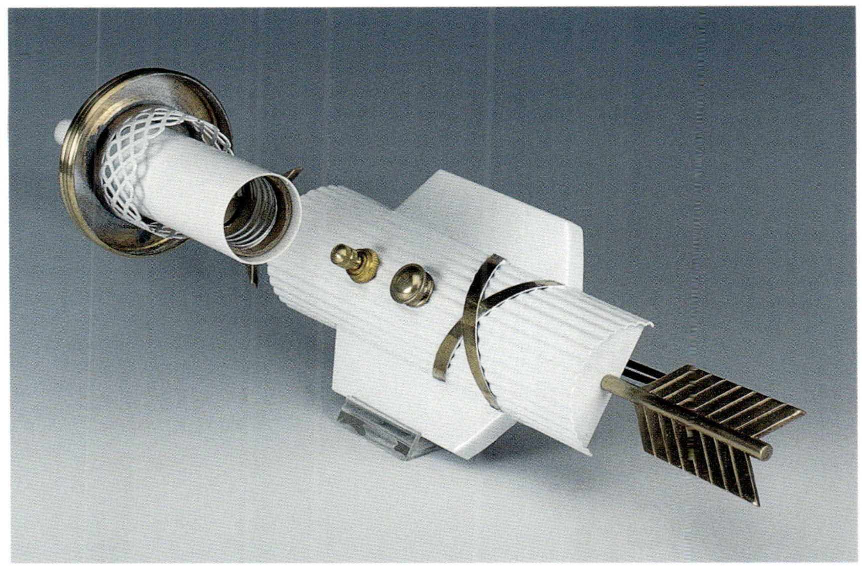

Top: Original Guild design sketch for "THE ELBA."

Bottom: Also in the Empire style, #1664 "ONE-LIGHT BRACKET." The alternate finish for this fixture was pewter and gold. 14" h. *Courtesy of John and Donna Thorpe*

Classic Modern

"In the opinion of many leading architects and decorators, no school of design expresses the spirit of the 20th Century with such exquisite taste as does Classic Modern. This new, and decidedly growing, period of decoration is in reality a successful blending of the classical forms which glorified the architecture of ancient Greece and Rome, with the functional designs of present-day furniture and furnishings.

"Nowhere in the field of design is the Classic Modern style more impressive than in lighting. Under the hand of the modern designer, electricity is not restricted to traditional forms. It becomes dramatic, appearing in designs that are unusually beautiful in proportion, and superb in their classic simplicity.

"The need for Classic Modern lamps and lighting fixtures has long been acute, principally because neither the mechanically severe nor ornate designs which have been available found favor in American homes. Few fixtures fill the function for which they were planned as well as Chase Classic Modern Lighting. Shielded by frosted and sandblasted glass, the illumination is scientifically diffused in a manner as pleasing to the appearance of the room as it is comfortable to the eye. In many fixtures, chromium reflectors intensify the light, directing it so that the light beams become decorative. Reflecting the last word in Classic Modern styling, Chase Fixtures are handsomely finished in either satin chromium or polished chromium. The combination of these brilliant finishes with frosted glass gives Chase Fixtures a decorative character which exquisitely reflects the spirit of modern interiors.

"Chase Classic Modern Lamps are finished in polished chromium, combined in certain cases with frosted glass discs, Royal blue glass, and crystal. Particularly welcome will be several lamps which have been scaled to suit the requirements of the dressing table and bedside table, for most modern lamps are too large for such use. In these scaled lamps, the spread of the arms and the flare of the shades have been carefully considered, so as to use a minimum of space, and yet provide a maximum of carefully shaded light.

"Chase Fixtures and Lamps are rich in the decorative details that make the Classic expression so pleasing a form of modern design. Original classic designs, such as the acanthus leaf, urn, swag, reeded column, arrow, and flame finial give these products a character and individuality that is not only Classic Modern, but essentially different from any designs yet offered in residential lighting.

"Chase Lighting offers types of Fixtures and Lamps to fit every room, every decorative scheme in the Classic Modern manner—each in perfect harmony with its companions, and each in harmony with its setting."

Left: Designed for "Classic Modern" interiors, # M 646 "THE PLANETARIUM." "Inspiration for the design of this beautiful and symbolic fixture came from an old astrolabe, or globe, mapping the position of the heavenly bodies, made about the year 1750." Clear glass stars dot the frosted glass globe. 45" overall height; fixture, 16-1/4" h., 13" d. *Photo by Jacqueline Jones-Ridge. Courtesy of Gary M. Piper*

Above: An "Armstrong's Linoleum Floors" advertisement, from the December 1936 issue of *Ladies' Home Journal*. "THE PLANETARIUM" hangs above the tub, with # M 529 "THE IMPERATOR" lighting the sink area, for a truly out-of-this-world effect!

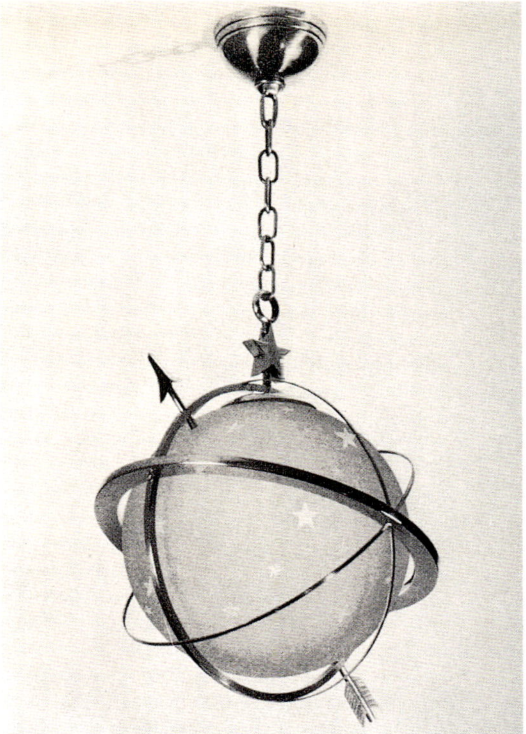

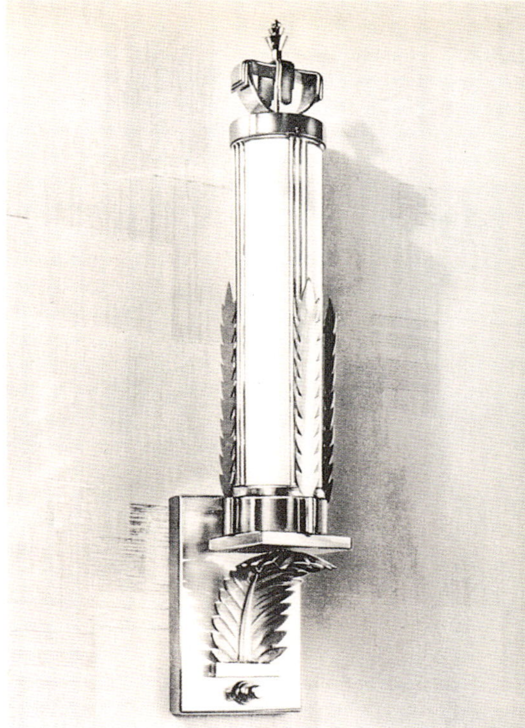

Top left: 1934 Lighting Fixtures catalog photo, "THE PLANETARIUM."

Top right: Also from the 1934 catalog, "THE IMPERATOR."

Bottom left: Another striking wall bracket from 1934, # M 523 "THE TROY." The Imperial leaf design is carved in the frosted glass. 11-1/2" h.

Bottom center: Ancient sea symbols render # M 534 "THE THESSALY," "particularly harmonious for the bath." A Greek wave design is etched on the circular plate glass disc, and the "shell" is finished in polished chromium. 7" h. x 7" w.

Bottom right: Another example of Classic Modern styling, # M 545 "THE AURORA," which incorporates elements of Georgian design. The six half circles of plate glass are etched with a lotus pattern, and arranged around a central frosted glass column. 45" overall height; 16" fixture height.

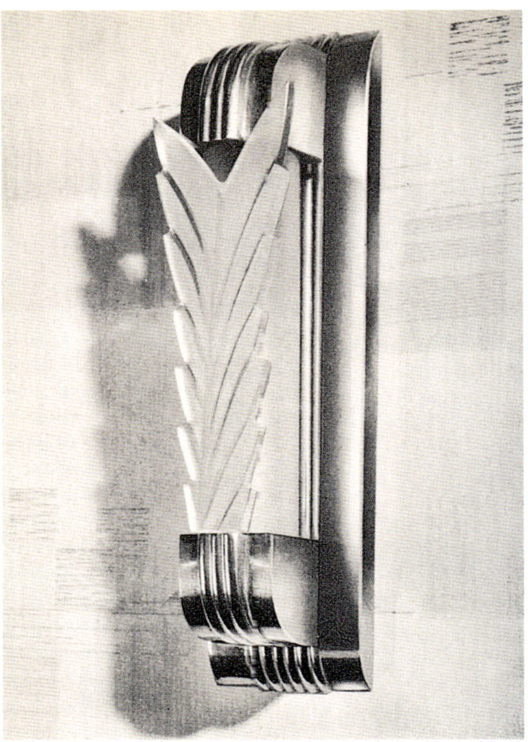

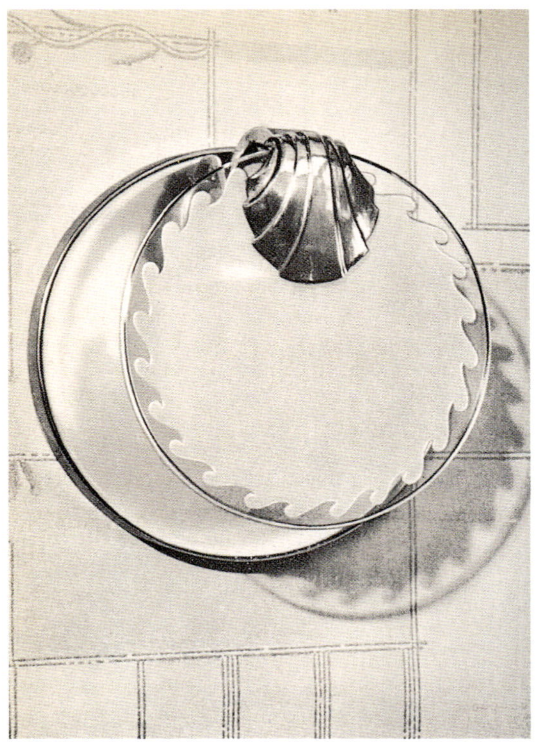

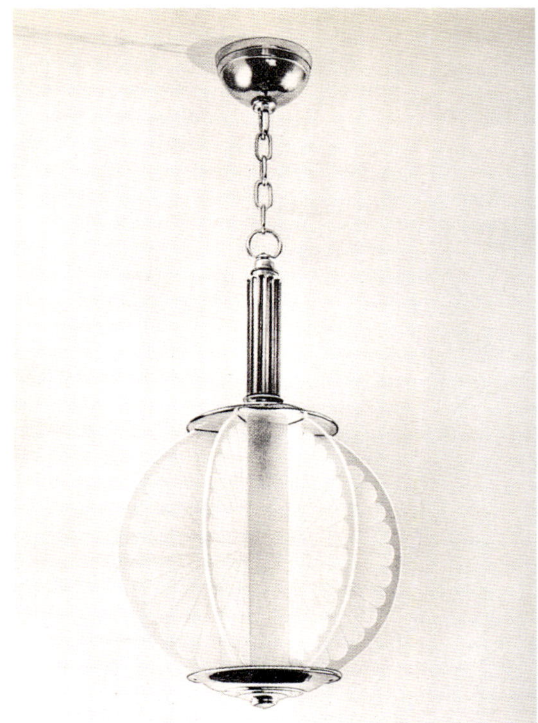

Neo Classic (1937 Fixtures only)

Making a brief appearance in the 1937 Lighting Fixtures catalog were "Neo Classic" fixtures. By 1938, this "successful blending of Ancient and Modern motifs" had itself been blended into the "Classic Modern" category.

"Neo Classic, or Modern style, although new, is decidedly growing in use. In reality, it is a successful blending of Ancient and Modern motifs. In presenting our Neo Classic designs, we offer ensembles of beautifully decorated and original looking wall brackets and ceiling fixtures that have a modern feeling and inspiration which makes them very striking. Unusual workmanship is apparent in every fixture, as is the excellent quality of materials, for we use nothing but the finest glass, and only lasting Chase Brass as the basic material.

"Each Chase Neo Classic design features cut glass chimneys and crystal trim. Available finishes are an equally elegant Bone White and Gold or Pewter and Gold."

American Adaptations

"Chase American Adaptations are primarily designed for the home that does not require lamps and fixtures of any particular period, yet deserves products of good design, reliable finish, materials, and workmanship, at reasonable prices. The Chase American Adaptations actually fill a great need. Strong, well-constructed, and made of non-rusting Chase brass, they offer unquestioned durability. Of good design, they will not only add to the appearance of any home, but will reflect good taste for many years to come.

"A majority of the Fixtures in the Chase American Adaptations group are styled for the principal rooms in the house—the living room, dining room, and bedroom. For these rooms Chase presents two ensembles of matching ceiling fixtures and wall brackets, each ensemble distinctly different in design, one adapted from Colonial styles while the other is patterned after Federal forms. A comprehensive selection of Fixtures for the smaller rooms of the home is also included. These represent the highest quality to be found among utility fixtures, many being finished in a choice of chromium, white enamel, or brass.

"In the Lamps of this group may be seen the work of several of the country's leading designers, who have given each design a character all its own—a character that depends upon the expression of the designer's idea rather than on period form. This group, therefore, is composed of exceptionally interesting and unusual designs seldom found in the field of residential lighting. The lamps have a wide range of finishes—polished chromium, satin chromium, copper, brass, English bronze, black enamel and white enamel—some of them applied singly but often in combination with other finishes.

"Decidedly inexpensive, when compared with products of similar style and price, Chase American Adaptations have a beauty that is far from being merely surface deep. Each one reflects such good taste that by day or night they will add decorative charm to any interior with which they are in harmony."

An example of a Chase "American Adaptation" ("exceptionally reasonable in price"), #A 1171 "THE CORNWALL." 45" overall height; 17" fixture height. *Courtesy of John and Donna Thorpe*

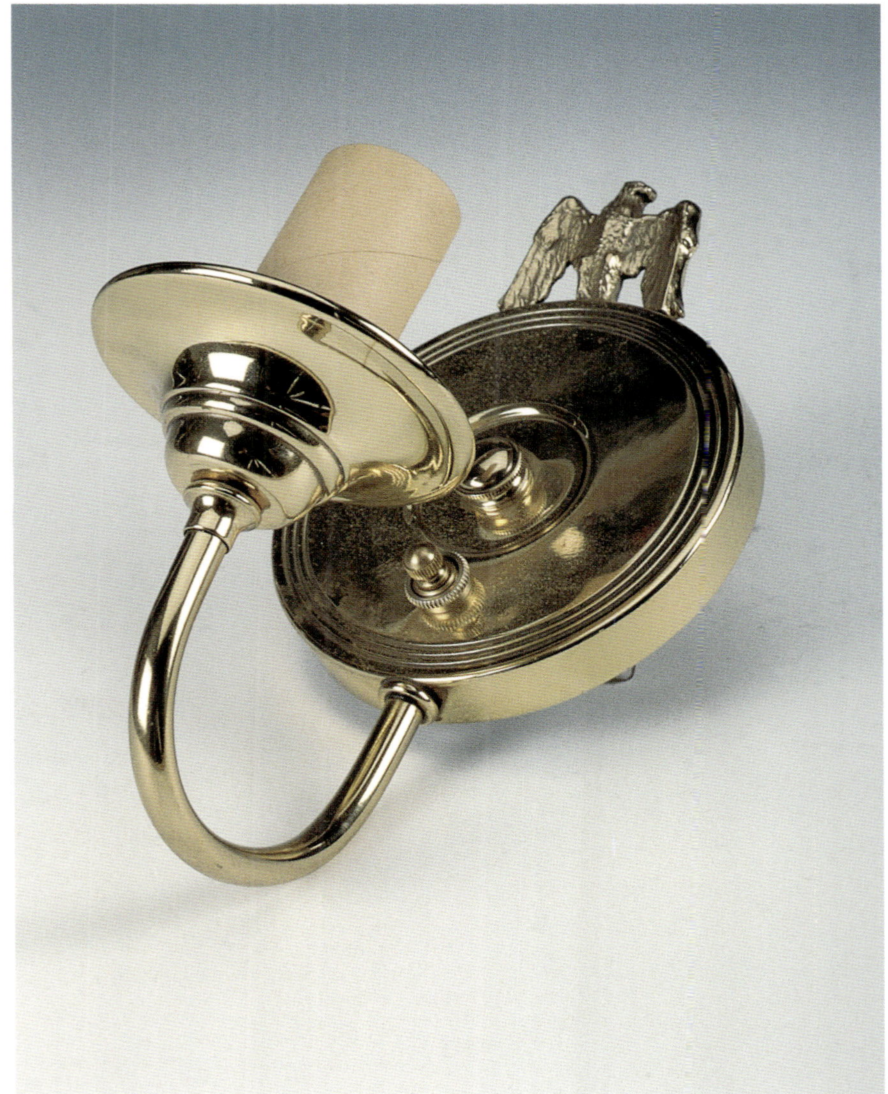

This American Adaptation, #A 1104 "THE FAIRFIELD," has "a simple dignity that gives it appropriate charm for living room, dining room or bedroom." 7-7/8" h. *Courtesy of John and Donna Thorpe*

Out of the shadows

While never officially promoted as specific design categories, two additional themes pop up with enough regularity in the Chase inventory to merit individual analysis. "Nautical" lamps were so prevalent—from the "ANCHOR" and the "BARNEGAT" to the "WINDJAMMER" and the "WHEEL"—that one can only marvel at the ability of the Chase copywriters to dredge up enough seaworthy terms to describe them, without being washed overboard in a flood of repetition. Equally popular were the "Novelty" lamps—quaint "COLONELS," "DRUMS," and "CONSTELLATIONS," destined, no doubt, for a career in the nursery or playroom. An oddly appealing combination of both genres was 1934's "THE FLYING CLOUD LAMP," #A 601. A central globe of green antique blown glass, modeled after the style of an old fishing-net ball, was topped with a small replica of the famed "Flying Cloud" clipper ship, sailing merrily in perpetuity around the lamp's perimeter. A definite must for the home that does "not require period styles."

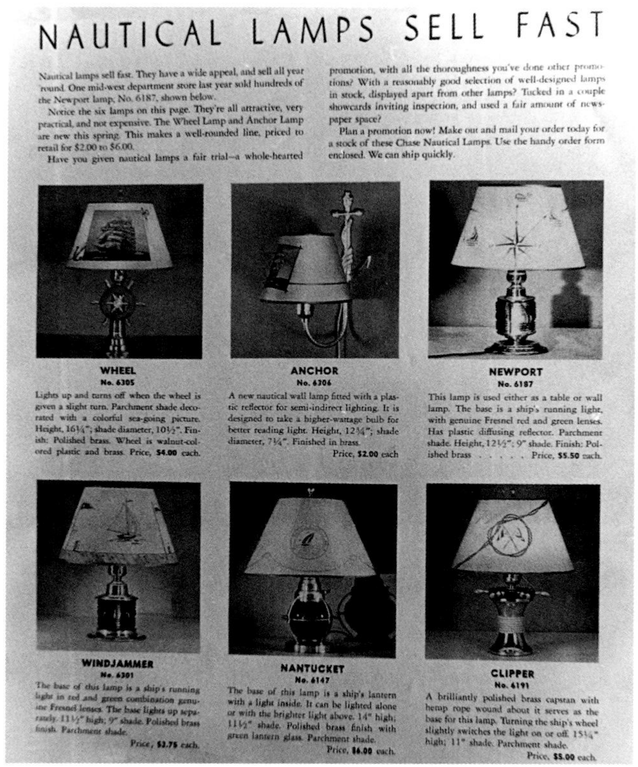

NAUTICAL LAMPS SELL FAST

Nautical lamps sell fast. They have a wide appeal, and sell all year 'round. One mid-west department store last year sold hundreds of the Newport lamp, No. 6187, shown below.

Notice the six lamps on this page. They're all attractive, very practical, and not expensive. The Wheel Lamp and Anchor Lamp are new this spring. This makes a well-rounded line, priced to retail for $2.00 to $6.00.

Have you given nautical lamps a fair trial—a whole-hearted promotion, with all the thoroughness you've done other promotions? With a reasonably good selection of well-designed lamps in stock, displayed apart from other lamps? Tucked in a couple showcards inviting inspection, and used a fair amount of newspaper space?

Plan a promotion now! Make out and mail your order today for a stock of these Chase Nautical Lamps. Use the handy order form enclosed. We can ship quickly.

WHEEL
No. 6305
Lights up and turns off when the wheel is given a slight turn. Parchment shade decorated with a colorful sea-going picture. Height, 16¼"; shade diameter, 10½". Finish: Polished brass. Wheel is walnut-colored plastic and brass. Price, **$4.00** each.

ANCHOR
No. 6306
A new nautical wall lamp fitted with a plastic reflector for semi-indirect lighting. It is designed to take a higher-wattage bulb for better reading light. Height, 12¾"; shade diameter, 7¼". Finished in brass. Price, **$2.00** each

NEWPORT
No. 6187
This lamp is used either as a table or wall lamp. The base is a ship's running light, with genuine Fresnel red and green lenses. Has plastic diffusing reflector. Parchment shade. Height, 12½"; 9" shade. Finish: Polished brass . . . . . Price, **$5.50** each.

WINDJAMMER
No. 6301
The base of this lamp is a ship's running light in red and green combination genuine Fresnel lenses. The base lights up separately. 11½" high; 9" shade. Polished brass finish. Parchment shade. Price, **$3.75** each.

NANTUCKET
No. 6147
The base of this lamp is a ship's lantern with a light inside. It can be lighted alone or with the brighter light above. 14" high; 11½" shade. Polished brass finish with green lantern glass. Parchment shade. Price, **$6.00** each.

CLIPPER
No. 6191
A brilliantly polished brass capstan with hemp rope wound about it serves as the base for this lamp. Turning the ship's wheel slightly switches the light on or off. 15¼" high; 11" shade. Parchment shade. Price, **$5.00** each.

SAILING, SAILING

NAUTICAL FURNISHINGS
by Chase
for Summer Cottages, Recreation Rooms, Clubs, Boys' Rooms, Bars.

NAUTICAL furnishings are especially popular at this time of the year for decorating summer homes and shore cottages. Marine decorations like anchors, ship's wheels and rope lend a carefree atmosphere to recreation rooms, bars and club rooms. They also make rooms look cooler in summer.

Here is a group of sixteen articles that will make an excellent display in your store window. Group the items as illustrated here and for a background for the display duplicate the attractive sailing drawing above, on a large white cardboard.

Reading, left to right, from the upper left hand corner, the nautical furnishings shown in the picture are as follows:

No.	Name	Retail Price
6305	Wheel Lamp	$4.00
90136	Weathervane	1.00
6310	Masthead Lamp	5.00
6306	Anchor Lamp	2.00
6191	Clipper Lamp	5.00
90142	Davey Jones Book Ends (pair)	2.50
15006	Clipper Bowl	2.00
90138	Pilot Book Ends (pair)	3.50
6301	Windjammer Lamp	3.75
90125	Tarpon Fish Bowl	3.00
90098	Ivy or Fish Bowl	1.00
25008	Masthead Lantern	2.50
6187	Newport Lamp	5.50
885	Riviera Ash Tray	1.50
856	Dolphin Box	.50
884	Whirligig Ash Tray	1.00

Left: Ahoy there! Chase turned out oceans of lamps and other products with a "Nautical." theme. Shown in this ad are #6305 "WHEEL;" #6306 "ANCHOR;" #6187 "NEWPORT;" #6301 "WINDJAMMER;" #6147 "NANTUCKET;" and #6191 "CLIPPER."

Above: And the flood continues! A flyer promoting the 1939 New York World's Fair carried this assortment of "Nautical Furnishings" on the reverse. Retailers were reminded that items with a nautical theme "lend a carefree atmosphere" and "make rooms look cooler in summer"!

When in doubt, call it a "novelty lamp." Among the Chase novelties is this "CONSTELLATION LAMP," #17048, designed by Walter Von Nessen, and introduced in the 1934 catalog. The top tilts in any direction to shade the frosted globe. 8-1/2" h., 7-1/2" d. *Courtesy of H. James Pierce*

Lurelle Guild's illustration of an Early American interior for the 1934 Fixtures catalog. On the desk at right is lamp #A 601, "THE FLYING CLOUD," a captivating Novelty lamp with a Nautical theme. 18" h.

Shifting focus

"While the design of Chase decorative fixtures has been inspired by historic periods of decoration, it is no longer the practice to restrict your choice of lighting fixtures to the same period as your room furnishings. It is realized today that a blending of period styles make a room look less stiff and formal, and more pleasing."

Chase Lighting Fixtures catalog, 1940

A "blending of period styles" was official Chase policy by 1940, but as early as 1937, change was in the air. Reflecting a new and more casual approach to home decor, 1934's detailed stylistic period descriptions, accompanied by their especially commissioned watercolor illustrations, were banished from the 1937 Chase Fixtures catalog. Replacing them were brief explanatory paragraphs (like that on the "Neo Classic" theme, given earlier), partnered with actual photos of Chase fixtures and lamps in model room settings. Function and practicality were now the major selling points, and the period-neutral Chase "Even-Glow" fixtures, (providing "science's best approach to daylight"), received prominent catalog coverage. Also by 1937, "American Adaptations" had vanished entirely as a separate category; its remaining listings were dispersed to such function-specific groupings as "Bathroom Brackets" and "Beam Lights."

"Through-design" had evidently lost its appeal. The 1938 Fixtures catalog lumped the remaining period descriptions together on one page, and the major copy emphasis was on just how interchangeable fixtures and lamps from the varied periods could be:

> You will find, for, example, that practically all the Federal and Georgian fixtures will be equally at home in houses of Colonial design, while a Colonial fixture, although it may be founded in Early American decoration, will look absolutely in keeping in an apartment of the Federal period. In other words, the design of the fixture may originate from Colonial or Empire decoration, but the use of the fixture is distinctly not limited to "period houses."

Whether such "mix-and-match" was a novel design idea, or simply a means of moving slow sellers in the Chase inventory, it was a far remove from Lurelle Guild's original plan: a complete lighting line designed "without violating in any way the traditions of the periods."[1] Still, Guild, the designer-businessman who knew that "beauty alone does not sell," would no doubt have understood the reasoning behind the change of focus—the need for Chase to provide products that *would* sell.

By 1940 the Fixtures catalog had removed almost every period designation. Generic categories ("Even-Glow Fixtures," "Decorative Fixtures," "Fixtures With Colored Glassware," and the like) were the catch-all replacements. The single holdover among the period groupings—"Classic Modern"—was now reborn as the presumably more user-friendly (and patriotic) "Modern American," "especially popular for use with American Modern, Swedish Modern, and other furniture where straight lines predominate." Fixtures were promoted for their suitability to specific rooms of the home ("Dressing Room," "Kitchen," "Entrance"), rather than for thematic compatibility within a single room.

For the remainder of the life of Chase Lighting, the emphasis was on practicality. Although the 1941 Fixtures catalog introduced a section on "Chase Colonial Fixtures," the reasoning behind this was clear-cut: "the great majority of new homes are of Colonial architecture." Overall though, the 1941 catalog stressed component elements as major selling points, from frosted bowls ("hand-cut"), to crystal trim ("the combination of highly polished metal and the sparkle of crystal-clear trimmings give an exquisite grace, delightful charm and splendor"). Even the copywriter's occasional flights of fancy ("the iridescent and amber etched bowls are blended together so delicately that the glass has a richness, restraint, and neutral coloring that will match any color scheme") were laced with common sense: "color in the glass also softens the light and helps eliminate any possible glare." The 1941 catalog introduction stated it bluntly: "the first consideration in lighting equipment today is given to eye comfort rather than to eye appeal—but you will find a good combination of both in Chase Lighting Fixtures."

Farewell to through-design: a style-neutral fixture from the 1937 catalog, #1569 "EVEN-GLOW ONE-LIGHT CEILING FIXTURE." 12" d., 11" l.

From "through-design" to "through with design," Chase changed with the times. By keeping pace with America's taste, the company managed to maintain its position as an industry leader.

"Of the many advantages Chase Lighting offers the home owner, architect, and decorator, probably none will be more welcome than the authentic designs for every important period of architecture and decoration. To the home owner, this means that it is now possible to select lamps and fixtures for a given type or style of home with full assurance that the pattern, form, and decoration are correct in every detail. Architects and decorators will likewise welcome Chase Lighting for the purity of the designs offered."

Chase Lighting Fixtures catalog, 1934

Chapter 4
"Bright Ideas: Marketing Chase Lighting"

"In these times of Depression, nothing changes the appearance of a room like a new lamp. A new lamp adds a crisp look to the home."
Chase Brass & Copper Co. advertisement, 1933

Whether appealing to the consumer's frugality with cost-conscious ad copy, or dazzling them with a 1934 Fixtures catalog bound in gold cloth, Chase explored every viable option in marketing its new Lighting division. Increased public awareness meant increased sales—and Chase Lighting achieved such awareness in a remarkably short time. Here's how:

Bright Idea #1: Catalogs and Brochures

Chase relied heavily on its Lamps and Lighting Fixtures catalogs to promote interest in the company's product. The catalogs themselves were "available to architects and decorators through Chase Lighting dealers." In the early years, ordinary folk could make do with brochures available through magazine coupons, highlighting specific design periods. Presumably, if your interest was only in "Early English," a complete catalog detailing all the periods would be a waste of your time and the company's money.

The 1934 Fixtures catalog was the most lavish, with its gold cloth binding, assorted color pages, and gold foil accents. In addition to Introductions by F. S. Chase and Lurelle Guild, the catalog featured effusive praise of the Chase Lighting line by sixteen "leading authorities," including magazine editors, architects, and the presidents of both General Electric and Westinghouse.

The Chase Specialties catalogs and pamphlets also did their bit to promote the company's lighting products; even pamphlets dating from prior to 1933 depict several available lamps. Later catalogs, in addition to regular lamp inventory listings, also included photos of suggested "product groupings," often incorporating lamps. Those interested in a "Nautical" or "Crescent" display, featuring lamps as well as Specialty items, could check the product groupings for ideas.

Bright Idea #2: Advertisements

How do you attract the homemaker's interest? Easy: you advertise in homemakers' magazines. That was the Chase theory in the 1930s, and it was one that worked successfully. From *The American Home* to *Woman's Home Companion*, enticing examples of the Chase lighting inventory were on view, reminding potential buyers that "it costs so little" for Chase lighting products that offer "a freshness, charm, and individuality all their own." Those on fixed budgets could "pay for it easily on the Chase Time-Payment plan" (which your Chase Lighting Dealer would "gladly explain").

Coupon-clippers could get in on the action, too: a pamphlet released by "United Profit-Sharing Coupons" offered the Chase "GLOW-LAMP" for just "100 Green Certificates or 500 coupons." For the "DESK LAMP," more diligence was required: the going rate was "265 Green Certificates or 1325 coupons."

Magazine covers were prime real estate. For its 1934 debut catalogs, Chase Lighting had commissioned prominent illustrators to depict model room settings, decorated to represent specific periods, and liberally stocked with Chase lamps and fixtures. During 1935, nearly every one of the paintings turned up on the cover of *Furniture Age*.

Bright Idea #3: The Chase Shops

"A "Chase Shop" is a modern shelving unit thoughtfully designed to display a reasonable selection of gifts. It is like a special department in your store which your customers will come to know and remember as gift headquarters. And they will come to it many times throughout the year."
Chase Specialties catalog, 1942

They could read the ads about Chase lamps. They could order the brochures about Chase lamps. But where could people actually buy them? The answer was "The Chase Shop," the store-within-a-store concept featuring Chase lamps and Specialty giftware, that blossomed at hundreds of retail outlets nationwide. Based on a sample shop in Chase Tower, the Chase Shops allowed merchandisers to concentrate their Chase products in one setting, making shopping simpler, and increasing Chase's name-brand recognition.

The Chase Shop designs were the brainchild of Chase Director of Design Harry Laylon. Their sleek, eye-catching lines meshed well with almost every store decor, attracting attention without overpowering nearby merchandise, and showing off the Chase product to its very best advantage.

Years after the last Chase lamp rolled off the production line, Mr. Laylon agreed to recreate a Chase shop design for the Tokyo firm, Art Deco Modern. A 1991 letter, accompanying his completed blueprints, offered some additional Chase Shop insights:

> I gave a lot of thought to this design. Being only 6 feet long by 3-1/2 feet high it can't be too complicated, and being free-standing, I have rounded the ends for easy movement around it. I made it 3-1/2 feet tall instead of 4 feet as the objects displayed on it will be more visible. I think it will look great when it's made, and capture the spirit of Chase and the period. White is the ideal color to display chrome, and the mirror backs in the center should add sparkle. You could save money making this of plywood and painting, but the Formica is so much more practical and better looking.

What better setting for a Chase lamp?

Bright Idea #4: "Better Light-Better Sight"

Although today's collectors relish them for their eye appeal, Chase lamps and fixtures were, of course, initially designed to perform a specific function. If they did not light an assigned area effectively and economically, the products would have fallen out of favor, regardless of their attractiveness. From the earliest days of the Chase Lighting division, functional effectiveness of was highlighted, with the 1934 catalog noting:

> That Chase believes in adequate diffused illumination in the home is seen in the drawing which appears by each fixture showing it in use, properly shaded to prevent glare.

By 1937, functional effectiveness had become a major emphasis of the Chase catalogs. A two-page Fixtures spread, bannered "The Advantages of Scientific Lighting" was accompanied by before-and-after photos of youngsters squinting over their homework in poor lighting, then enjoying the miraculous changes wrought by Chase "Even-Glow" fixtures. Those who felt that any sort of light would do were simply not reading their Chase catalog thoroughly enough:

Glare Blinds and Darkness Strains the Eyes

> The wrong kind of light is injurious to the eyes and is just as bad as not having enough light. For example, too bright a light concentrated in a small spot with the rest of the room improperly lighted or in darkness, is harmful to the eyes because of the extreme contrasts between the intense light and dark areas, and causes nervousness and fatigue.

Scientific Light Saves Eyesight

> Scientific light is diffused, glareless light, light that is evenly distributed throughout a room, so that there are no areas of semi-darkness. A large percentage of defective eyesight is caused by improper light, and is a reason for many a backward school child.

Diffused Light is Restful to the Eyes

> Tired feet make a tired body, but tired eyes make one mentally and physically weary. Under the right kind of light, the eyes are relaxed, and can see without effort. Diffused light is science's best approach to daylight. It is so natural to the eyes that it makes reading and working indoors easy on the eyes and restful.

Needless to say, Chase light was diffused light!

Chase continued to stress the benefits of proper lighting with increasing frequency during the ensuing years of the Lighting division. The missionary fervor reached its zenith with the release of a 1936 booklet, *Saving Your Eyes With Correct Lighting*. Among more photos of poorly-lit folk blundering about and awaiting the intervention of Chase were admonitions, such as this one from M. J. Julian, President of the Better Vision Institute, Inc.:

> Don't neglect or trifle with your most priceless possession. The stakes are too high and the odds too much against you. Look out for your eyes now, and they will look out for you for life. Remember, you can't buy new eyes.

But you *could* buy new lamps and fixtures—and thanks to its ongoing advertising campaign, Chase made sure you knew of the best place to buy them. For nearly one dozen years, the company's marketers worked overtime, keeping Chase Lighting in the forefront of public consciousness—and keeping prospective buyers reaching for their pocketbooks.

"Chase: For Better Light. . .Better Sight. . .and Better Taste in your home."
Chase Lighting advertisement, 1936

PAST . . PRESENT . . FUTURE

BY

F. S. CHASE

When I first came to work at the Manufacturing Plant of the Chase Companies in 1889 there was no such thing as electric fixtures.

Edison had invented the electric light in 1879, but the commercial manufacture of electric bulbs and sockets was still in the experimental stage. There were 30 or more different designs of electrical sockets each with its designer's claims for particular advantages of locking or screwing the bulb into its socket, and all of us despaired of ever getting one standardized design that would make possible the commercial manufacture and use.

But even in those days, 50 years ago, we were in the lighting fixture business, for candlesticks, oil lamps, and gas jets were the lighting fixtures of that day, and we were making them. A few years later we were making Welsbach burner parts, and then, very quickly, electrical sockets and electrical fixture parts. From then on we made electrical parts; made them for manufacturers and assemblers, who put them together and sold the completed product under their name and through their own salesmen.

But when we bought our old customer, The American Brass & Copper Co. in 1925, we found ourselves for the first time in the business of selling completely assembled electrical fixtures. And during the following years we became increasingly interested in the design and appearance of our products.

During these recent years we have seen the electrical fixture business become more and more disorganized, both in its system of distribution and in its price structure, while the quality of its products showed little improvement in design or taste.

4

We have watched other industries suffer from the same weaknesses, and solve them at last, intelligently and courageously, with benefit to themselves, their customers and to the consumer of their products.

The furniture business for example got away from its "mission" and "bird's-eye maple" monstrosities, and produced furniture of period designs that rank with the best hand-made reproductions. Wall papers, textiles, pottery, glassware, and other things for the inside of the house, each in its turn has redesigned its products, and turned out honestly made articles of good design at moderate prices.

Houses themselves have changed over night from jig-saw nightmares with bulging windows and darkening porches to the attractive, cheerful, well-thought out homes of today.

We have seen no such change in lighting fixtures. The garish colored glass of 1910 is still with us. Pink roses with polychrome gold leaves still disfigure some commercial lighting fixtures. Many a wall bracket that started out to be of a simple design ends up daubed with gilt and chocolate paint with pink and green glass inserts. It is a fair criticism to say that at least among low-priced fixtures the lack of good taste is apparent to all. In fact the intelligent man who goes to buy moderately priced fixtures of good design for his living room is hard put to it to find them. In this statement every architect and decorator will agree.

Further, the price that should be paid for electrical fixtures has become a puzzle to the average man. Most buyers have found that a little argument will get them a discount from the listed price, so have most contractors and dealers. Under the strain of competition many manufacturers have sold to both jobbers and retailers, and many times to consumers too.

It is a fair statement to say that the present price structure of commercial lighting fixtures is in a chaotic condition.

Into such conditions we introduce our new line of Chase Lighting Fixtures. They are well designed. We have used the very best of materials. The line is large and diversified both in design and in price, and they are made and sold as cheaply as the best of modern production methods will allow. Further, they will be sold only at their advertised prices, and our dealers will be assisted in their sales promotion, and protected in their territories.

Under such policies of manufacture and distribution we believe the effect will be to stabilize prices and to benefit all who have the interests of the lighting fixture industry at heart. To this end we ask the friendly interest of the industry in our efforts to be of aid to us all.

F. S. Chase

PRESIDENT

5

Most lavish of the Chase catalogs were those issued by the Lighting division in 1934, announcing the new Guild line. In his Introduction to the 1934 Lighting Fixtures catalog, company president F.S. Chase outlines the need for well-designed lighting fixtures "made and sold as cheaply as the best of modern production methods will allow."

What leading authorities say about Chase Lighting

Emily Post

"The Chase Exposition was a dream that came true, every style of fixture for every style of room at prices that make buying possible, even for those with very moderate purses. I think you have done a splendid thing and I do send my very best congratulations to the artist with vision and the manufacturer with taste who made this really notable contribution to the beauty of American homes."

EMILY POST
Famous Writer and Lecturer

"I have just seen the line of interior lighting fixtures which has been developed by your Company, and I think it meets the demand for well designed and attractive fixtures that can be sold at a reasonable price. It fits in very well with the national campaign that is being carried on under the caption 'Better Light—Better Sight'. I congratulate the Chase Brass & Copper Company, and it has my best wishes for success in the sale of this line."

WALTER CARY, *President*
Westinghouse Lamp Company

Stewart Beach

"Well designed fixtures at reasonable cost have always been difficult to find, particularly outside the great metropolitan centers. Your program for nation-wide distribution of a wide selection of fixtures and lamps in handsome period designs from Early English to Classic Modern will go a long way toward solving this problem."

STEWART BEACH, *Editor*
House Beautiful

"I can sincerely say that I think the new Chase lighting fixtures the most important contribution to American homes in many years. Appreciating the difficulties of selecting types for all popular domestic architectural styles, I think they have done a remarkably complete job. The designs are excellent, the prices sensibly within reach of every homemaker. I congratulate you on a much-needed job well done!"

JEAN AUSTIN, *Editor*
American Home

"The Chase Company has proved that it is unmoral to make the small home owner pay for fixture manufacturers' excess overhead and lost motion as a penalty for having decent taste. Furthermore you have so far the only fool-proof display I have ever seen; to have put in no junk, just to make it harder, may be iconoclastic in the trade but it is a blessing to the client and a rare tribute to design."

HARVEY STEVENSON, *Architect*

"It is most gratifying to an architect to see that the Chase Brass & Copper Company have produced an extensive list of beautifully designed lighting fixtures, applicable to any style of architecture, at a price within the reach of the average pocketbook. In the past it has always been discouraging to the architect to find the larger companies which naturally market extensively, foisting such ugly fixtures, and we are extremely grateful to you."

HENRY M. POLHEMUS, *Architect*

Alon Bement

"It is not a very difficult matter to improve the appearance of a contemporary machine-made object when no restrictions are laid down. But it is exceedingly difficult to reduce production costs, meet constantly changing consumer taste, and at the same time improve style and beauty. The Chase Brass & Copper Company is to be congratulated upon its outstanding achievement in creating the first authentically designed group of lighting fixtures and lamps at reasonable prices."

ALON BEMENT, *Director*
National Alliance of Art and Industry

"I send my heartiest good wishes to the Chase Company for the success of their new electrical fixture line. Any well made line of electrical merchandise that is to be sold by constructive policies of distribution and merchandising should be of great benefit to the industry."

GERARD SWOPE, *President*
General Electric Company

8

"I have seen the pictures of your electrical fixtures, and I certainly shall go over and see the display very soon. But these designs are so good, and the reputation of the Chase Companies is such that I know I will not be disappointed when I see the actual fixtures. May I congratulate you on good designs well carried out?"

JAS. GAMBLE ROGERS, *Architect*

"Nothing has needed art direction more than our lighting fixtures. They have been very bad, moderately bad, and anæmic. Realizing this, the Chase Company has collaborated with Lurelle Guild, an authority in design, intelligent as to periods, and generally understanding of what Americans of discernment like in their homes. The result is a wide variety of sound form, expressed in interesting media and spirited color."

AUGUSTA OWEN PATTERSON
Associate Editor, Town & Country

Augusta Owen Patterson

"Lighting the home has been handicapped in the past by a gaudy and impractical assortment of fixtures, possessing neither design merit nor effective efficiency for home lighting. There is therefore a need for a study of fixtures intended for general illumination, for reading, for dining and working. Fixtures developed for these purposes, of the right material and correct in color, will revolutionize the lighting methods in domestic architecture."

A. LAWRENCE KOCHER, *Managing Editor*
The Architectural Record

"Only a good designer and a sympathetic manufacturer working together could produce the splendid and diverse patterns that comprise Chase fixtures and lamps. Behind the designs lies the romance of tradition, and something of that romance and awareness of tradition will pass over to those who select them for their homes. They are calculated, in the finest sense, to stimulate a justifiable pride of ownership."

RICHARDSON WRIGHT, *Editor*
House & Garden

Richardson Wright

"Welcome, Chase! That is the sentiment of the trade upon the entry of the Chase Brass & Copper Company into the lighting fixture business. Their new fixtures reflect credit upon the industry. They conform to every principle of good taste—are authentic in design and charming in their effect. What is more they can be obtained readily by householders through a plan of financing—something never before attempted. Now there can be no excuse for neglect of this important feature in home decoration."

JAMES KRIEGER, *Editor and Publisher*
Lighting & Lamps

"It is refreshing to find in one collection so many good lighting fixtures—true in design to the periods which inspired them, excellently finished, and priced most reasonably."

RUBY ROSS WOOD
Interior Decorator

"We send our very best wishes for your success in the line of electric lighting fixtures. We have been to see your display of these and find among them many which seem to us of excellent character, both in design and execution."

DELANO & ALDRICH, *Architects*

"American industry at its best is exemplified by the new Chase lighting fixtures. Chase has combined distinction in creative design with integrity of materials and workmanship in a way hitherto available only in custom-made work. The development of six complete groups of stock fixtures and lamps in the vital spirit of six authentic styles is a contribution to the stimulation of good taste in America. With the advent of these designs, the architect and decorator can create interiors harmonious in every detail at a cost within the means of the main body of American home owners."

KENNETH K. STOWELL, *Editor*
The Architectural Forum

Kenneth K. Stowell

9

What better way to promote your new line than to call in the experts? Chase did just that, and the results were included in the 1934 Lighting Fixtures catalog. From architect Henry M. Polhemus, to General Electric Co. president Gerard Swope, all were effusive in their praise. Alon Bement, Director of the National Alliance of Art and Industry, summed it up best by congratulating Chase for "creating the first authentically designed group of lighting fixtures and lamps at reasonable prices." *1934 Lighting Fixtures catalog courtesy of John Myhre*

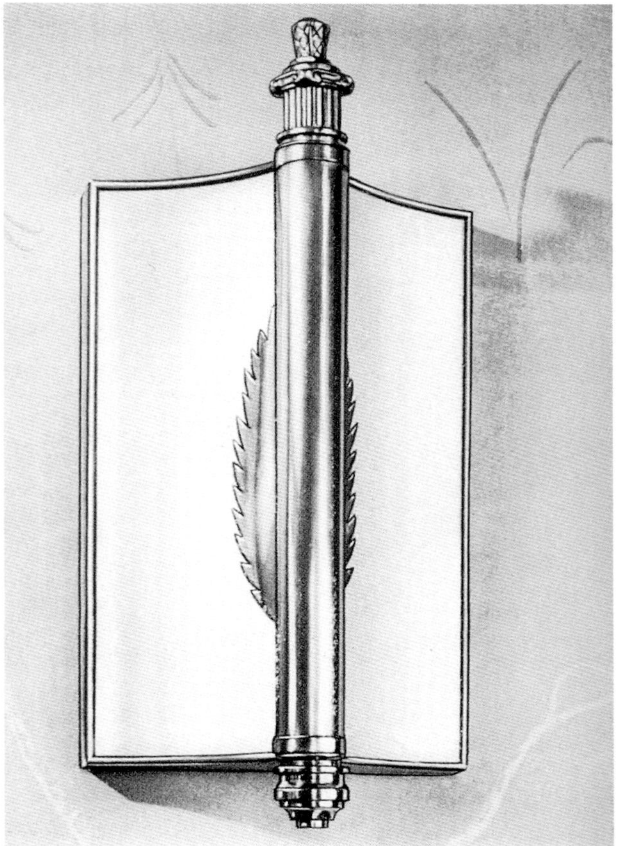

Left: Close-up photos, showing each lamp and fixture in all its detailed glory, were a major attraction of the 1934 catalogs. "THE VESTA," # M 530, a Classic Modern design, features an "interesting stylized decoration of wheat silhouetted against plain panels of frosted glass which are framed in metal with a rope design." 9" h.

Bottom left: Another in-depth view from 1934, this of ceiling fixture # M 546, "THE AUGUSTA." Although the pattern of raised reeds and a star carries out the Classic Modern theme, the design is simple enough to complement other decorative schemes. 6-1/2" w.

Left: Just the basics: earlier Chase product photography resisted the frills. Among the lighting items given a rudimentary depiction in this 1931 Specialties holiday pamphlet are the "SAF-CANDLE," #11256; the "CANDLELIGHT," #11150; and #11255, the "PILGRIM LIGHT."

Above: With the passage of years, a more sophisticated approach emerged. The 1942 Specialties catalog strikes up the band, with this complete "Drum" grouping, featuring the "DRUM LAMP," #6324; #90156 "DRUM BANK;" #894 "DRUM CIGARETTE SERVER," and #893 "DRUM ASH TRAY."

Soldiers on parade! Also from the 1942 catalog, the "SENTINEL LAMP," #17112, with matching book ends, #17109.

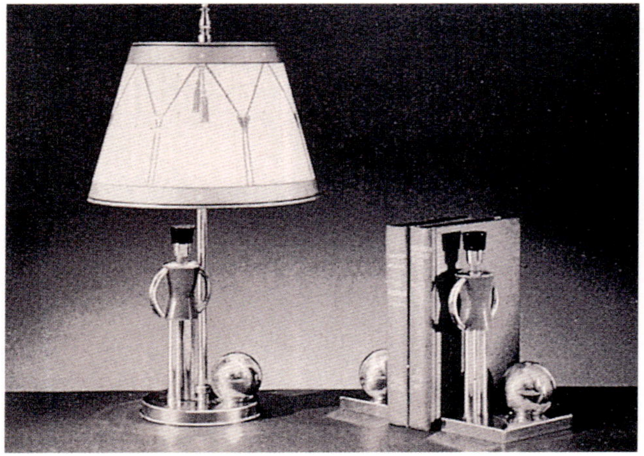

From 1940, another matched set, the "CRESCENT LAMP," #6156, with "CRESCENT BOOK ENDS," #90137. Also shown: #879 "RIBBED ASH RECEIVER."

Everything's shipshape in this 1942 grouping of #6309 "FARRAGUT LAMP;" #889 "THREE ANCHORS ASH TRAY;" and #90142 "DAVEY JONES BOOK ENDS."

Still sailing the marketing seas. From 1941, #6314 "BARNEGAT LAMP," #884 "WHIRLIGIG ASH TRAY," and #887 "BRIGANTINE CIGARETTE SERVER."

Bon voyage! 1940s "WHEEL LAMP," #6305, surrounded by #90138 "PILOT BOOK ENDS," #872 "TOWER LIGHTER," and #885 "RIVIERA ASH TRAY."

CHASE Check List

FIFTEEN BRILLIANT ANSWERS TO YOUR CHRISTMAS GIFT QUESTIONS

$1.00

Who wouldn't welcome such a stunning, useful gift as the Chase Smokestack! Perfect for bridge and dinner tables. Holds twenty cigarettes. Finished in gleaming non-tarnishing chromium, in bronze, and in black nickel. Just $1.00.

Since everybody needs and welcomes a really good-looking ash-tray, let the Chase Aristocrat solve dozens of your Christmas Gift problems. It's new, practical and really beautiful, whether you select it in brilliant chromium or in rich copper and brass. Only $1.00.

Here is a gift that few men have—all men want—the Chase Jigger and Swizzler Set. The High Hat Jigger holds the correct 1½ oz. The niblick Swizzlers are perfect for mixing and stirring. Complete set, only $1.00.

Whether they serve lemonade, tea, highballs, or punches they need a long-stirring spoon and a pair of ice tongs. Chase makes both in non-tarnishing chromium, and packs them in an attractive gift box at the cheerful price of $1.00 for both.

This good looking Chase Candy Dish has a three-compartment glass container which makes it practical for serving varied sweets, nuts, after-dinner mints. Comes in four beautiful finishes—nickel and black, brass and copper, all brass or all copper. Only $1.00.

$1.50 to $3.00

Whether she serves chocolates, mints, nuts or olives in it, she will always remember receiving this useful and lovely gift. The Chase Bon Bon Dish is finished in copper and white enamel, copper and green, or in gleaming chromium and black. And it is just $1.50.

Here is a gift that will delight a man 365 mornings a year—the Chase Newspaper Rack. Keeps the daily news out of the breakfast butter. So good-looking that even wives like it. In English bronze, or brass and copper. And it costs only $1.50.

The Chase Drum Lamp is a grand gift for boy, girl, man or woman. An excellent night light. Soft light shines through both drum heads. Colorfully finished in red and blue, also in white and black. Complete, with cord, $1.50.

One of the smartest and most useful of all Chase gifts is this modern Mint and Nut Dish. Perfect for serving two kinds of olives, nuts, candies, mints and appetizers. In non-tarnishing Chase Chromium. Also in brass and copper. $2.50.

This practical Chase Breakfast set is a welcome gift for it can be used every day. For breakfast trays, after-dinner coffee, tea and luncheon, it is ideal. Finished in modern Chromium, it will never tarnish. The set (creamer, sugar and tray) is modestly priced at $3.00.

$4.00 to $4.50

The person who receives this stunning Chase Sauce Bowl will be delighted with it. First, because of its beautiful design, and gleaming chromium finish. Second, because it is ideal for serving all salad dressings, gravies, hot chocolates and other sauces. Complete with ladle—but $4.00.

This smart, modern Chase Ice Bowl and Tongs will be welcomed many times because it has so many uses. For potato chips, crackers, marshmallows, nuts, as well as ice, it is ideal. Beautifully finished in silvery chromium, also in brass and copper. $4.50, including tongs.

This modern Chase cocktail shaker in gleaming, non-tarnishing chromium is as easy to look at as it is to shake. The sleeve top fits snugly and a good strainer makes it practical. Finished in polished chromium with red, green or black enamel rings. A beautiful gift, $4.50.

Whoever gets this clever Chase Pancake and Corn Set will bless your generosity. So useful. The Chromium pitcher for serving syrup, hot chocolate sauce, melted butter, cream. The Chromium Spheres for sugar, salt, pepper and other condiments. Tray, in blue glass and chromium. $4.50 for the four pieces.

The Chase Desk Lamp is a superb gift because it does what few lamps do—makes reading and writing easy. Swivels in all directions. Smartly finished in chromium or bronze. With ivory shade—only $4.50.

If you have any difficulty in buying these or any other Chase gifts write directly to Chase Brass & Copper Co., Dept. A-3, Chase Tower, New York

THE AMERICAN HOME, DECEMBER, 1934

3

14

A. F. Sozio

Christmas

Below—Attractive and useful set of accessories for the bar that are made of Chromium plated Copper. This group includes a Stir-it pitcher, ice bucket and tongs, an ice crusher and a bar caddy. The bar caddy is a very practical article that combines the best features of a measuring jigger, bottle opener, cork screw and ice breaker

Above—Salesclerk of a big department store is shown here demonstrating to a customer some of the lovely and brilliant giftware articles made of Copper, Brass and Bronze or plated with gleaming Chromium. Among the attractive items there are undoubtedly many that will solve some of your gift problems. Shown here are candlestick sets, floral accessories, bowls, buffet servers, cocktail sets, coffee percolators, condiment sets, salt and pepper shakers, ash trays, ice buckets, serving trays and a host of other articles to gladden someone's heart . . .

Below—Here is a splendid group of holiday gift suggestions for the man or woman whose hobby is boats. The wheel on the polished Brass lamp turns the light on or off when it is turned. Together with the Pilot book ends and the Riviera ash tray, this makes a really appropriate ensemble. The wheel in the ash tray revolves and, as it is numbered, guests can amuse themselves by spinning the wheel . . .

Above—Unusual selection of table accessories combining the attractive, brilliant finish of Chromium with clear ribbed glass. In this group are a cruet set, Jubilee jam jar, Jubilee syrup jug and an Arcadia water pitcher. In the front is a three-layer candy box, consisting of three sections stacked one on the other with a cover

Left—The base of this Masthead table lamp is a ship's lantern that is lighted by a separate bulb and switch independent of the main reading lamp. It is polished Brass with a choice of red or green lantern glass. A pair of these lamps, one with green glass and one red are most effective

COPPER & BRASS BULLETIN

Left: Making a list, and checking it twice! The holiday season was a prime marketing time for Chase lamps and gift items. This "Chase Check List" from the December 1934 issue of *The American Home* includes the "DRUM LAMP" night light, #01010, and the "DESK LAMP" #01003.

Above: Holiday gift-giving was made easy with this sampling from the December 1939 *Copper and Brass Bulletin*. Among the Chase items shown are, at bottom left, the "WHEEL LAMP," #6305, and, bottom center, the "MASTHEAD LAMP," #6310.

ONE CERTIFICATE EQUALS 5 COUPONS

CHASE

2302—Electric Utility Lamp. Stand and base chromium finish. Parchment finish shade. Adjustable to any angle. Complete with cord and plug. Height 14½ inches. 265 Green Certificates or 1325 Coupons.

2689—Sugar and Creamer. Chromium plated finish. Black handles. Height of Sugar Bowl 4¼ inches. 160 Green Certificates or 800 Coupons.

2118—Electric Glow Lamp. Polished copper. Without bulb. Complete with cord and plug. 100 Green Certificates or 500 Coupons.

2691—Jam Set. Hob-nail glass jar. Chromium plated finish lid and tray. Glass spoon. Height 5¼ inches. 170 Green Certificates or 850 Coupons.

2117—Automatic Table Lighter. Height 3¼ inches. White enamel with chromium plated finish top and base. 80 Green Certificates or 400 Coupons.

2687—Smoker's Set. Polished nickel plated finish. Black enamel trim. 7 inch glass bottom tray, two ash trays and cigarette server. 85 Green Certificates or 425 Coupons.

2688—Cocktail Shaker. Bright chromium finish with black enamel rings. Equipped with strainer. Height 11½ inches. Diameter 3¾ inches. 265 Green Certificates or 1325 Coupons

2686—Ash Tray. Polished nickel plated. Diameter 3½ inches. 22 Green Certificates or 110 Coupons

2701—Devonshire Water Pitcher. Polished chromium plated finish with white metal lining. Capacity 2 quarts. 230 Green Certificates or 1150 Coupons.

2690—Mint and Nut Dish. Polished chromium plated finish. Height over all 4½ inches. Trays are 4 inches in diameter. 165 Green Certificates or 825 Coupons.

PAGE 45

Coupons will get you anything—even Chase lamps! "United Profit-Sharing Coupons" offered various Chase items in its 1935-36 catalog, including the "DESK LAMP," #01003, and the "GLOW LAMP," #01001. *Courtesy of Barbara Endter*

Chase got plenty of mileage out of its 'theme room" illustrations. Besides appearing in pamphlets, catalogs, and advertisements, this rendition of an "Empire" setting turned up on the December 1935 cover of *Furniture Age*. The original painting is by Pierre Brissaud.

"Early English" made the cover of *Furniture Age* in January 1935. English artist Ernest Walker was commissioned by Chase to create this illustration.

CHASE SHOP BOOK

A CHASE SHOP INCREASES SALES - - - ALL YEAR ROUND

The Chase Shop shown above was installed by the May Co. Dept. Store, Cleveland, Ohio. The free Chase Shop book gives you plans and directions for constructing and finishing many different types and sizes of shops similar to this one.

Grouping items in display units is becoming more and more popular. It gives the impression of larger store stocks, adds to the appearance of the store, and increases sales, as the "Chase Shop" has for so many of our dealers.

A "Chase Shop" makes one of the best group displays we have seen. It is a well designed modern shelving unit. A Chase Shop is like a special department which your customers come to know and remember as gift headquarters. There are hundreds in use today by small stores and stores as large as Marshall Field's.

A "Chase Shop" can be built for as little as $25.00.

The "Chase Shop" Book gives all the necessary plans and information you need to build any size unit. Several designs and sizes of shops with approximate costs are shown. And if your requirements are unusual our own designer will plan a Chase Shop especially for you.

Write today for your free copy. Address Advertising Department, Chase Brass & Copper Co., Waterbury, Connecticut.

WRITE FOR THIS FREE BOOK OF GIFT DISPLAY PLANS AND SUGGESTIONS

2 •

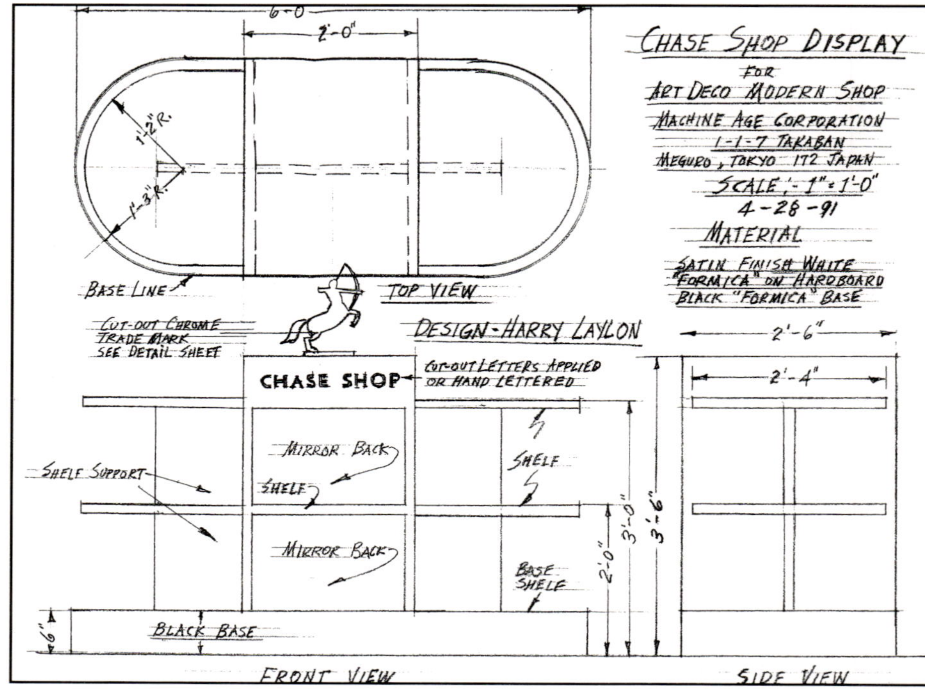

Left: "A Chase Shop Increases Sales—All Year Round!" Retail stores featuring these free-standing displays of Chase products noted a marked increase in sales of Chase lamps and giftware items. The eye-catching "Chase Shops" were the work of the company's Director of Design, Harry Laylon. The shop pictured was designed for Cleveland, Ohio's May Company.

Above: In 1991, Harry Laylon embarked on one of his final design projects: recreating a proposed "Chase Shop" for the Tokyo, Japan decor firm, Art Deco Modern. Shown is Mr. Laylon's design for the "Chase Shop" unit. *Courtesy of Tetsumasa Suda*

Poor Lighting

Below, is the same living room as the well lighted one on the right. But it is lighted with exposed bulbs that glare in your eyes. Look at the heavy shadows caused by poor light distribution. The brightest spot is right around the fixture itself and because there is nothing to diffuse the light, it never reaches very far. The result is eyestrain if one attempts to read in a poorly lighted room like this one.

Good Lighting

The living room above is lighted with a Chase "Even-Glow" fixture. Notice how well lighted it is even to the far corner behind the bookcase. There are no shadows, no glare from bare bulbs, nothing to cause eyestrain. The room is lighted so that you can read with comfort in any part of it.

CHASE

Page 5

"Poor light, poor sight." A major Chase selling point over the years was the health benefit provided by the company's lamps and lighting fixtures. The 1940 Residential Lighting Fixtures Catalog provided a visual walk-through of a typical home, illustrating how each room could be markedly improved with the addition of the right Chase fixtures. The grumpy couple, at left, seem to find a touch of Chase, at right, does wonders for their outlook. Similar miracles of modern lighting occur in the photos that follow. *1940 Residential Lighting Fixtures catalog courtesy of Peter Linden and Eric Menard.*

Front Door

Placing two lanterns, one on each side of the door, is the most effective way to light up a doorway. The fixtures balance each other well, and relieve the plain look and emptiness of the large wall spaces. Chase lanterns are made in many sizes and types for all styles of architecture.

Porch

Outdoor lanterns should be made of copper, either in stained copper, or in a black finish that will hold up under climatic changes. A hanging lantern is a good choice for a high porch ceiling because it brings the light closer and it is easy to reach and keep cleaned.

CHASE Page 59

Entrance

The hall lantern is the first fixture your guests see as you welcome them at the front door, and the last as they leave. You want the first and last impression of your home to be a good one, so be choosey about the fixture you use. Any Chase hall lantern will add charm to your hall. The fixture shown here is the No. 1379 illustrated in large size on page 45.

Hall

A hall lantern at the top of the stairs is a decorative and practical light. Here the Chase lantern No. 1235 (shown on page 44 in larger size) lights up both the hall and stairway. It also dresses up a large ceiling area that would look very bare without it. For small halls with low ceilings, any of the close-up ceiling fixtures among the decorative fixtures on pages 48 and 49 could be used.

CHASE Page 43

Living Room

The living room below is furnished in Swedish Modern furniture. A lighting fixture with the same severe lines as the furnishings might have been used, but it wouldn't add the charm to the room that this Early American fixture does. This is a good example of how periods can be mingled to get a more interesting room.

Dining Room

This dining room is an example of how period furnishings can be used together to make a more interesting looking room. Here is a Sheraton dining room set, an eighteenth century period, but the lighting fixture is an Early American design. Yet the two seem to be made for each other for they look so well together.

CHASE Page 13

Bedroom

For bedrooms, colored glassware comes in both iridescent glass and floral designs in beautiful colors on light cream colored glass. Every bedroom should have a ceiling fixture for good general illumination so that there is ample light at the full-length closet door mirror, the vanity, and bureau drawers, to distinguish between colors of socks and ties, without carrying them to the light.

Dining Room

Here is a colored glassware fixture in a dining room with grey tinted walls in stucco finish. Notice that the iridescent glass, while it is colorful, has no predominating colors to clash with the tinted walls, but blends in harmoniously. The translucent glass gives semi-indirect lighting. The strong light rays are softened not only by reflecting them from the ceiling, but also filtering them through the translucent glass. There is no glare and no dark area directly beneath the fixture. The mellow light makes the dining room more cheerful and the meals more enjoyable.

CHASE Page 33

Hallway

Beam Lights are usually used to light up narrow hallways as illustrated below. They fit close to the ceiling, take up no headroom, and are out of the way when large pieces of furniture are moved through the hall. Chase Beam Lights are available in a variety of finishes to blend with tinted ceilings and wall papers.

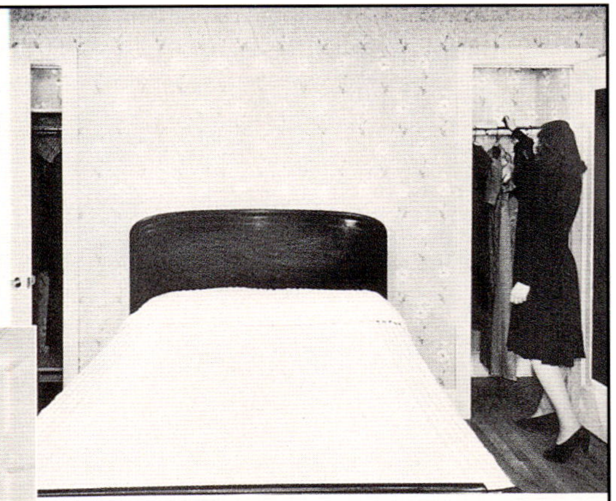

Clothes Closet

It is easy to pick out clothes that vary in color and fabric designs in a well lighted closet, but it is difficult to tell them apart in a poorly lighted closet. That's why we recommend Chase Beam Lights for clothes closets. The style of the fixtures is not as important as it is in other rooms, but we have a number of attractive Chase Beam Lights at moderate prices for you to pick from. They are illustrated on the two pages following.

CHASE
Page 47

Dressing Room

The soft indirect lighting from these modern Chase fixtures gives intimacy and charm to these dressing rooms. Notice how ideally suited these fixtures are to this Modern American interior, not only in lighting effect, but in symmetry and smartness.

Vanity

This scene is typical of many up-to-date well-appointed bedrooms. The modern effect is accented by the plain round mirror, and hassock, and the simplicity of Chase lighting fixtures. This is a pair of No. 526 lighting fixtures illustrated on page 40.

CHASE
Page 39

Bathroom

Besides a center ceiling fixture for uniformly lighting the bathroom, wall brackets should be used at the mirror. Sometimes a single light is placed over the mirror, but for best results lights should be installed on each side. Most Chase bathroom brackets are made with a convenience outlet for electric shavers and curling irons.

Kitchen

No home would be complete without a kitchen and no kitchen, no matter how attractive it is, is complete without scientific lighting. The kitchen light should give no irritating glare, and no shadows on badly lighted corners. Chase kitchen fixtures give ample and diffused light all around the kitchen, and make it easier to see your work.

CHASE
Page 51

CHASE

Game Rooms

The three Chase fixtures on the next page are especially made for game rooms. They are a combination of decorative and practical lighting. The marine rope and anchor trim on the No. 1338 ceiling light and the No. 1339 matching wall bracket are popular decorations for game rooms. For these nautical symbols are usually associated with fun and recreation, an atmosphere you will want for your game room.

For practical purposes, Chase game room fixtures fit close to the ceiling. They do not hang low or take up much headroom. Notice, too, that the enclosing globe is used because it keeps out dust and is easier to keep clean.

For children's playrooms, or for game rooms with very low ceilings where the lighting fixture is apt to be accidently hit, the No. 1380 fixture is guarded with a strong wire grille to protect the glass globe.

The translucent globes filter the intensity of the light bulbs. There is no harmful glare in anyone's eyes, no matter where they sit, but instead there is plenty of restful light for reading cards, playing games, or "just looking on."

CHASE
Page 56

Every room ablaze with Chase! The cover of the 1940 Residential Lighting Fixtures catalog.

Chapter 5
"The Chase Lamps Gallery"

"Brilliant in style and authentic in design—Chase presents a complete line of period lamps at prices within reach of all."

Chase Lamps brochure, 1934

Chapter 5 boasts a shining array of Chase lamps—those produced from the dawning of the Specialty division in 1930, straight through to the twilight of the Lighting division in 1942. Each and every known lamp released by Chase is pictured in this book. Most of the lamps sold through the Specialty catalogs are pictured in this chapter; some, used to illustrate specific points in other chapters, can be located by referring to the Index. (The Lurelle Guild lamp designs of 1934 comprise Chapter 6.)

For useful comparison and reference, the Chase lamps have been categorized by shape (e.g., "Urn-shaped"), theme (e.g., "Early English") or function (e.g., "Dual-Purpose"). If more than one category was applicable, the lamp has been placed in the one most pertinent.

The centaur, trademark logo of the Chase Brass & Copper Co. While a ready identifier of Chase products, the centaur did not begin showing up on lamps with great regularity until the mid-to-late 1930s.

Illuminating Information

Even with the assistance of photos, many collectors on the prowl may locate a likely candidate, but still find themselves asking "is this *really* a Chase lamp?" With the passage of years, many shadeless, tarnished lamps on the secondary market look nothing like the pristine originals. And the Chase "centaur" trademark, a sure giveaway on many Chase giftware items, is often impossible to locate on a Chase lamp. For the puzzled collector, hints for reliable identification are offered by John and Donna Thorpe, of the Chase Collectors Society:

> Most early Chase lamps and fixtures are not marked with the familiar Chase name and centaur logo. However, a longtime Chase collector will often find a familiar part or piece on the lamp, to help in identifying it. Parts from the Chase giftware division were sometimes re-thought, re-designed, and re-used as components for Chase lamps and fixtures.
>
> The base metal will always be brass or copper. A small magnet will help determine this—it won't stick. All of the Chase lamps that we've taken apart to re-wire have the model number stamped somewhere on one of the parts. It could be on a metal washer, trim piece, or on the top of the weighted base piece. As this is usually a hidden number, it won't help you in the antique store, but can prove provenance after a purchase. If the number is different than the inventory number given for that lamp, don't worry: Chase often mixed and matched parts, especially bases. Chances are, the number you located will be found as the identification number for another Chase lamp.

By the mid-to-late 1930s, the centaur was showing up on lamps with greater regularity—making identifying a find as "Chase" much easier!

Shedding Some Light

What could potential customers expect from a Chase lamp? Most importantly, they were made of "lasting Chase brass," which was not only impervious to rust, but also the ideal base for applied finishes. (Among the finishes offered by Chase were chrome, copper, English bronze, nickel, and black nickel.) In addition to their novel designs, the lamps also featured detailed craftsmanship in their construction, from wiring "bearing the label of approval of the National Board of Fire underwriters," to finely executed shades of "metal, Bakelite ('plastic'), parchment, crepe, faille taffeta, or Clair de Lune." An essay accompanying the 1934 Chase Lamps brochure managed to hit all the high points of their appeal:

> Fresh in inspiration and carefully styled for the needs of the American home, Chase table and floor lamps possess an individuality—a beauty—that sets them apart from all other lamps. Now it is possible for you to select lamps for a particular period, room, or style of home, with full assurance that the finish, decoration and type are traditionally correct. And the prices

are truly reasonable! Ranging from $4.50 to $59.50, you are sure to find the particular style you want—at the price you want to pay.

These beautiful lamps are scaled to fulfill every lamp requirement, in both period style and sizes. In the following pages you will find tall, 'important' lamps for the spacious room, medium-sized lamps for the average room, and smaller lamps for occasional tables, dressing tables, and hall tables.

So that greater harmony may be achieved in all interiors, Chase has designed its floor lamps and bridge lamps to agree with the table lamps in basic design and decoration. Thus, when Chase table lamps and floor lamps are used together in one room, they form a pleasing relation to each other.

Representing a choice of the best designs of previous generations, these lamps will always be in style, and, made of durable Chase brass, they will give lasting satisfaction for years to come.

Presenting: the Chase Lamps Gallery!

Ball Shapes

Left: The prototypical Chase "ball" shape on #01001 "GLOW LAMP," which made its debut prior to 1933. Adapted from a toilet float by Ruth Gerth, the "GLOW LAMP" was a staple of the Chase line through the 1941 catalog. 8-1/4" h. *Courtesy of John and Donna Thorpe*

Right: Another Gerth design, the "BALL TABLE LAMP," #11235. The base is brass, the ball copper. In its final catalog appearance, 1936, the "BALL" inventory number was changed to #01002. 15" h. *Courtesy of John and Donna Thorpe*

Above: Two "ball" designs that first appeared in the 1939 catalog. *Left:* #6146 "WESTBROOK," an "inexpensive lamp with smart lines." 15" h. *Right:* #6166 "ALDEN," a dual-purpose lamp, for use on either table or wall. 14-1/2" h. *Courtesy of John and Donna Thorpe*

Left: "A small lamp for the radio, hallway, or dark corner" (and a close relative of the "BALL" lamp), #6184 "HAMPTON." 10-3/4" h.

Right: Designed by Walter Von Nessen, the "PLANET LAMP," #01015. The 1938 catalog described this as a "good all 'round table lamp that is attractively designed for appearance, and mechanically constructed to give the correct amount and kind of light for reading." 18" h. *Courtesy of John and Donna Thorpe*

Top left: The "SHELTON," #6162, was also available in bronze. 12" h. *Photo courtesy of John and Donna Thorpe*

Top center: The variations are limitless: "three fluted columns support a sphere." #6161 "CARLTON." 22" h. *Photo courtesy of John and Donna Thorpe*

Bottom left: A longer stem, but the "ball" shape remains constant: #6167, "BRISTOL." 16-1/4" h.

Right: The sphere flattened, on #6165 "DISCUS." 10-3/4" h. *Courtesy of John and Donna Thorpe*

Urn Shapes

Top left: The classic "trophy urn" shape of the "BEVERLY," #6143, is supported by a square stepped-up base. 17" h.

Bottom left: Another narrow urn, this one with a fluted tapered base. #6186 "BURTON." 17-1/2" h.

Right: A somewhat narrower urn shape distinguishes the "BEDFORD," #6177. 21" h. *Courtesy of John and Donna Thorpe*

Put them on a pedestal: #6175 "WINTON." Bakelite bands on the "WINTON" body and pedestal were available in colors to complement almost every decor. 15-1/2" h. *Courtesy of John and Donna Thorpe*

Top center: Softer lines, and a rounded pedestal. #6181, "MARLBORO." 21-1/2" h.

Bottom center: Another rounded pedestal, but a narrower urn, to harmonize with "Empire, Federal, Early American, or Modern furnishings." The "LOMBARD," #6321, 22" h.

Top right: Decorated in a manner suitable for Empire settings. #6157 "EMPIRE," 21-1/2" h. *Photo courtesy of John and Donna Thorpe*

Bottom right: A slumped urn shape, found only in the 1939 catalog. #6144 "GEORGIAN." 17" h.

Central Cylinders

Bottom center: #01009 "REEDED LAMP." The reeded pattern of the lamp column is followed through in the accordion-pleated parchment shade. 10-3/4" h.

Bottom left: A less ornate use of the reeded pattern, plus globes at top and bottom of the cylinder stem, distinguish #6182, the "TREMONT." 23" h. *Photo courtesy of John and Donna Thorpe*

Right: A fluted column, and a pedestal, too! #6136, "FORUM," 19-1/2" h.

Far right: Bakelite inserts add interest to the "AMBASSADOR," #6300. 23-1/2" h. *Photo by Jacqueline Jones-Ridge; courtesy of Gary M. Piper*

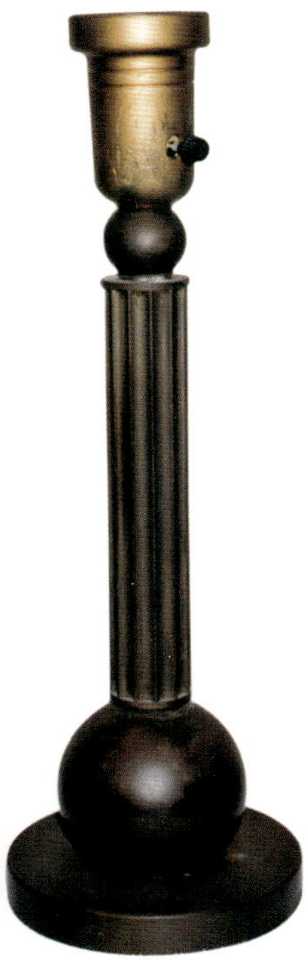

Top: The three-tube base of #6171, the "SENTINEL," was available in either white or bronze. (This 1939-only design bears the same name, but no other similarity, to #17112, the 1941 and 1942 "SENTINEL.") 24-1/2" h.

Bottom: A 1939-only design, the "ESSEX," #6149. 12" h.

A sleek central column of white plastic, with a metal accent band: #17118, "MELISSA." 16-3/4" h. *Photo by Jacqueline Jones-Ridge. Courtesy of Gary M. Piper*

A simple central column offset by a fluted white Bakelite base. The "AQUILLA," #6326, 18-1/2" h. *Photo by Jacqueline Jones-Ridge. Courtesy of Gary M. Piper*

Introduced in 1939, the "COMMANDER," #6170 had an etched plant design on its square columnar base. In addition to the coppertone finish with tortoise shell trim shown, the "COMMANDER" was available in satin silver with white Bakelite trim. 24-1/4" h. *Courtesy of John and Donna Thorpe*

Detail, "COMMANDER" etched design.

Top: Its narrow column and graceful base made the "PENELOPE," #17110, ideal for dressing table use. 18" h.

Bottom: Swirl ribbing on the glass bowl, and fluting on the upright tube, are hallmarks of #6319, the "VICTORIA." Aptly named, the lamp was designed for Victorian-style bedrooms. As the 1942 catalog notes, the brass finish "goes so well with maple." 18" h.

The central column of #6183, the "PLY-MOUTH," is segmented into an adaptation of a Colonial "three-candle lamp." 20-1/4" h.

Similar to the "PLYMOUTH," except for trim and shade: the "MALDEN," #6185. 20-1/4" h.

The "three-candle" look again, this time with an "Empire" styling. The "D'ORSAY," #6317. 18-1/4" h.

'Round and 'round she goes: #01004, the "CIRCLE LAMP." The shade's swivel attachment meant the lamp could be adjusted to the angle most convenient for reading. 14" h. *Courtesy of Stephen and Joanne Klender*

The "CIRCLE" and its predecessor the "RING LAMP," #11242. With shade, the "RING" height was 17". *Courtesy of John and Donna Thorpe*

Curved Stems

Making its first appearance in 1939 was the "CLIFTON," #6164. This dual-purpose lamp was very similar in styling to Von Nessen's "THE LAMP," #NS-597. 14-1/2" h. *Photo by Jacqueline Jones-Ridge. Courtesy of Jackie and Harry Ridge*

Top center: One of the earliest "curved-stem" Chase lamps, dating prior to 1933, the "SIGMA LAMP" #11244, designed by the Gerths. 20" h.

Bottom center: Similiar in style, and also pre-1933, the "DELTA LAMP," #11243. 17" h.

Top right: Slightly taller than the Clifton, and joining the line in 1940, #17102 "ATHENA VANITY," also a dual-purpose lamp. 16-1/2" h. *Photo courtesy of John and Donna Thorpe*

Bottom right: Chase advertisement for the "ATHENA."

Top left: Most basic in the Chase "Colonial" line was an electrified version of the Early American spindle lamp. Tallest, with a reverse base, was the "CHATHAM," #6192. 21-3/4" h.

Bottom left: #6316 "MT. VERNON HURRICANE." Just like in Colonial times, but electrified! The 1941 catalog notes that the "MT. VERNON" was "popularly used in pairs on the buffet or mantelpiece." A non-electrified version was also available. 8-1/2" h.

Top center: Appearing only in the 1939 catalog, "PRISCILLA," #6131 was an adaptation of a Colonial candle light. 11-1/2" h. (Another "PRISCILLA" candle light, #11144, appeared prior to 1933, and was a companion piece to the "PILGRIM" battery lamp, #11255.)

Bottom center: A hurricane for the wall: #6199 "WILLIAMSTOWN." The circular mirror is gun-metal. (The "HURRICANE WALL BRACKET" #24010 is the non-electrical version of this.) 11" h.

Spindle adaptations. *Left:* #6168 "LENOX," 12" h. *Center and right:* #6179 "BREWSTER," in polished brass and English bronze. 17-1/4" h. *Courtesy of John and Donna Thorpe*

Top left: A prism lamp, the "JAMESTOWN," #6312. The lamp's swivel harp made it possible to tilt the shade for better reading light.

Top center: Another Colonial lamp "well used in pairs:" #6325 "FALMOUTH," 10-1/2" h.

Right: The "FALMOUTH" (lower left) was one of the products featured in this *Better Homes & Gardens* holiday preview dating from December 1941.

28

Hang a Stocking for Your Home!

$5 and under

Gifts of Lasting Beauty

By Christine Holbrook

RIGHT alongside your Christmas stocking—and Dad's and those for the small fry—*do* hang a whopping big sock for Santa to fill for that most precious spot in the whole world these days—your home! Start now to help the old boy shop for it thoughtfully and lovingly. Gifts of lasting beauty, like these we've assembled and others they'll inspire, will make this Yuletide remembered long after the turkey and tinsel have disappeared.

$10 and Under

6 Santa suggests, for that room of yours with the Colonial flavor, a walnut banjo clock with a self-starting electric movement ($8.80, Sessions Clock Co.) **7** A three-in-one smoothie! It's a back- and front-door chime replacing doorbells. And it's a thermometer and a humidity gauge to boot! ($6.95, NuTone Chimes, Inc.) **8** Hunting a spot for your treasured bits or books? These Early American maple shelves would be charming alone or in pairs for dining-room, living-room, or bedroom ($7 each, Heywood-Wakefield) **9** This hurricane lamp with its fine slim lines comes in ruby, crystal, or sapphire blue. Lovely in pairs or all by itself ($8 each, Lightolier) **10** Safe harbor for those phonograph records that are always getting bumped about! Space for 12 albums with a shelf for singles ($9.90, Duo-Use Cabinet by Georgian Cabinet Shops) **11** Do go peasant in your informal furnishings—it's lots of fun. This buxom miss is gay wi color, merry contrast for the simple sha To make a matching pair, there's a peasa mister ($10 each, Royal Haeger Lamp C **12** No end of travel spots for such a thr rug in hooked design or the new textur weave. Welcome before your hearth, do or couch ($5.75, Bigelow-Sanford Carp Co.) **13** Even clocks are growing air-min ed! Hands, dial, and "wing" base of t mahogany timer suggest the modern a liner. It's an electric self-starter ($7. Seth Thomas) **14** For your Early Americ bedroom or downstairs dressing room yo love this mirror with carved wood fra and inner stripe of gold ($6.95, Nu Companies, Inc.) **15** Delicate and delig ful—this Eighteenth Century piece over the sofa in the living-room, or may a pair in the dining-room or flanking yo mantel ($7.95, Montgomery Ward)

$5 and Under

1 Ivy in this chubby copper pot trains gracefully around the white or green scroll. Wall hook comes, too ($1 per pair, Chase Brass & Copper Co.) **2** Short on timekeepers? Here's a self-starting alarm clock—yours in ivory or brown plastic ($2.95, Warren Telechron Co.) **3** Today countless etchings by acknowledged artists are inexpensively priced. These three: top, "Across the Point," by Ettinger; middle, "Fog Bound," by Grant; bottom, "Memories," by Castellon ($5 each; framed, $8.25, Associated American Artists, Inc.) **4** Twin lamps like this brass-footed beauty would be handsome on buffet, mantelpiece, or dresser. One's lovely on hall table or bedside stand ($3 each, Chase Brass & Copper Co.) **5** It's a dainty streamliner just three inches high in your choice of white or black. Three or four pulls of the button and your little clock's wound! ($1.95, Westclox)

From left: #6307 "SETTLER'S HURRICANE" (called the "HURRICANE" in 1940), 7-1/4" h.; #6311 "POTOMAC," 15-1/2" h.; #6178 "LEXINGTON," 12" h. A candle version of the "SETTLER'S HURRICANE," #16006, was also available. Prism lamps, such as the "POTOMAC" and "LEXINGTON" complemented both Colonial and Victorian decors. *Courtesy of John and Donna Thorpe*

Swirled glass globes are a feature of all three lamps shown. *From left:* #6313 "IPSWICH, 18-1/4" h.; #1310 "FIVE- LIGHT CEILING FIXTURE," 36" overall length; #6302 "PUTNAM," 13-1/4" h. The "PUTNAM" was a dual-purpose lamp; chandelier #1310 appeared only in the 1938 Lighting Fixtures catalog. *Courtesy of John and Donna Thorpe*

Top left: #6194, the "CHESTER." This reproduction of an old oil lamp originally came with a parchment shade featuring an appliqued rural scene. 11-3/4" h. *Photo by Jacqueline Jones-Ridge. Courtesy of Gary M. Piper*

Top center: A Colonial "oil pot lamp" in polished brass, the "CONCORD," #6138. 10-3/4"h. *Photo courtesy of John and Donna Thorpe*

Top right: The "KINGSTON," #6188. This lamp is identical to the "CONCORD," but available in white, red, or green, "with Tole characteristics." 10-3/4" h.

Bottom left: Another oil lamp reproduction, this with a frosted glass chimney. #6193 "NEWTON," 8 3/4" h.

Bottom center: A central wood ball accents the polished copper or polished brass finish of the "MILTON," #6180. 10-1/4" h.

Bottom right: Hand-rubbed wood also highlights the unusual shape of Colonial-style lamp #6142, the "BRUNSWICK." "Because of its maple finish, it is a good lamp to use with maple furniture." 15" h.

Right: Earliest of the nauticals, the "BINNACLE LIGHT," #25002. The "BINNACLE," produced from 1933 through 1938, was also available in battery version #25001. 5-1/2" h. *Courtesy of John and Donna Thorpe*

Above: Shaded version of the "BINNACLE," #01006 "SHIP AHOY." 10- 1/2" overall h.

Facing page: Shiver me timbers! Three selections from the vast Chase array of "Nautical" themed lamps. *From left:* #6187 "NEWPORT," 12-1/2" h.; #6310 "MASTHEAD," 16" h.; #6314 "BARNEGAT," 11-1/2" h. The "lantern" portion of each lamp could be illuminated separately from the top light. The "NEWPORT" was a dual-purpose lamp. *Courtesy of John and Donna Thorpe*

This page:
Top left: The "MASTHEAD," cast adrift. Edges of the original shade were "lashed with cord, much as a sail is fastened," and buyers had a choice of red or green lantern glass. *Courtesy of Stephen and Joanne Klender*

Top center: A predecessor to the "BARNEGAT," which debuted in 1941, is the "WINDJAMMER," #6301, featured in the 1939 and 1940 catalogs. 11-1/2" h.

Top right: From 1939 only: #6147, the "NANTUCKET," another ship's lantern, but more globular in shape. 14" h.

Bottom: Real hemp rope is wrapped around the base of the lamp at left, the "CLIPPER," #6191, 15-1/4" h. A slight twist of the "wheel" turned the lamp on or off. At right, another wheel-operated lamp, the aptly-named "WHEEL," #6305. 16-1/4" h. *Courtesy of John and Donna Thorpe*

More maritime fun! *Left:* #6306 "ANCHOR," a wall lamp. 12-3/4" h. *Right:* Another dual-purpose lamp, the "FARRAGUT," #6308. 12-3/8" h. *Courtesy of John and Donna Thorpe*

Is it the "FARRAGUT"? The design is similar, but the base is unmarked, has concentric circles, and "ship's wheel" handles. The anchor's rough casting and blue color are also not found in the Chase "FARRAGUT" listings. *Photo by Jacqueline Jones-Ridge. Courtesy of Jackie and Harry Ridge*

A portion of a Chase promotional brochure showing, center, the original "FARRAGUT." Also pictured: #6319 "VICTORIA." *Courtesy of Barbara Endter*

Novelties

Top: Something for the younger set: #6160. the "KIDDIE" lamp. "A toy military band marches around the shade, and a like design is stamped in the base." 11-1/2" h.

Bottom left: Let the drums roll out! The perfect addition to the "SENTINEL," "COLONEL," "COLONEL'S LADY," and "KIDDIE" lamp roster: the "DRUM LAMP," #6324. The drum motif was a popular one at Chase and included the "DRUM" nightlight, #01010, a bank, and smoking accessories. (1934's Lamps catalog also featured a drum lamp in the Empire style, # E 600, "THE SCARLET DRUM.") 10" h. *Photo courtesy of John and Donna Thorpe*

Right: The "SENTINEL," #17112. His stalwart stance appeared on the cover of 1942's final Chase Specialty catalog. The "SENTINEL's" uniform was available in red or blue plastic, and the original shade was decorated to represent a drum. 15-7/8" h. *Photo by Jacqueline Jones-Ridge. Courtesy of Gary M. Piper*

More militia: #27014 "COLONEL'S LADY" greets her cohort, #27013 "COLONEL." He debuted in 1934, she followed in 1935. The painted-face bulbs of the Lurelle Guild designs were listed as "standard, available everywhere"! Each, 9-3/8" h. *Courtesy of John and Donna Thorpe*

A change of outfit for the military pair. Green and white was offered as a third color choice. *Courtesy of John and Donna Thorpe*

Top: The "COLONEL" and his lady guard a nursery, in this Metal Lath ad from the 1937 edition of *Homeowners' Catalogs*.

Bottom left: Cheers! The Chase "BEER MUG," #90042, is converted into #01007, the "TANKARD LAMP." The "TANKARD" appeared only in the 1934 catalog, which noted the lamp "makes a timely debut for use at 3.2 parties, and for decorating private bars." 11" h.

Bottom right: Uncataloged, but clearly marked "Chase" is this clever novelty: the "MR. PEANUT LAMP." How did it get its nickname? A quick comparison with the mascot on a can of Planters Peanuts™, and the answer should be obvious. There's a rotating celluloid panel behind "MR. PEANUT'S" eyes. When the lamp is lit, symbols of the four playing card suits—clubs, hearts, spades, and diamonds—are displayed in succession. *Photo by Dale Endter. Courtesy of Barbara Endter*

Walter Von Nessen's "CONSTELLATION" lamp, #17048, in polished copper. The pierced stars of the metal shade were lit by the globe beneath. 8-1/2" h. *Courtesy of John and Donna Thorpe*

Desk Lamps

An early version of the "DESK LAMP," #01003. Unlike models that appear in the Chase catalogs, this variation has different fittings at top and base, and the stem is not fluted. 14-1/2" h. *Photo by Jacqueline Jones-Ridge. Courtesy of Gary M. Piper*

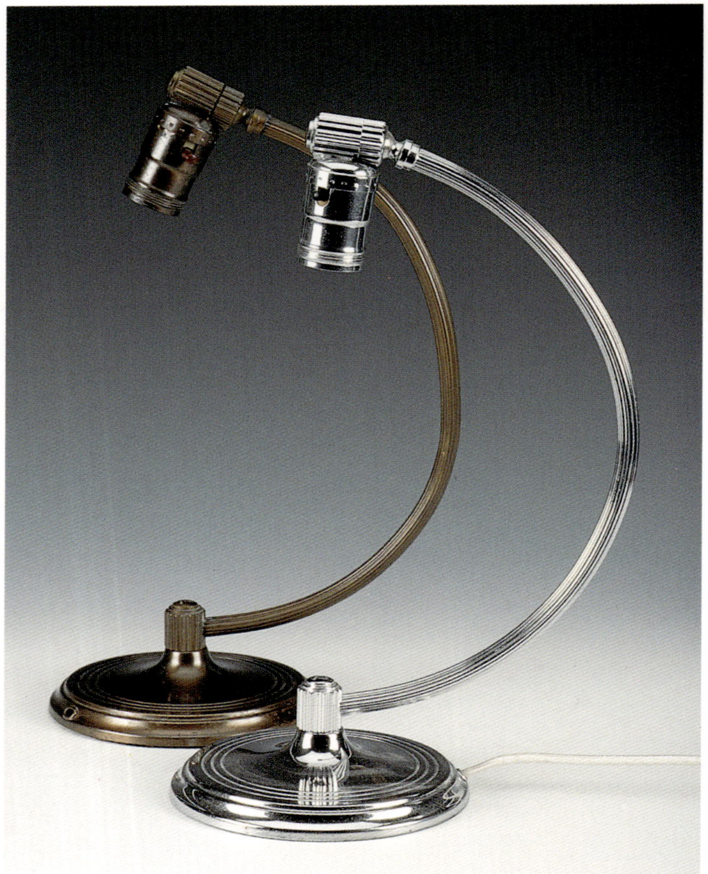

Catalog version of the "DESK LAMP" in English bronze and polished chromium. *Courtesy of John and Donna Thorpe*

Top: The "DESK LAMP" goes presidential. It's shown here gracing one of the bedrooms in the former residence of President and Mrs. Franklin D. Roosevelt, Hyde Park, New York.

Bottom: "All the comforts of reading in bed." The "DESK LAMP," at left center, is one of the bedroom lighting options featured in this ad from the January 1934 *Woman's Home Companion*.

Another curved-stem desk lamp, the "COUNCILOR," #6173, came equipped with a push-button socket. 13" h.

Left: #6154 "COMET," a dual-purpose desk lamp. The original shade of #6154 was translucent white plastic. #6151, with metal shade, was also available. 8-1/2" h. *Right:* #6176 "SUTTON," suitable for desk or table use. 14" h. *Courtesy of John and Donna Thorpe*

"Just right for a boy's room or a home craftsman's work bench." #6320 "SUNBIRD" featured a convex plastic base, and an adjustable opaque metal shade. 9-1/4" h. *Photo by Jacqueline Jones-Ridge. Courtesy of Gary M. Piper.*

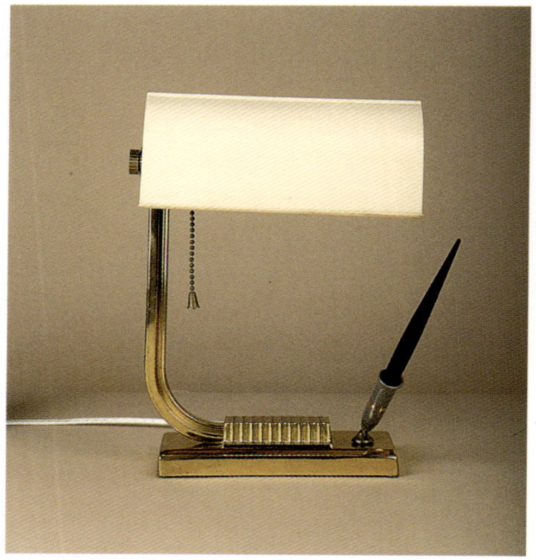

Top left: #01011, the "QUILL LAMP," named for the embossed design of crossed quills that decorates its base. 10" h. *Courtesy of Stephen and Joanne Klender*.

Top right: Another decor variation of the "QUILL," with a combination black and nickel base. *Photo by Jacqueline Jones-Ridge. Courtesy of Jackie and Harry Ridge*

Bottom left: The "BOND," #6172, came equipped with an adjustable translucent plastic shade. The lamp's grooved base prevented pens and pencils from slipping away. 10" h. *Photo by Jacqueline Jones-Ridge. Courtesy of Gary M. Piper*

Bottom center: Sheaffer Pen Co. adapted the "BOND" to promote the company's writing products. This "BOND" still carries the Sheaffer label. *Photo by Jacqueline Jones-Ridge. Courtesy of Gary M. Piper*

Bottom right: High? Low? Adjust the socket stem to any height desired on the "WINTHROP," #6155! 11" h. *Courtesy of John and Donna Thorpe*

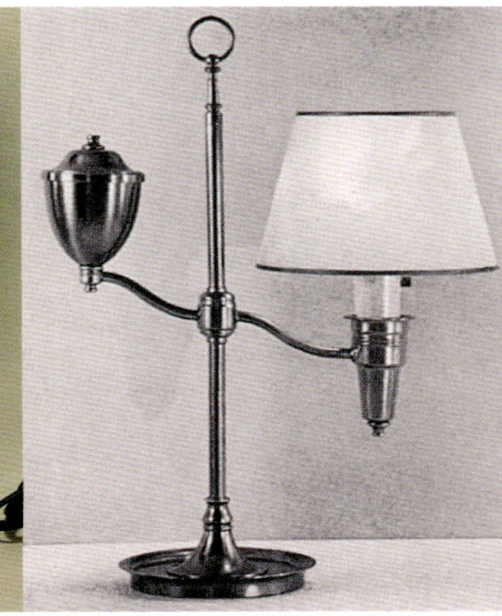

Left: Stationery or memos could be kept close at hand with the "WRITING PAPER LAMP," #01014. In addition to English bronze with walnut, #01014 was also offered in polished copper with blond maple. The shade shown is original. 13" h. *Courtesy of Danny Kaplan*

Above left: For the scholar with a sense of style: #6323 "ACADEMY." The four-column central stem was available in white or walnut-color Bakelite. 15-3/4" h. *Photo by Dale Endter. Courtesy of Barbara Endter*

Above center: #6196 "ADAM STUDENT LAMP." Adding a Colonial flavor to this desk lamp were an oil pot and candle arm. 19-1/2" h.

Above right: One of the loveliest Chase desk lamps: the "CHANCELLOR," #6189, a classic in bronze, with translucent white plastic shade. A "specially designed Holophane prismatic light director" distributed the "CHANCELLOR'S" light properly, protecting eyes from glare. 17" h.

Dual-Purpose Lamps

A wedge of Bakelite forms the body of dual-purpose lamp #6156, the "CRESCENT." "A star cluster design on the parchment shade adds to its astronomical look." With a plastic reflector, the "CRESCENT" was available as #6303. 11-1/2" h. *Courtesy of John and Donna Thorpe*

As decor accents, Chase also offered the "CRESCENT BOOK ENDS," #90137. *Courtesy of Stephen and Joanne Klender*

Top: A late addition to the dual-purpose line: 1942's "LEXICON," #6322. For unobstructed lighting, the "LEXICON's" diagonal bracket can be pushed forward through the ball on the base. 11-5/8" h. *Courtesy of John and Donna Thorpe*

Bottom: A wood-and-metal dual-purpose combo, #6190, the "WESTWOOD." 14" h.

Right: *From left:* Two urn-shaped dual-purpose lamps. #6195 "BERKELEY, 15-1/4" h.; #6153 "WARWICK," 13-3/4" h. When hung, both lamps appear free-floating, grasped by their metal arms. *Courtesy of John and Donna Thorpe*

Left: The maple ball of the "EDGEWOOD," #6159, turns on its axis for conversion from table to wall lamp. 14" h. *Courtesy of John and Donna Thorpe*

Above: Shown with a reverse view of the "WRITING PAPER LAMP," #01014 is, at left, dual-purpose lamp #6174, the "PRESTON." Like the "EDGEWOOD," the "PRESTON" features a maple ball body. 10-1/2" h. *Courtesy of John and Donna Thorpe*

A 01005 "FLUTED BASE TABLE LAMP." "The light reflects from the polished chromium fluted sides of the base, giving brilliant kaleidoscopic refractions." 16" h. *Courtesy of John and Donna Thorpe*

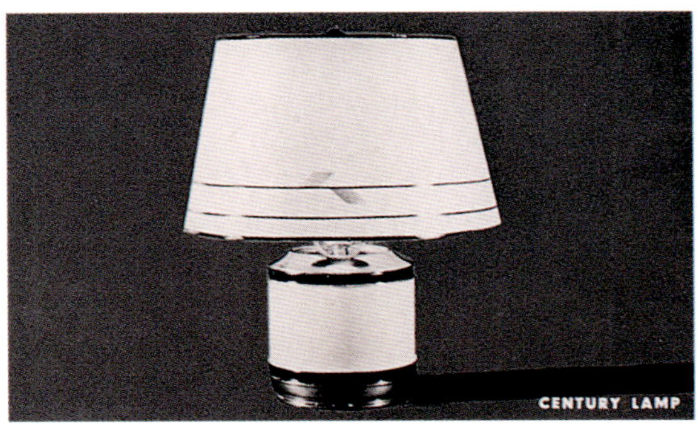

Top: 1934 catalog debut photo of the "CENTURY LAMP" # A 01008, in black enamel with chromium banding. 15" h.

Bottom: As shown in the 1935 catalog, the "CENTURY LAMP" in white enamel.

Designed by Lurelle Guild, the "CONSOLE LAMP," #27010, "reflects the colors of the room, and while modern in design, harmonizes quietly with any style of decoration." Homemakers were advised to display it next to brightly-colored objects, which would reflect in the lamp's mirror-like surface. 17" h. (Another "CONSOLE LAMP," #11250, designed by Walter Von Nessen, appears in Chapter 2.) *Courtesy of John and Donna Thorpe*

Left: "Conceived from a fragment of Greek classical art:" # M 500 "THE ARCADIA." The drapery pattern on the lamp body was repeated in the design of the original blue Clair de Lune shade. 18-1/2" h. *Photo by Jacqueline Jones-Ridge. Courtesy of John Myhre*

Above: "Deriving its name from the crystal flame finial that sparkles between the candle cups:" # M 503 ""THE FLAME." When in use, the finial "sparkles and finds reflection in the highly polished chromium about it." 15" h. *Photo courtesy of John and Donna Thorpe*

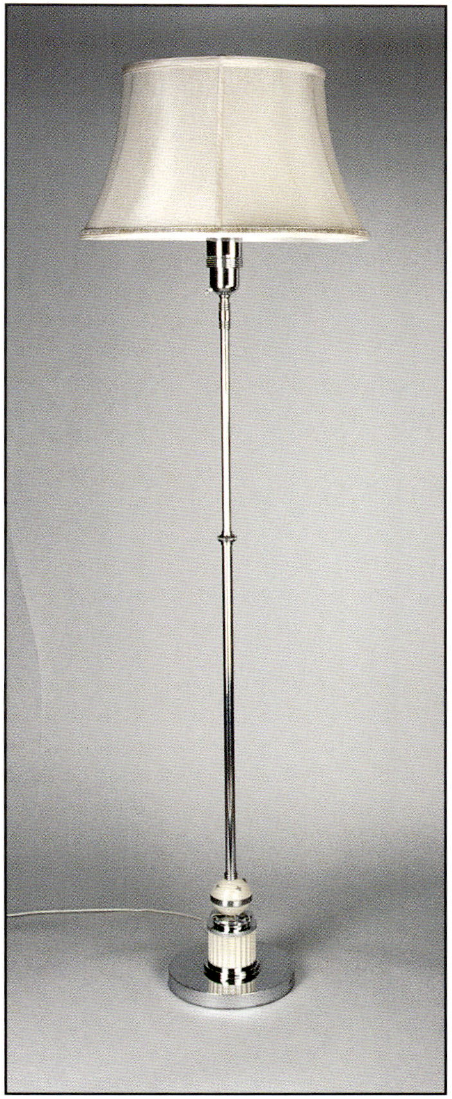

"THE DELPHIC" floor lamp, # M 350 "combines polished chromium and white in a charming manner." Adjustable height. *Photo by Jacqueline Jones-Ridge. Courtesy of Gary M. Piper*

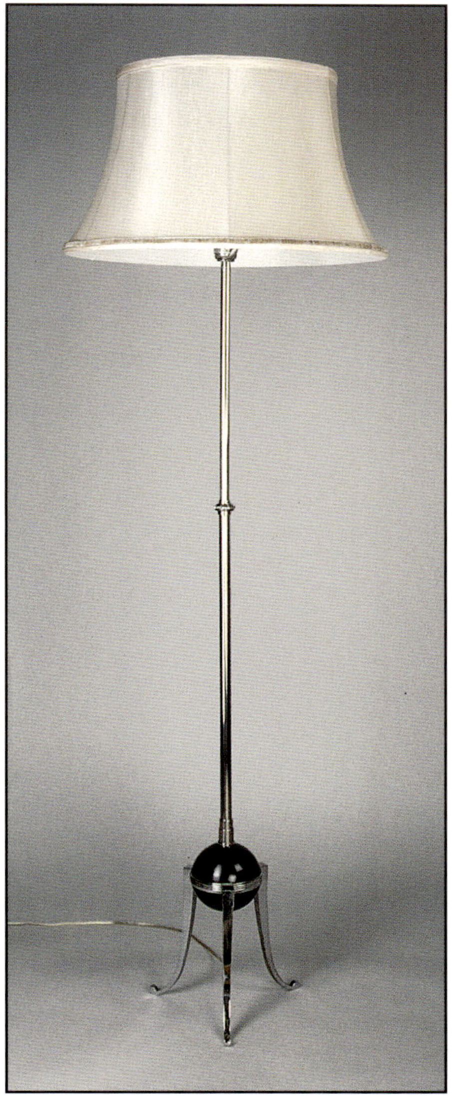

M 250 "THE HELLENIC" floor lamp is "strikingly finished in polished chromium and black," and came with an indirect metal reflector. Adjustable height. *Photo by Jacqueline Jones-Ridge. Courtesy of John Myhre*

THE NEW LAMPS

give light as well as beauty

For years the only qualifications people have asked for in buying a lamp were in respect to its looks. If it was attractive in appearance and the shade was the right proportion to the base, well and good. That was all that was necessary. Today, however, the picture has changed. Decorative qualities still count but, in addition, there is something else that matters, an that something is the light-giving qualitie: Does this lamp give enough light to rea by? Will that lamp light my desk sufficiently? Is that the lamp I should get t light my card table? Those are the kin of questions we hear today when the ale man or woman goes forth to buy a lam

By revolving the arm, the modern floor lamp to the left can be used as either a bridge lamp or reflector type. From Russell Wright Studios. Below it a double-duty lamp in modern design which can serve as floor or bridge lamp. The height is adjustable. Rembrandt Lamp Corp.

Dana B. Merrill

The semi-indirect reflector floor lamp above, in polished chrome with white has scientifically designed light-giving quality. At right: chromium, with black trim; indirect metal reflector. Chase Brass & Copper Co.

Albert M. Leach

LET'S look back at the really amazing strides that have been taken during the last few years in "light engineering," as the science of illumination is called. About three or four years ago, lamp manufacturers began to realize that there was something to be considered in bringing out new lamps besides their mere appearance. They had heard numerous complaints from various sources in regard to the need of better lighting but they had done nothing about it. So they began to experiment with different kinds of lighting equipment, looking for a means to aid in giving a stronger and more direct light. And they hit upon the reflector.

Table lamp at right, in untarnishable silver, has a new device: a switch control for three degrees of light. Shade of stretched eggshell silk. The Lightolier Company

The reflector lamp, as you probably all know, is th lamp with the inverted metal cone, at the bottom of whic is placed a high-wattage bulb. This reflector throws th light against the ceiling and it is reflected down in a even, shadowless light. That was the first step in bette illumination and it was one which has practically don away with a type of lamp once very popular—the plain candle-arm floor lamp Today we hardly ever see these lamp on the market. The candle-arm reflecto with its greatly improved lighting, ha replaced it.

From then on, experiments were mad by the dozen. Every company began bringing out improved reflector lamps, addin new features or making variations tha they thought would increase their light giving qualities. However, so far most c this light engineering was confined to floo lamps. Table [*Please turn to page 18*

Below: Table lamp, modern in feeling. Shade ca be lowered or raised t meet any need. Mutual Sunset Lamp Mfg. C

170

The "DELPHIC" and "THE HELLENIC" are among the lamps profiled in this February 1935 article on new designs from *The American Home*.

Uncataloged Lamps

Some lovely Chase lamp variations were never cataloged. This lamp bears a striking design resemblance to the Empire-themed # E 402 "THE CARROLLTON," shown in Chapter 6. However, here a central globe and eagle have replaced "THE CARROLLTON's" dangling prisms. Similar globes appear on # E 400 "THE D'ORSAY," and # M 506 "THE DORIC." *Courtesy of John and Donna Thorpe*

Central globe detail.

A New Lamp Adds A Crisp L
To The H

CHASE

In these times of depression nothing changes the appearance
like a new lamp. Nowadays one can buy a complete lamp, sha
for less than the shade alone used to cost. And so women buy s
bases together, getting the advantage of having them harmoni
they are designed as a unit.

Ship Ahoy Light No. 01006

While this lamp is particularly designed for Summer resorts, seashore, and lake and stream cottages, it is also a lamp for a boy's bedroom, or a guest room. It carries with it a salty sea atmosphere from the old ship's lantern base
of brightly polished brass t
and up-to-date looking mar
that harmonizes with it.
The over-all height of the l
inches, and it retails for $
priced at $14.40 per dozen

Circle Lamp No. 01004

This lamp works on a swivel, which allows the light to be adjusted to a convenient angle for reading. The graceful design creates an impression of weight and size without actually taking up much room for it is only 14 inches high, and
12 inches in diameter. It is
and design for use on an
Furnished in polished chro
lish bronze, or Patina green
with shade it retails for $5.
each wholesale.

Fluted Base Table Lamp No. 01005

Here is a beautiful and unusual lamp that will harmonize with almost any period of decoration. From early Victorian and Biedermeier to Colonial and Modern, this lamp will fit and blend, and yet be strikingly beautiful in itself. The light reflects from the polished
fluted chromium sides of th
ing a beautiful mirror-like
Height 16 inches, diameter
inches. Furnished in brillian
dull English bronze, and
green. Complete with shac
for $7.50. Price $3.75 each

CHASE

Chase Brass & Copper Co., Incor
Specialty Sales Dept. — 200 Fifth Ave., New Yo
Printed in the United States

"In these times of Depression, nothing changes the appearance of a room like a new lamp." Chase lamps of every design and style period helped brighten the lives of 1930s consumers. *The Gift And Art Shop*, March 1933.

Chapter 6

"The 1934 Chase Lamps Brochure"

*"Of course, you want to know more about Chase Lamps than we can possibly tell you here. So send the convenient coupon below. It will bring you a beautiful **free** booklet showing **all** Chase Lamps, prices, and where to see them."*

Chase Lighting advertisement, 1935

How many homeowners of the 1930s anxiously awaited receipt of their promised Chase brochure, eager to begin redecorating? Well, you don't have to wait! Reprinted here in its entirety is the 1934 Chase Lamps brochure, featuring primarily the designs of Lurelle Guild. (And it's ***free***, too!) *1934 Chase Lamps brochure courtesy of Barbara Endter*

The Flying Dolphin (left)

The Flying Dolphin comes either in antique tin or in pewter. A little red dolphin is poised on the edge of the base. It has a 12 inch parchment shade. Lamp height, 18 inches. Price, $12.00. Base only, $10.00.

The Gloucester (right)

Colorfully finished either in Barn Red or Laurel Green, the Gloucester is copied from an old whale oil lamp. The 10 inch white parchment shade carries a Colonial sunflower decoration. Lamp height, 17 inches, $7.25. Base only, $6.00.

The Mt. Vernon (left)

Finished in Colonial brass, the Mt. Vernon has two adjustable metal shades that come in either Barn Red or Colonial brass. It makes an excellent reading lamp. Height, 18 inches. Price, $13.50.

The Admiral (right)

Designed from an old Colonial ship's lamp, the Admiral is finished in Colonial brass and is fitted with a 16 inch parchment shade in an antique egg shell finish with dull gold binding. Lamp height, 22¾ inches. Price, $14.25. Base only, $12.00.

The Barnett (left)

This old historical desk light is finished in Colonial brass with pewter rings on the stem. The quaint reflector is finished either in Barn Red or Laurel Green, the inside being in cream. Lamp height, 17 inches. Price, $12.00.

The Danforth (right)

Copied from an early model by William Danforth, this lamp is finished in Colonial brass with the laurel decoration on the base, in silver. The ivory parchment shade is 12 inches wide. Lamp height, 18 inches. Price, $8.75. Base only, $7.00.

The Washingtonian (left)

Symbolical of the classic spirit of 1810, this lamp is finished in Federal brass and black. The pale gold faille taffeta shade has black corners and is 13 inches wide. Lamp height, 22 inches. Price, $28.50. Base only, $16.50.

The Patriot (right)

Commemorating the achievements of George Washington, the Patriot is finished in Federal brass and has a 14½ inch pale gold faille taffeta shade, self binding and gold piping. Lamp height, 19½ inches. Price, $23.25. Base only, $13.50.

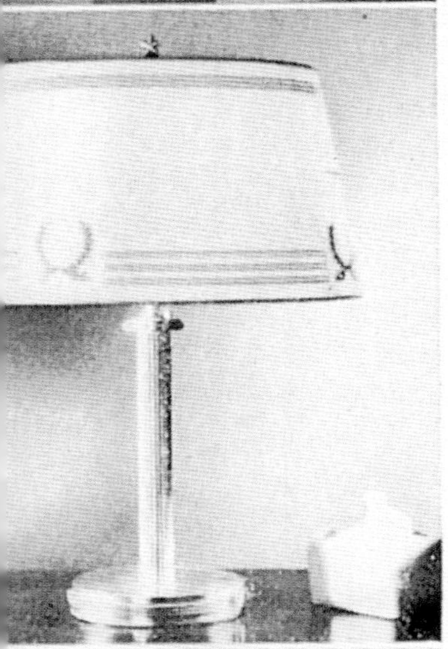

The Columbia (left)

This gracefully styled lamp is finished entirely in Federal brass, and is surmounted by a 14 inch white parchment shade with decoration in gold and an antique gold binding. Lamp height, 19 inches. Price, $11.75. Base only, $10.00.

The Ipswich (right)

This charming and authentic lamp is finished in Federal brass and decorated with an eight-pointed star. The 10 inch shade is white parchment with the stars, lines and binding in dark blue. Lamp height, 17 inches. Price, $13.50. Base only, $12.00.

The Victory (left)

The lovely patriotic design of the Victory is heightened by its Federal brass finish. The 12 inch shade is of pale gold pleated faille taffeta with gold binding and black piping. Lamp height, 17¼ inches. Price, $16.00. Base only, $12.50.

The Maryland (right)

Carrying out the rich gleam of Federal brass in the lamp itself, the 13 inch oval shade is appropriately made of gold faille taffeta with gold binding and a gold and white cord. Lamp height, 17 inches. Price, $22.50. Base only, $12.00.

The Continental (left)

The Continental is a colorful lamp, being finished in Federal brass with a gray green base. It is topped by a 15 inch white pleated faille taffeta shade, gold binding, green piping. Lamp height, 22¼ inches. Price, $17.00. Base only, $12.50.

The Republic (right)

Smartly styled and distinguished by its bound arrows, the Republic Lamp is finished in Federal brass. The 12 inch white parchment shade is decorated with gold, antique gold binding. Lamp height, 16½ inches. Price, $10.75. Base only, $8.75.

The John Paul Jones (left)

Finished in Federal brass and mounted on a toned black base, the John Paul Jones lamp is typical of its era. The oval shade, 15½ inches wide, is of egg shell faille taffeta. Lamp height, 21 inches. Price, $37.00. Base only, $25.00.

The Constitution (right)

This lamp, with its lovely crystal prisms, has a Federal brass finish combined with black. It is topped by a 16 inch gold faille taffeta shade, self binding, reefed with black. Lamp height, 21¾ inches. Price, $35.00. Base only, $20.00.

The Georgetown (left)

A classic urn in Federal brass and a white fluted column give the Georgetown a majestic appearance. It has a 20 inch yellow faille taffeta shade, red and black binding and a red cord. Lamp height, 28¾ inches. Price, $39.50. Base only, $22.00.

The Liberty (right)

This beautifully proportioned Federal lamp is finished entirely in Federal brass. It is topped by a 14 inch white faille taffeta shade with gold binding and a gold and white cord. Lamp height, 18½ inches. Price, $19.50. Base only, $11.50.

The Windsor (left)

The high pedestal base, in Georgian brass, beautifully sets off the antique white urn. The 19 inch shade is of gold faille taffeta with a white and gold grosgrain binding. Lamp height, 26½ inches. Price, $45.50. Base only, $27.50.

The Victor Hugo (right)

Colorfully finished in either Regent Red, Adam Green or Black, with trimmings in Georgian brass, this lamp is beautified by a 12 inch white faille taffeta shade trimmed with gold galleon. Lamp height, 18¾ inches. Price, $28.50. Base only, $15.00.

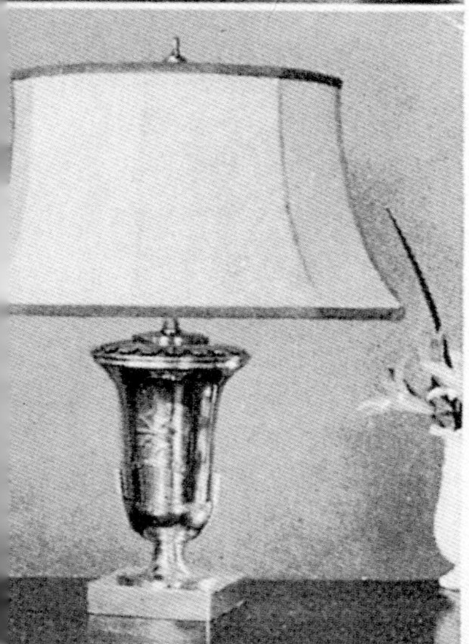

The Hammond (left)

Graced by a lovely urn, decorated with a heraldic design, this lamp is finished in Georgian brass. It has a 15 inch white faille taffeta shade with dark gold grosgrain ribbon binding. Lamp height, 19¼ inches. Price, $17.00. Base only, $13.00.

The Melton (right)

This smart table lamp is finished in Georgian brass and is adaptable to any size room. It is fitted with a 12 inch toned parchment shade with brown and gold lines and drapery. Lamp height, 16½ inches. Price, $9.00. Base only, $6.50.

The Princess Anne (left)

This lamp comes in two finishes, either in Georgian brass or in Georgian brass with an Adam Green base. The 19 inch shade is of gold faille taffeta, self binding and green piping. Lamp height, 25 inches. Price, $43.00. Base only, $25.00.

The Wedgwood (right)

Finished in Georgian brass with the genuine Wedgwood plaque in green and white, or in silver with the plaque in blue and white, this lamp has 5¾ inch faille taffeta shades with ruffled tops. Lamp height, 16 inches. Price, $47.00. Base only, $40.00.

The Girandole (left)

The Girandole Lamp, authentically Georgian in style has a Georgian brass finish which is accented by crystal prisms and etched crystal chimneys. It will add great distinction to a Georgian living room. Lamp height, 15½ inches. Price, $25.50.

The Mirabeau (right)

Mounted on a black base and colorfully finished in Republic Red and Empire brass the Mirabeau has a 15½ inch oval shade of egg shell taffeta with gold binding and red piping. Lamp height, 18½ inches. Price, $34.00. Base only, $22.00.

The Cheltenham (left)

Entirely finished in Georgian brass, this lamp has a simplicity that makes it an excellent choice for any room. The 12 inch shade is white pleated faille taffeta with a gold binding. Lamp height, 18½ inches. Price, $12.50. Base only, $8.50.

The Swan (right)

This lamp is finished in either Republic Red, Directoire White or Corsican Green, with Empire brass trim. The 12½ inch shade is of egg shell faille taffeta, binding and cord to match. Lamp height, 18 inches. Price, $22.50. Base only, $15.00.

The Chippendale (left)

This authentic lamp is finished in Georgian brass with either Adam Green or Regent Red beneath the fretwork. It has a 16 inch coffee colored faille taffeta shade, piping of red or green. Lamp height, 22 inches. Price, $32.00. Base only, $20.00.

The Navarre (right)

Gaining distinction from its broad, round lines and interesting decoration, this lamp is finished in Empire brass, and topped by a 12 inch shade of red parchment with gold binding. Lamp height, 19 inches. Price, $12.00. Base only, $10.00.

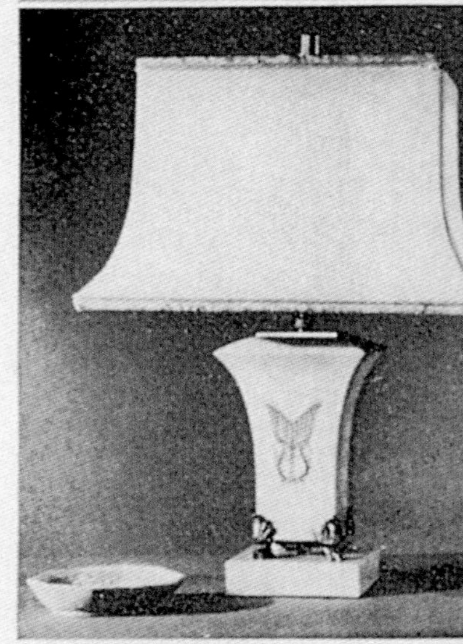

The Carrollton (left)

In tones of crystal, white and gold, this lamp commands attention. It is finished in Empire brass and has a 16 inch white pleated faille taffeta shade, white and gold rolled binding. Lamp height, 22½ inches. Price, $37.50. Base only, $22.50.

The Savoy (right)

Finished in Empire brass, the Savoy is a charming lamp for many types of interiors. The 16 inch oval shade is of egg shell faille taffeta with gold binding, piped with red. Lamp height, 17¼ inches. Price, $18.50. Base only, $13.50.

The Lady Godey (left)

A hand of the finest porcelain holds this lamp, which is finished in Empire brass. The 12 inch shade is of Wedgwood-blue Clair de Lune, trimmed with white braid and chromium balls. Lamp height, 21 inches. Price, $30.50. Base only, $18.50.

The Chalfonte (right)

Smartly executed in Empire brass and black the Chalfonte is topped by a 14 inch black Clair de Lune shade with gold cord binding. It will give a brilliant and distinctive accent to any room. Lamp height, 21 inches. Price, $28.50. Base only, $16.50.

The Mayhew (left)

The Mayhew offers new and interesting lines in lamp design. It is finished entirely in Empire brass and has a 12 inch egg shell faille taffeta shade with light green binding, dark green piping. Lamp height, 16¾ inches. Price, $13.00. Base only, $9.50.

The Bordeaux (right)

This French Provincial lamp is finished in Directoire White, Corsican Green or Republic Red, Empire brass trim. It has a 12 inch egg shell faille taffeta shade, self binding, piped with red. Lamp height, 18 inches. Price, $17.00. Base only, $8.50.

The Scarlet Drum (left)

Inspired by a Revolutionary drum this lamp is finished in Republic Red and laced with Empire brass. The 14 inch shade is red Clair de Lune decorated with gold cord. Lamp height, 17½ inches. Price, $22.50. Base only, $12.00.

The Carolinian (right)

The base of this tall lamp is in Empire brass, the column in Directoire White and the 19 inch shade is white pleated faille taffeta bound with gold and white grosgrain, gold bows. Lamp height, 29 inches. Price, $40.50. Base only, $22.50.

The Argonne (left)

Beautifully decorative, the Argonne is finished in Republic Red, Empire brass and black. The 14 inch shade is of white parchment and banded with red, top and bottom. Lamp height, 18 inches. Price, $10.50. Base only, $8.50.

The d'Orsay (right)

This striking Empire lamp is exceptionally smart. It is finished in Empire brass and black and topped by a 14 inch beige colored cane cloth shade with black binding, piped with gold. Lamp height, 22½ inches. Price, $39.00. Base only, $22.50.

The Victoria (left)

This charming lamp has a column in Directoire White supported by a base finished in Empire brass and black. The 14 inch shade is of black Clair de Lune, with gold cord. Lamp height, 20½ inches. Price, $27.00. Base only, $15.00.

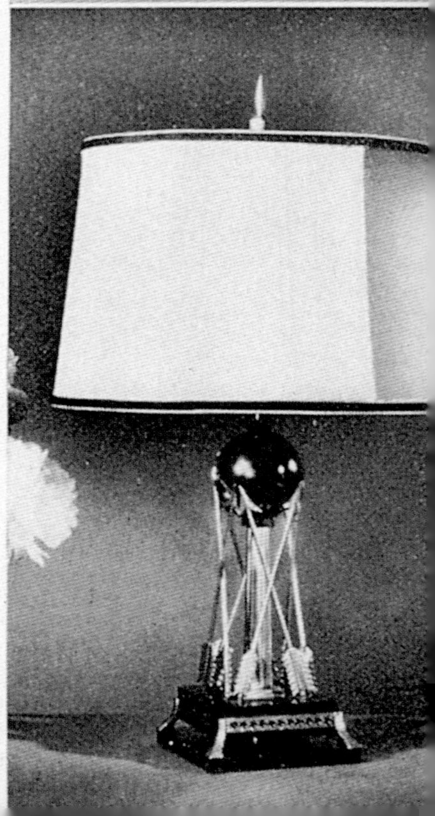

The Ionic (left)

Resting on a gracefully turned Ionic base, this pleasing lamp is finished in polished chromium and graced by a 15 inch oval shade of moonstone Claire de Lune with white ribbed bands. Lamp height, 18 inches. Price, $33.50. Base only, $18.50.

The Flame (right)

Two graceful candle arms give distinction to this lamp, in polished chromium. The 14 inch shade is of yellow faille taffeta lined with white, with a silver and white grosgrain binding. Lamp height, 15 inches. Price, $21.00. Base only, $12.00.

The Sparta (left)

With its cylindrical chromium body relieved by banded lines, this lamp has true Classic Modern distinction. The 14 inch shade is white parchment, ringed with silver lines. Lamp height, 19¾ inches. Price, $11.75. Base only, $10.00.

The Plato (right)

Thoroughly unusual in design, the Plato is finished in polished chromium. The 10 inch oval shade has a closed top. White self-striped crepe, with self binding and silver piping. Lamp height, 13¼ inches. Price, $18.00. Base only, $10.00.

The Ulysses (left)

The attractive cylindrical body of the Ulysses is finished in polished chromium and is topped by a 12 inch white Clair de Lune shade trimmed with braided white and gold cord. Lamp height, 18 inches. Price, $22.00. Base only, $15.00.

The Arcadia (right)

Rich ornamentation gives the Arcadia unusual distinction. Made of lasting brass and finished in highly polished chromium, this lamp has a 14½ inch oval shade of blue Clair de Lune. Lamp height, 18½ inches. Price, $33.50. Base only, $17.50.

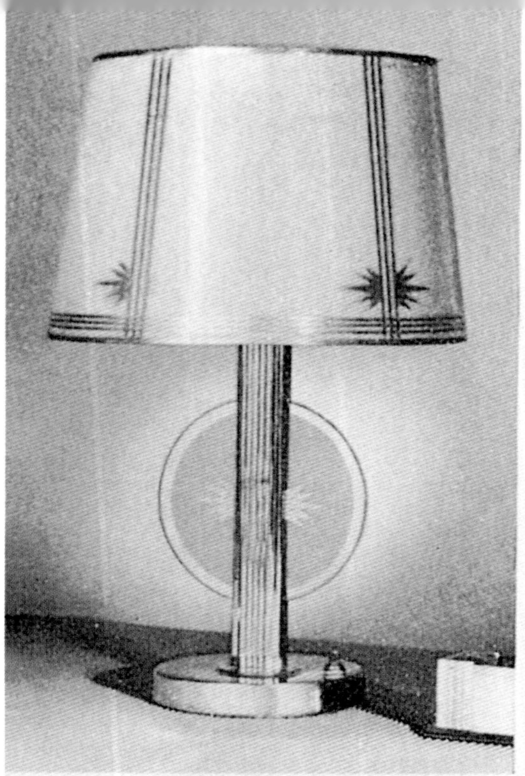

The Luna (left)

Decorated with a "camphor glass" disc and finished in polished chromium, the Luna has true individuality. It has a 10 inch white parchment shade with lines and decorations in silver. Lamp height, 15¾ inches. Price, $11.75. Base only, $10.00.

The Desk Lamp (right)

Finished in either polished chromium or English bronze, the Desk Lamp can be adjusted to nearly any position. The 8½ inch shade is supplied in a choice of old ivory parchment or beige parchment. Lamp height, 14½ inches. Price, $4.50.

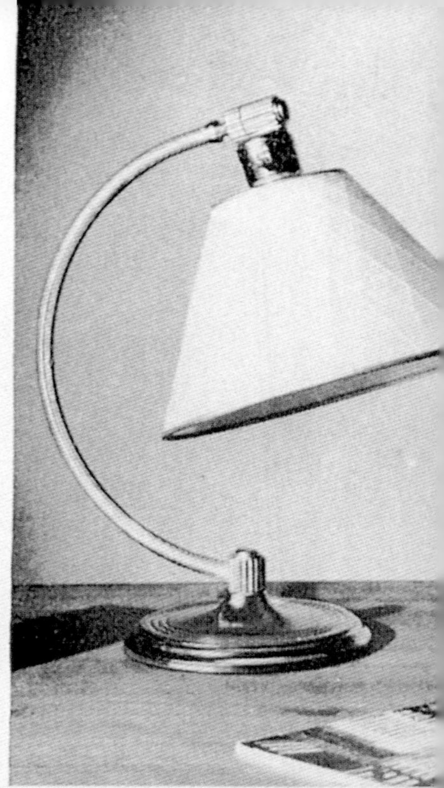

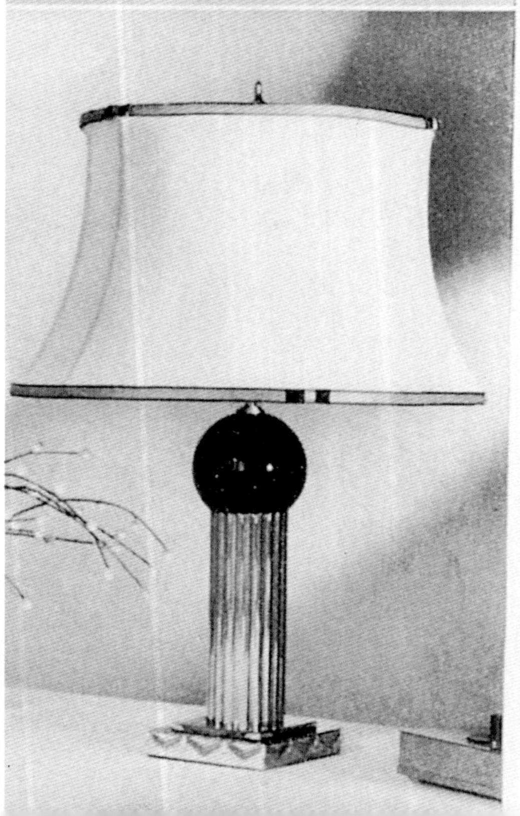

The Doric (left)

The Doric has a lovely fluted column of polished chromium supporting a blue Biedermier glass ball. The 15 inch egg shell faille taffeta shade has a silver binding piped with blue. Lamp height, 22¾ inches. Price, $25.00. Base only, $12.00.

The Flying Cloud (right)

Finished in antique brass, with the center glass ball of green glass, the Flying Cloud's nautical interest is completed by the dark green cord on the 10 inch pale gold faille taffeta shade. Lamp height, 18 inches. Price, $24.00. Base only, $15.00.

The Zodiac Lamp (left)

With the signs of the Zodiac on the center ring and the globe in sky blue, the Zodiac is topped by a 16 inch oval shade of gold faille taffeta, blue binding. Lamp height, 17 inches. Price, $24.75. Base only, $15.00.

The Fluted Base Lamp (right)

The fluted column which gives this lamp distinction, is finished in polished chromium and mounted on a black base. A 12 inch white parchment shade with black and silver lines completes the color scheme. Lamp height, 16 inches. Price, $7.50.

The Century Lamp (left)

The Century Lamp is finished either in black enamel with chromium band or white enamel with chromium band. The 12 inch natural parchment shade has line decorations in black and silver. Lamp height, 15 inches. Price, $6.00.

The Ball Lamp (right)

The Ball Lamp comes finished in polished chromium, or in polished copper with a polished brass base. Its 12 inch white parchment shade is decorated with lines in colors to match the base. Lamp height, 15 inches. Price, $7.50.

The Console Lamp (left)

This lamp is finished either in satin chromium with a polished chromium base, or, in English bronze. A 12½ inch rectangular shade of white parchment or beige parchment matches the base. Lamp height, 17 inches. Price, $10.00.

The Circle Lamp (right)

The Circle Lamp is finished either in polished chromium or English bronze. Matching these finishes is an 8½ inch shade which is supplied in old ivory parchment or in beige parchment to match the base. Lamp height, 14 inches. Price, $5.50.

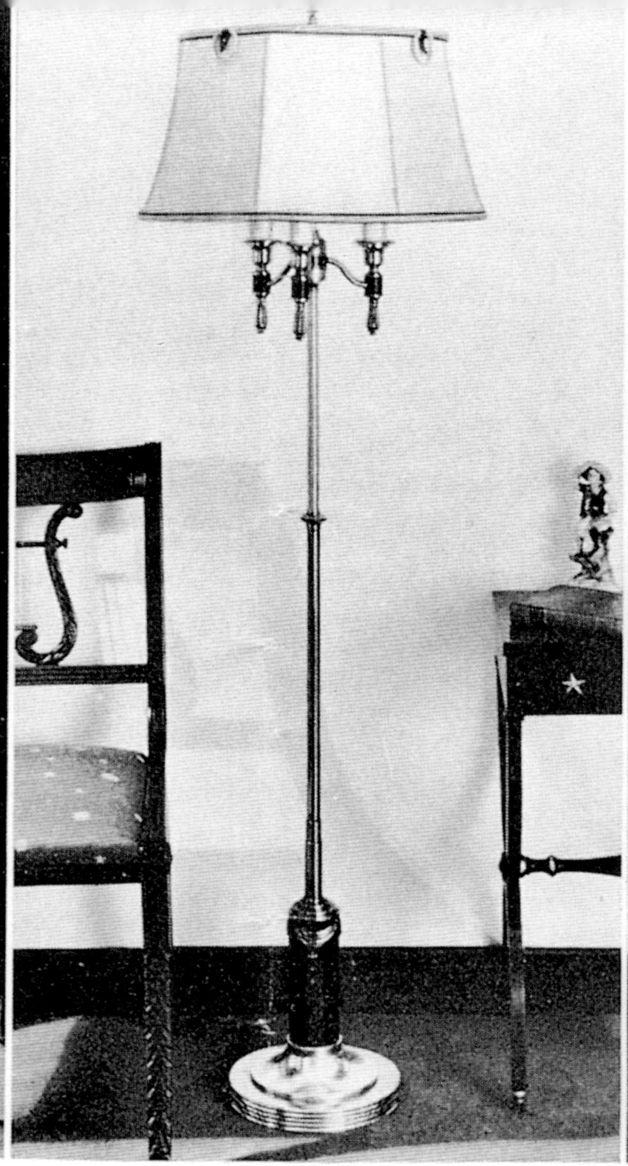

The Dedham

Inspired by a candle stand of the Pilgrim Century, this lamp is finished either in black iron or in polished steel combined with Colonial brass. So beautifully have these early finishes been applied that even the early forge marks have been reproduced. The 18 inch oval toned parchment shade has a gold binding. Price, $28.00. Base only, $25.00.

The Virginian

Finished in Federal brass and black, this lamp has an 18 inch gold faille taffeta shade with self binding, black piping. Height, adjustable. Price, $48.50. Base only, $35.00. Alternate: Virginian Three-Lite-Indirect Floor Lamp. In addition to three lights it has a metal indirect reflector. Shade: same as above. Price, $56.00. Base only, $42.50.

The Adams

This lamp is supplied in polis chromium and black or Fede brass and black. It has an 18 i white faille taffeta shade, black silver binding. Height, adjusta Price, $43.50. Base only, $30.0 Alternate: Adams Semi-Indi Floor Lamp. With semi-indirect flector. Shade: same as above. Pr $46.00. Base only, $32.50.

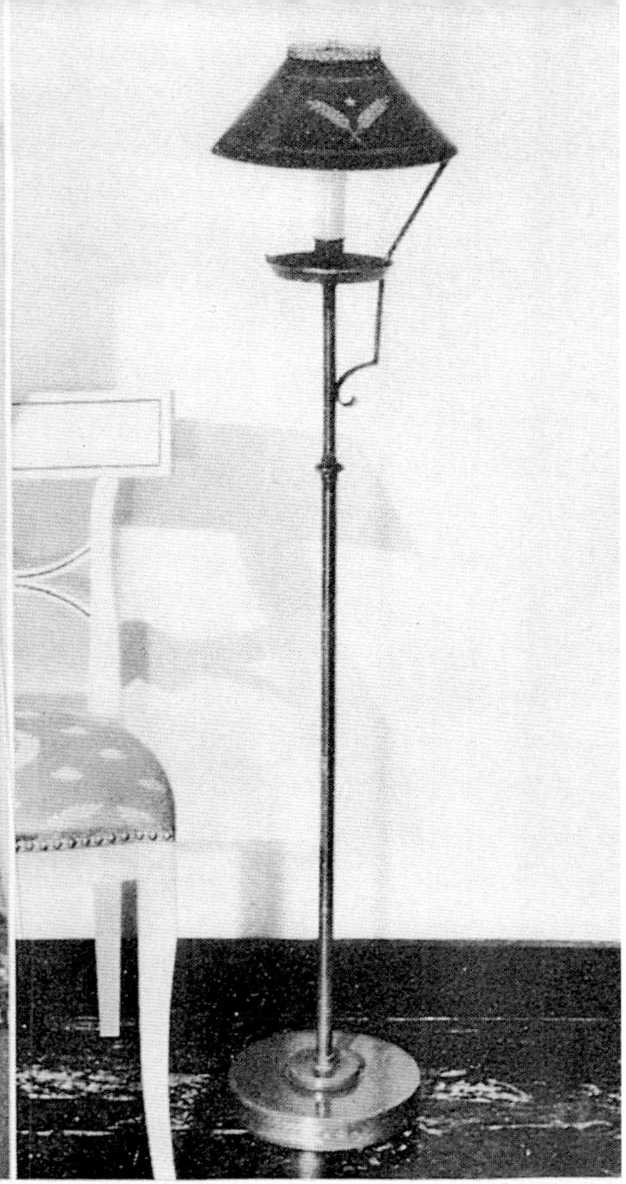

The Arrow

ısually striking in design, with starred octagonal base and arrow ı, this Federal bridge lamp has implicity that makes it suitable many other decorative schemes. ish, Federal brass and black. It itted with a 10 inch shade that nished in Federal brass. Height, ustable. Price, $27.00. Base only, .00.

The Paddington

This lamp is finished in Georgian brass and has an 18 inch white pleated faille taffeta shade, white and gold binding. Height, adjustable. Price, $46.50. Base only, $30.00. Alternate: Paddington Semi-Indirect Floor Lamp. Fitted with white diffusing glass semi-indirect reflector. Shade: same as above. Price, $49.00. Base only, $32.50.

The Trianon

An excellent choice for the bedroom as well as the living room or library, the Trianon is an authentic copy of a French Empire lamp and comes finished either in Republic Red, Directoire White or Corsican Green with trimmings of Empire brass. The 11¼ inch shade is of metal, in colors to match. Height, adjustable. Price, $27.00.

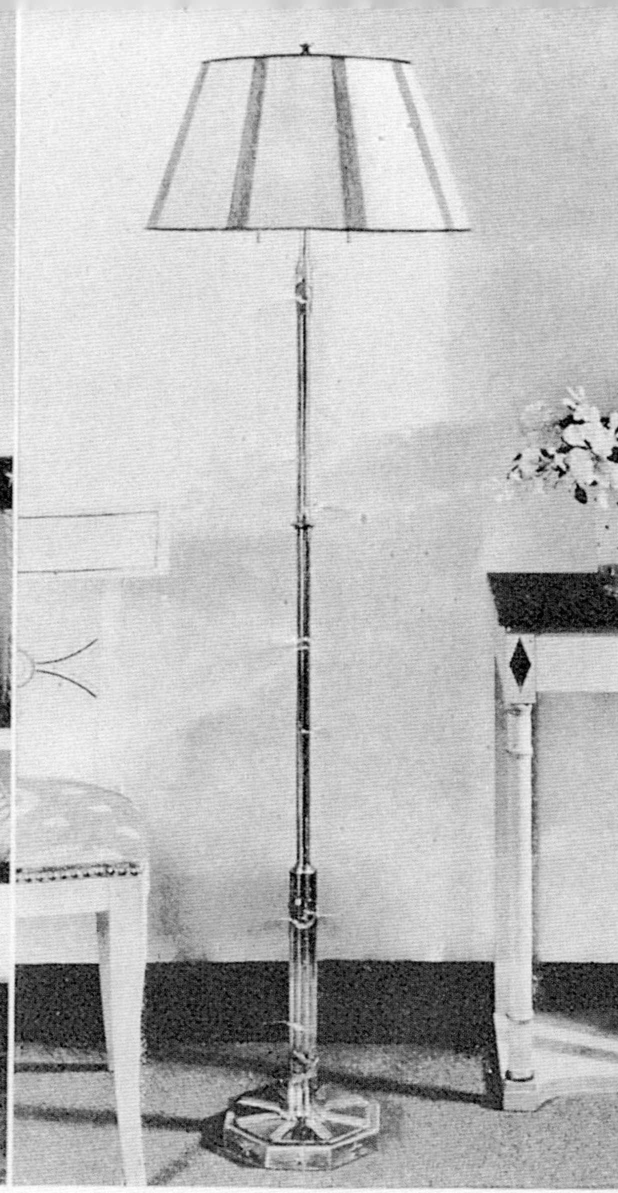

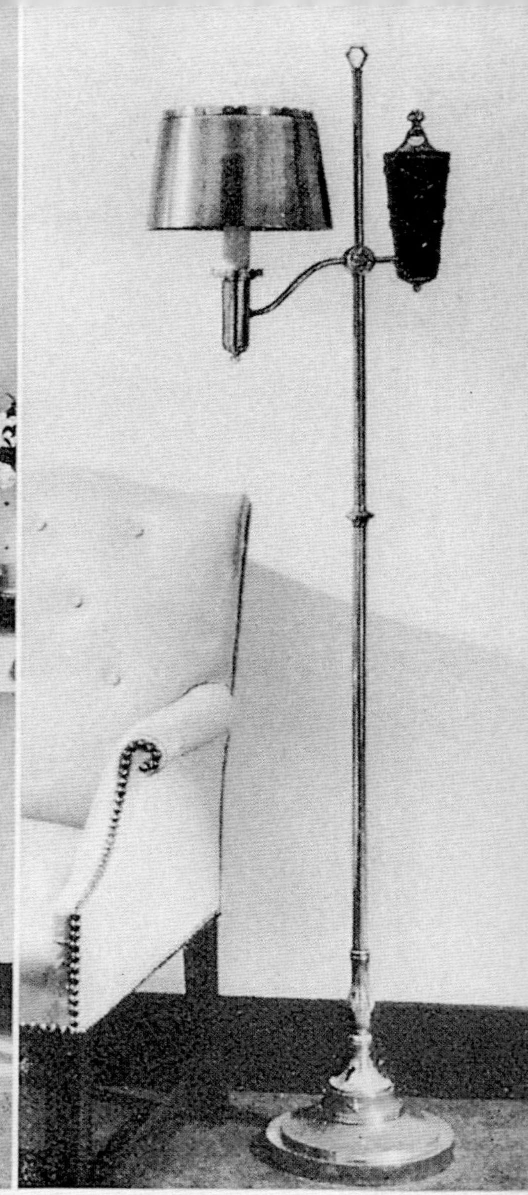

The Chantilly

The slender tapering shaft and delicate galleries of this lamp give it a trim appearance that is lacking in many bridge lamps. The Chantilly is finished entirely in Empire brass and has a 10 inch pale gold faille taffeta shade with blue and gold binding. Lamp height, adjustable. Price, $36.00. Base only, $30.00.

The Avignon

Decorated with the reeds and stars of the Empire period, this lamp is finished in Empire brass. It has an 18 inch toned parchment shade, with reeded bands. Height, adjustable. Price, $28.00. Base only, $25.00. Alternate: Avignon Semi - Indirect Floor Lamp. Fitted with semi-indirect reflector. Shade: same as above. Price, $30.50. Base only, $27.50.

The Lafayette

Comes in Corsican Green, Repul
Red or Directoire White, Emp
brass trim. It has a 10 inch shad
Empire brass. Height, adjusta
Price, $38.00. Base only, $32.00.
Alternate: Lafayette Semi-Indi
Floor Lamp. Without bridge ar
fitted with semi-indirect reflec
It has an 18 inch parchment sh
Price, $31.00. Base only, $25.00.

The Cherbourg

e base of this lamp is finished in
sican Green with the trim in
pire brass. It has an 18 inch gold
le taffeta shade, dark green bind-
Height, adjustable. Price, $43.25.
se only, $27.50.
ernate: Cherbourg Semi-Indirect
or Lamp. Fitted with semi-indi-
t reflector. Shade: same as above.
ce, $45.75. Base only, $30.00.

The Delphic

The Delphic floor lamp combines polished chromium and white. It has an 18 inch white faille taffeta shade with rolled silver and gray binding. Height, adjustable. Price, $40.75. Base only, $25.00.
Alternate: Delphic Semi-Indirect Floor Lamp. Fitted with semi-indirect reflector. Shade: same as above. Price, $42.75. Base only, $27.00.

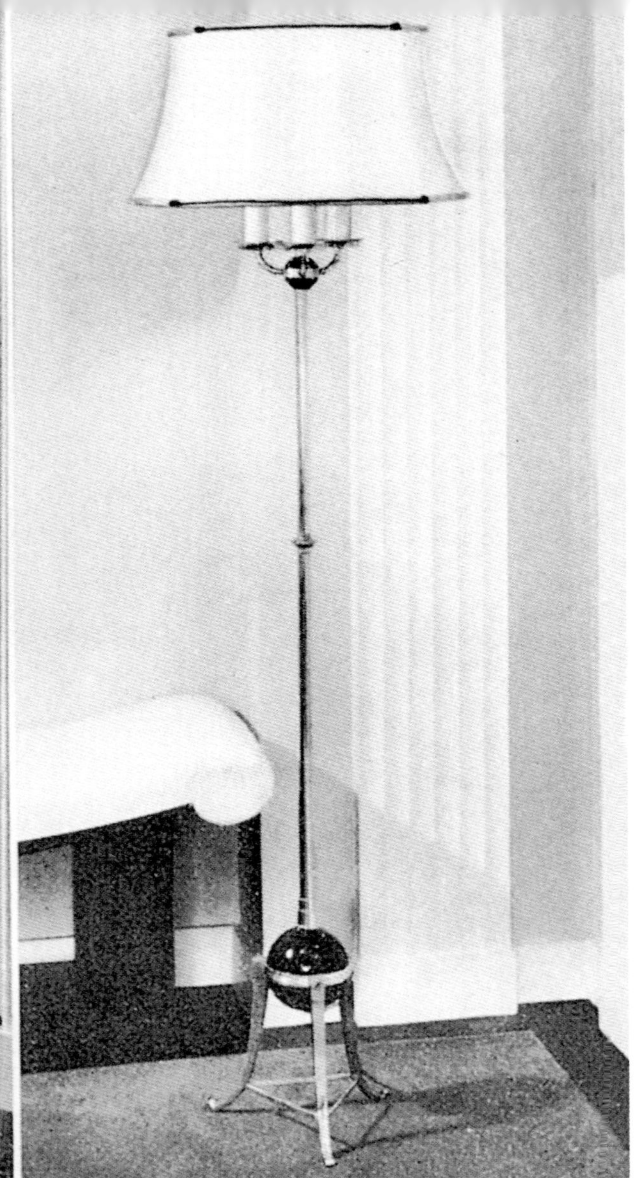

The Hellenic

Finished in polished chromium and black. The 18 inch shade is of white faille taffeta, silver gray binding, black cord. Height, adjustable. Price, $52.50. Base only, $37.50.
Alternate: Hellenic Three-Lite-Indirect Floor Lamp. In addition to three lights has a metal indirect reflector. Shade: same as above. Price, $59.50. Base only, $44.50.

Chapter 7
"Carrying A Torch: Chase Battery Lights"

"Such a cunning and convenient little bedside lamp to use when you haven't a lamp close at hand. And can't you imagine that a child of six or seven, just beginning to go about the house in the dark, would simply love it? Going up to bed alone in the dark would lose all its terrors if this were at hand."

House Beautiful
May, 1930

Mobility, as *House Beautiful* pointed out in its analysis of the "CANDLELIGHT," #11150, was a major selling point of the Chase battery lights. Wired lamps were not always practical—and a battery light could come in handy, whether you were a child creeping about in the dark, or a householder searching for a burnt-out fuse.

Battery lights were among the earliest Chase lighting devices, some appearing in advertisements prior to 1933's first formal Specialties catalog. Many had "wired" counterparts: the "BINNACLE (#25001 battery, #25002 wired); the "FARMER'S LANTERN" (#25006 battery, #25007 wired); the "SCONCE LIGHT" (#16004 battery, #16005 wired), and the "SKIPPER"S LANTERN" (#25004 battery, #25005 wired). One pair received different names: the battery-powered "PILGRIM CANDLELIGHT," #11255 ("a graceful, self-contained light for the guest-room bedside table, or to light a small son or daughter safely upstairs to bed"), and its less-mobile counterpart, the "PRISCILLA," #11144. The Chase Specialty division also produced several battery-operated flashlights: the "AIRALITE," #22003; the "BOMB," #22001; and (just in case of a blackout) the "ILLUMINATED PENCIL," #9012.

While most Chase battery lights flickered briefly, as remnants of the pre-Specialty and Lamps divisions era, a few proved remarkably durable. As late as 1939, the "BINNACLE LIGHT" was still providing a "salty sea atmosphere to city homes, summer cottages at the shore, outside porches, and terraces. And small boats, too."

Facing page: One of the very earliest Chase battery lamps was the nautical-themed "BINNACLE LIGHT," #25001. The globes of some "BINNACLES" were decorated in observance of Chicago's 1933-34 "Century of Progress International Exposition." *Courtesy of Stephen and Joanne Klender*

This page:
Left: The "BINNACLE" was also available in a wired version, #25002, shown here in brass and chromium flanking #16004, the "SCONCE LIGHT (BATTERY)."

Right: As noted in this July 1932 ad from *The Gift And Art Shop*, the "BINNACLE" "gives a steady light, or flashes for signaling." 5-1/2" h.

This Chase promotional flier touts the "new battery SCONCE LIGHT," #16004. In addition to battery and wired, a "SCONCE LIGHT (CANDLE)," #16003 could also be ordered. Each, 7-7/8" h.

Top: The "SCONCE LIGHT" (WIRED), #16005, and its battery counterpart, #16004. The battery version bears a promotional logo for the 1939 New York World's Fair. *Photo by Dale Endter. Courtesy of Barbara Endter*

Bottom: #11255, "THE PILGRIM CANDLELIGHT," just "$7.20 the dozen, complete with flame bulb and standard batteries." *Photo by Dale Endter. Courtesy of Barbara Endter*

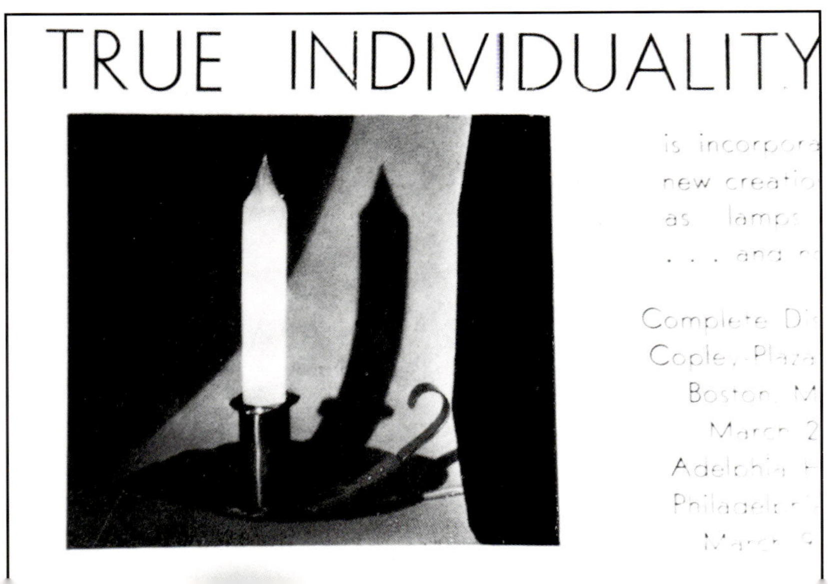

Top left: Although "THE PILGRIM" never graced the Chase catalogs, it did appear in early advertisements such as this one, from the April 1931 issue of *The Gift And Art Shop*.

Bottom left: Wired companion to "THE PILGRIM" was "THE PRISCILLA," #11144. *The Gift and Art Shop*, March 1931.

Above: "THE PRISCILLA," far right, joins three other Colonial- themed lamps. *From left:* #6307 "SETTLER'S HURRICANE," 7-1/4" h.; #16007 "MT. VERNON HURRICANE LAMP" (non-electric), 9-5/8" h., shown with the "MT. VERNON CANDLE SNUFFER," #90149; "FARMERS' LANTERN (BATTERY), #25006, 5-1/2" h. *Courtesy of Stephen and Joanne Klender*

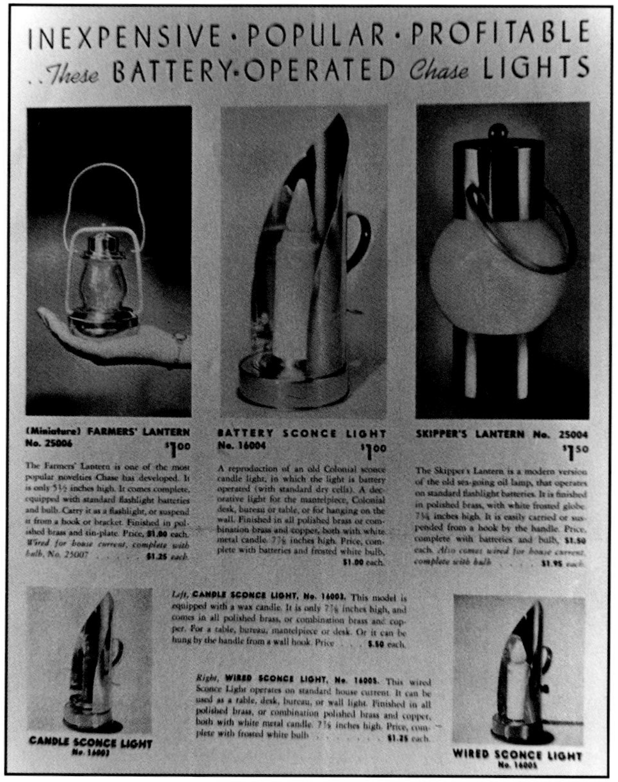

INEXPENSIVE · POPULAR · PROFITABLE
. . *These* BATTERY-OPERATED *Chase* LIGHTS

(Miniature) FARMERS' LANTERN No. 25006 $1.00

The Farmers' Lantern is one of the most popular novelties Chase has developed. It is only 5½ inches high. It comes complete, equipped with standard flashlight batteries and bulb. Carry it as a flashlight, or suspend it from a hook or bracket. Finished in polished brass and tin-plate. Price, **$1.00** each. *Wired for house current, complete with bulb, No. 25007* . . . . . . **$1.25** *each.*

BATTERY SCONCE LIGHT No. 16004 $1.00

A reproduction of an old Colonial sconce candle light, in which the light is battery operated (with standard dry cells). A decorative light for the mantelpiece, Colonial desk, bureau or table, or for hanging on the wall. Finished in all polished brass or combination brass and copper, both with white metal candle. 7⅝ inches high. Price, complete with batteries and frosted white bulb, **$1.00** each.

SKIPPER'S LANTERN No. 25004 $1.50

The Skipper's Lantern is a modern version of the old sea-going oil lamp, that operates on standard flashlight batteries. It is finished in polished brass, with white frosted globe. 7¼ inches high. It is easily carried or suspended from a hook by the handle. Price, complete with batteries and bulb, **$1.50** each. *Also comes wired for house current, complete with bulb* . . . . **$1.95** *each.*

Left, **CANDLE SCONCE LIGHT, No. 16003.** This model is equipped with a wax candle. It is only 7⅝ inches high, and comes in all polished brass, or combination brass and copper. For a table, bureau, mantelpiece or desk. Or it can be hung by the handle from a wall hook. Price . . . . **$.50** each.

Right, **WIRED SCONCE LIGHT, No. 16005.** This wired Sconce Light operates on standard house current. It can be used as a table, desk, bureau, or wall light. Finished in all polished brass, or combination polished brass and copper, both with white metal candle. 7⅝ inches high. Price, complete with frosted white bulb . . . . **$1.25** each.

CANDLE SCONCE LIGHT
No. 16003

WIRED SCONCE LIGHT
No. 16005

Above: "Inexpensive–popular–profitable." Shown in this dealer flier for battery-operated Chase lights are all three versions of the "SCONCE LIGHT," the "FARMERS' LANTERN," and, at right, the "SKIPPER'S LANTERN," #25004. 7-1/4" h.

Right: The "SKIPPER'S LANTERN" in its wired variation, #25005, complete with original box. Although it looks like a head in a pillbox hat, the design theme was that of an "old sea-going oil lamp." 7-1/4" h. *Courtesy of John and Donna Thorpe*

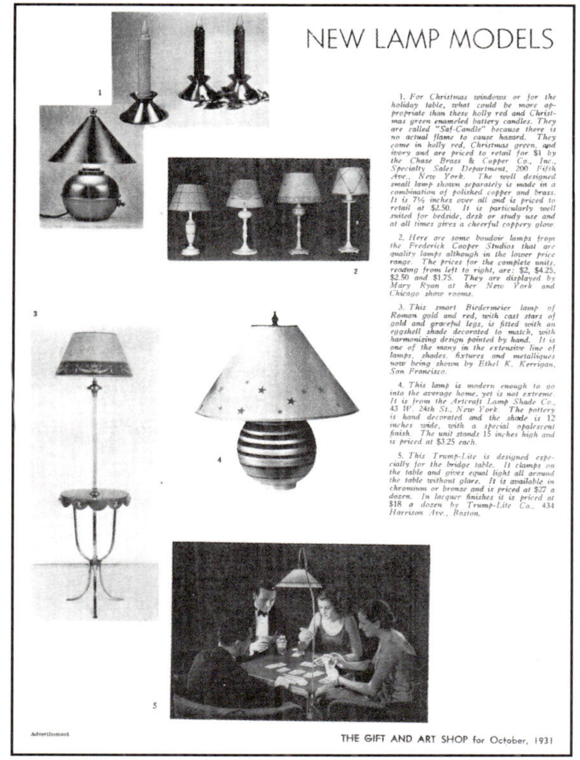

NEW LAMP MODELS

1. For Christmas windows or for the holiday table, what could be more appropriate than these holly red and Christmas green enameled battery candles. They are called "Saf-Candle" because there is no actual flame to cause hazard. They come in holly red, Christmas green, and ivory and are priced to retail for $1 by the Chase Brass & Copper Co., Inc., Specialty Sales Department, 200 Fifth Ave., New York. The well designed small lamp shown separately is made in a combination of polished copper and brass. It is 7½ inches over all and is priced to retail at $2.50. It is particularly well suited for bedside, desk or study use and at all times gives a cheerful coppery glow.

2. Here are some boudoir lamps from the Frederick Cooper Studios that are quality lamps although in the lower price range. The prices for the complete units, reading from left to right, are: $2, $4.25, $2.50 and $1.75. They are displayed by Mary Ryan at her New York and Chicago show rooms.

3. This smart Biedermeier lamp of Roman gold and red, with cast stars of gold and graceful legs, is fitted with an eggshell shade decorated to match, with harmonising design painted by hand. It is one of the many in the extensive line of lamps, shades, fixtures and metalliques now being shown by Ethel K. Kerrigan, San Francisco.

4. This lamp is modern enough to go into the average home, yet is not extreme. It is from the Artcraft Lamp Shade Co., 43 W. 24th St., New York. The pottery is hand decorated and the shade is 12 inches wide, with a special opalescent finish. The unit stands 15 inches high and is priced at $3.25 each.

5. This Trump-Lite is designed especially for the bridge table. It clamps on the table and gives equal light all around the table without glare. It is available in chromium or bronze and is priced at $27 a dozen. In lacquer finishes it is priced at $18 a dozen by Trump-Lite Co., 434 Harrison Ave., Boston.

Advertisement

THE GIFT AND ART SHOP for October, 1931

Left: After exhausting the possibilities inherent in ship's lanterns, Chase went for the ultimate in nautical design: the "LIGHTHOUSE LAMP," #16002. Appearing only in the 1935 Specialty catalog, the "LIGHTHOUSE" was "furnished in satin brass or satin nickel." The light, naturally enough, shone through the windows of the cupola. 6-1/8" h. *Courtesy of John and Donna Thorpe*

Above: "For Christmas windows or for the holiday table." The Chase "SAF-CANDLE," #11256, shown at top, was an early Chase innovation designed to prevent fires caused by flame candles. Available colors included "holly red, Christmas green, and ivory." Also featured in this photo from the October 1931 issue of *The Gift And Art Shop* is the "GLOW LAMP," #01001.

Enjoying wider distribution was another battery candle, the "CANDLE-LIGHT," #11250. A decorated version of the Chase "CANDLELIGHT," offered for sale by Rhode Island's Pohlson Galleries, gave rise to the misnomer, "Pohlson Candle." 5-1/2" h.

Top: A "CANDLELIGHT" pair, shown with original boxes. Colors are given as blue and "old rose." *Photo by Dale Endter. Courtesy of Barbara Endter*

Bottom: Keeping spirits bright: "Candlelight by Chase," box logo detail.

CHASE CHROMIUM • BRASS • COPPER PRODUCTS

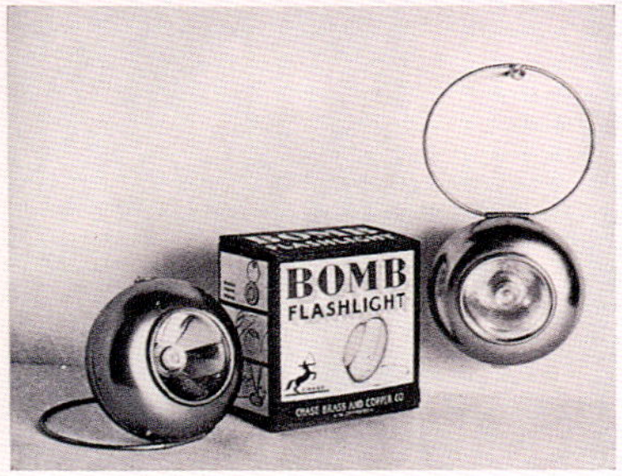

Bomb Flashlight No. 22001

"BOMB" FLASHLIGHT

No. 22001

A new type flashlight that will stand by itself, slip over the wrist or hang from a hook. Neat and compact; fits the coat pocket, takes little space in a car pocket. Diameter 3½ inches, 1¾ inches thick. Finished in polished nickel and packed separately in an illustrated box as shown or in an attractive 3-color counter display container that holds six lights. Complete with batteries and bulbs. Price, $1.00 each.

"AIRALITE"

No. 22003

A smart and handy companion to the powder compact; a small vest pocket flashlight. It measures but 2 x 2½ inches. Airalite has the candlepower and switch equipment of a much larger flashlight. It hangs on a hook or stands on its own base. Finished in polished nickel with colored enamel inlays to give it smartness and beauty. Takes a standard pen-light battery. Has unbreakable lens. Packed in individual gift box, or six Airalites to a display card designed for window or show case use. Complete with batteries and bulbs. Price, 75c each.

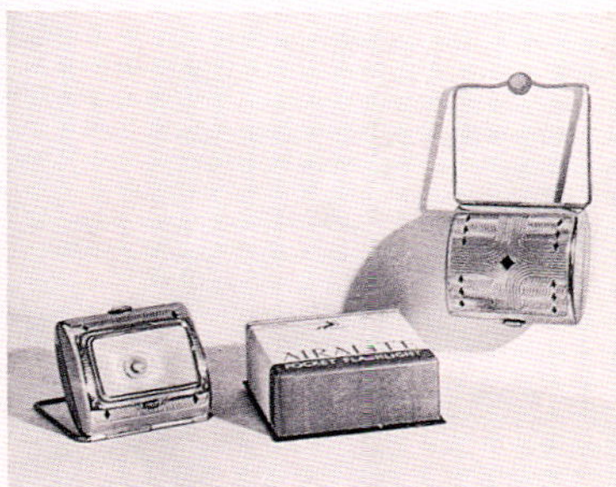

Airalite No. 22003

Page 34

May 23, 1933. A. MITCHELL Des. 89,969

PORTABLE BATTERY LAMP

Filed May 28, 1932

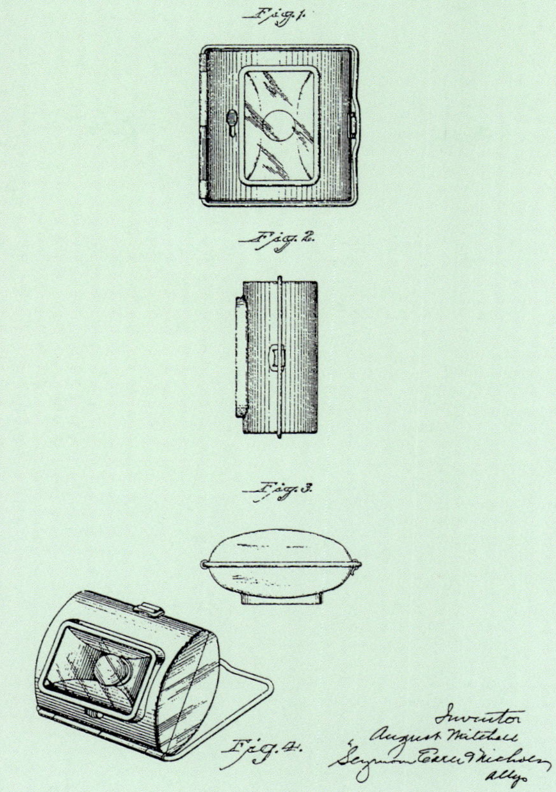

Top left: Lighting the way: Chase's enduring flashlight designs, shown on an original page from the 1934 catalog. #22001, "BOMB FLASHLIGHT," 3-1/2" d.; #22003, "AIRALITE FLASHLIGHT," 2" w. x 2-1/2" h. "The first really beautiful flashlights—as smartly designed as jewelry."

Top right: August Mitchell's 1933 patent for a "Portable Battery Lamp," soon to be on the market as the "AIRALITE."

Bottom: Chase lighting inventiveness knew no bounds: here's the original 1942 catalog entry for #9012, the "ILLUMINATED PENCIL," a flashlight and writing implement combo. Just the thing for rooms without the benefit of diffused Chase lighting! 5-5/8" l.

ILLUMINATED PENCIL No. 9012B

Patented U. S. Pat. Off. No. 2,204,136

Size: 5⅝" long; diameter, ⅝ inch.

Finish: Assorted finishes.

Price: Each, $.50
Sold in dozen lots only.

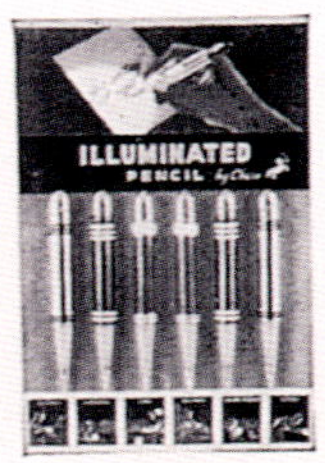

This pencil is invaluable for writing at night! It lights up the area around the pencil point just where the light is needed. It operates on a standard pen-lite battery cell. The flashlight bulb is in the white plastic part just above the point. The cap is turned to right to light up the point, and reversed to turn off the light. It also propels and repels lead. Six illuminated pencils in assorted finishes mounted on an attractive counter display card, as illustrated.

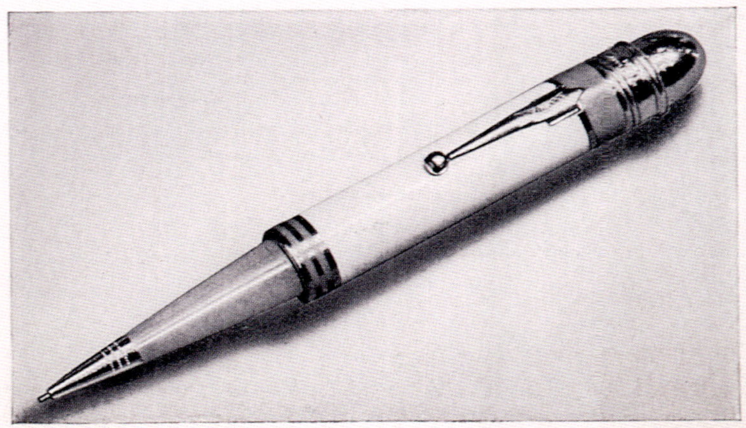

• 23

Chapter 8
"The Chase Lighting Fixtures Showroom"

"Now you may light your home beautifully and inexpensively—with lovely, new Chase Fixtures. No longer need you put up with unattractive, old-fashioned lighting fixtures that spoil the beauty of your home. Plan ***now*** *to replace the fixtures in one or more rooms. Refixturing is so easy—and costs far less than you may think! It is as simple as changing your curtains."*
Chase Lighting advertisement, 1934

Even for cash-strapped Depression buyers, "refixturing" was a bargain. With Chase prices ranging from $2.75 to a high of $50, it was possible, as the ads said, to "have the very finest fixtures in your living room—or your entire home."

The 1937 edition of the *Home Owners' Catalogs* featured this no-nonsense introduction to the section on Chase Lighting Fixtures. *Courtesy of Barbara Endter*

Lighting Up the Room

Designed by Lurelle Guild, over 170 separate Chase lighting fixtures were introduced in 1934. The first fixtures were available in the decorative styles of seven periods (full descriptions of each period can be found in Chapter 3). Classifications included "Early English" (J); "Early American" (C); "Federal" (F); "Georgian" (G); "Empire" (E); "Classic Modern" (M); and "American Adaptations" (A). The code letters shown preceded each inventory number, simplifying category identification; coordinating lamps by Guild were also offered for each period grouping.

In later years, as decorating by period began to lose its appeal, new fixtures were grouped by function, (e.g., "Hall Fixtures"), rather than by style. Descriptive fixture titles were abandoned; eventually, even the "PINE TREE SHILLING SCONCE" became just another "ONE-LIGHT COLONIAL BRACKET."

Scientific Lighting with "Even-Glow"

As function gained precedence in the Chase lighting line, a new arrival grabbed center stage: the Chase "Even-Glow" fixture. The 1936 pamphlet, *Saving Your Eyes With Correct Lighting* summarized the "Even-Glow" advantage:

> We introduce the new Chase "Even-Glow" lighting fixtures, which with astonishing economy give diffused light and eliminate glare entirely! The downward shaft of light from the bulb is filtered through the Plastic Bowl. But most of the light is thrown to the ceiling from where it is deflected and spread evenly throughout the room in diffused light. Chase "Even-Glow" lighting fills the room with light. It is a mellow light that is easy on the eyes. Protect your eyes and the eyes of your children from the ruin of improper lighting!

While the message wasn't subtle, and the "Even-Glow" bowl stylings were often repetitive, the public didn't seem to mind: "Even-Glow" remained an important part of the Chase inventory through the remaining life of the Lighting division.

Where Are They Now?

Even among today's seasoned collectors, Chase lighting fixtures, whether Guild or "Even-Glow," are in short supply. The reason is simple: unlike lamps, which could be easily removed when tastes changed, lighting fixtures were literally a part of the house itself. While the ads assured "refixturing is so easy," it really wasn't. Many homeowners, with little interest in rewiring, let old fixtures remain in place. If a major remodeling project did occur, the old fixtures were usually discarded rather than offered for resale. Who knew?

Additionally, at first glance it may be difficult to recognize a vintage fixture as "Chase." A new chandelier, shown hanging and brightly burnished in its catalog photo, appears much different than a dusty, tarnished piece, nestled among its loose wires on an antique dealer's shelf. Although Chase, in the early years, used paper labels glued to the canopies of chandeliers, and on the back of wall sconces, very few of these labels survive. Also generally missing in action are the paper hang tags that accompanied new sconces. Because of this, absolute authentication of a fixture as "Chase" is often not possible until the fixture can be taken apart for rewiring after purchase, and a model number hopefully found on one of the interior parts. As noted in Chapter 5's analysis of lamp identification, such numbers can be stamped on a metal washer, trim piece, or on the base. Early pieces will usually not carry the Chase "centaur" mark. When in doubt, study the original photo against the object to find as many points of similarity as possible, then make an educated guess. If the price is right, buy it. You may not see another.

At Starkweather

With the passage of years, many Chase fixtures have no doubt landed on the scrap heap. Fortunately, however, some homes have maintained their period decor. One such is "Starkweather," the original Watertown, Connecticut, home of Mr. and Mrs. Rodney Chase. Mr. Chase was a member of the Chase Brass & Copper Co.'s founding family, and a company officer. It's only natural that "Starkweather" would prove a safe haven—perhaps one of the last—for a host of Chase fixtures in their intended surroundings. The "on location" photos in this chapter were taken at "Starkweather," with the gracious cooperation of the home's current owners.

Welcome to the Lighting Fixtures Showroom

In addition to the "Starkweather" photos, our "showroom" features a sampling of newly photographed Chase fixtures drawn from private collections. A complete photo inventory of all Chase fixtures through 1937, as taken from original catalogs and brochures, appears in the chapters that follow. There's no doubt that, as more collectors become familiar with the "look" of a Chase fixture, more fixtures will surface. For now, as the 1934 Fixtures catalog promised, "a cordial welcome awaits you at the Chase showroom."

> *"Chase Fixtures introduce an entirely new and inexpensive way of adding charm to your home—for when you change the lighting of a room, you improve its whole appearance!"*
>
> Chase Lighting advertisement, 1934

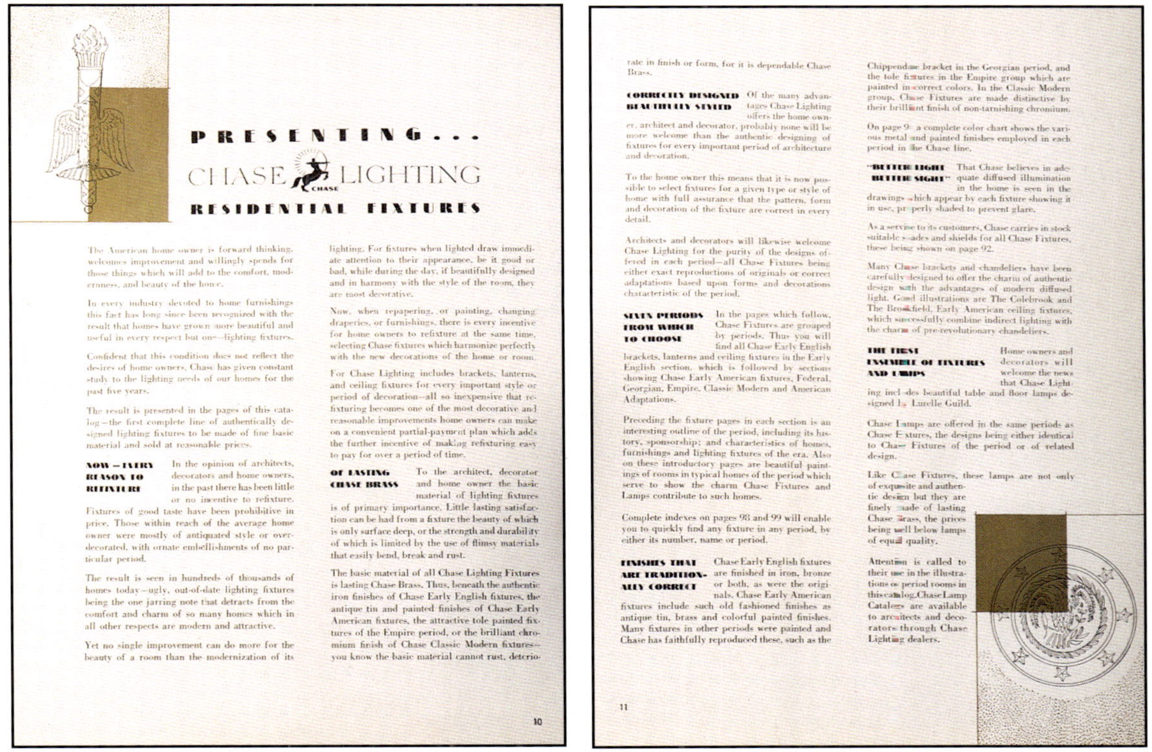

PRESENTING...

CHASE LIGHTING

RESIDENTIAL FIXTURES

The American home owner is forward thinking, welcomes improvement and willingly spends for those things which will add to the comfort, modernness, and beauty of the home.

In every industry devoted to home furnishings this fact has long since been recognized with the result that homes have grown more beautiful and useful in every respect but one—lighting fixtures.

Confident that this condition does not reflect the desires of home owners, Chase has given constant study to the lighting needs of our homes for the past five years.

The result is presented in the pages of this catalog—the first complete line of authentically designed lighting fixtures to be made of fine basic material and sold at reasonable prices.

NOW—EVERY REASON TO REFIXTURE In the opinion of architects, decorators and home owners, in the past there has been little or no incentive to refixture. Fixtures of good taste have been prohibitive in price. Those within reach of the average home owner were mostly of antiquated style or overdecorated, with ornate embellishments of no particular period.

The result is seen in hundreds of thousands of homes today—ugly, out-of-date lighting fixtures being the one jarring note that detracts from the comfort and charm of so many homes which in all other respects are modern and attractive.

Yet no single improvement can do more for the beauty of a room than the modernization of its lighting. For fixtures when lighted draw immediate attention to their appearance, be it good or bad, while during the day, if beautifully designed and in harmony with the style of the room, they are most decorative.

Now, when repapering, or painting, changing draperies, or furnishings, there is every incentive for home owners to refixture at the same time, selecting Chase fixtures which harmonize perfectly with the new decorations of the home or room.

For Chase Lighting includes brackets, lanterns, and ceiling fixtures for every important style or period of decoration—all so inexpensive that refixturing becomes one of the most decorative and reasonable improvements home owners can make on a convenient partial-payment plan which adds the further incentive of making refixturing easy to pay for over a period of time.

OF LASTING CHASE BRASS To the architect, decorator and home owner the basic material of lighting fixtures is of primary importance. Little lasting satisfaction can be had from a fixture the beauty of which is only surface deep, or the strength and durability of which is limited by the use of flimsy materials that easily bend, break and rust.

The basic material of all Chase Lighting Fixtures is lasting Chase Brass. Thus, beneath the authentic iron finishes of Chase Early English fixtures, the antique tin and painted finishes of Chase Early American fixtures, the attractive tole painted fixtures of the Empire period, or the brilliant chromium finish of Chase Classic Modern fixtures—you know the basic material cannot rust, deteriorate in finish or form, for it is dependable Chase Brass.

10

CORRECTLY DESIGNED BEAUTIFULLY STYLED Of the many advantages Chase Lighting offers the home owner, architect and decorator, probably none will be more welcome than the authentic designing of fixtures for every important period of architecture and decoration.

To the home owner this means that it is now possible to select fixtures for a given type or style of home with full assurance that the pattern, form and decoration of the fixture are correct in every detail.

Architects and decorators will likewise welcome Chase Lighting for the purity of the designs offered in each period—all Chase Fixtures being either exact reproductions of originals or correct adaptations based upon forms and decorations characteristic of the period.

SEVEN PERIODS FROM WHICH TO CHOOSE In the pages which follow, Chase Fixtures are grouped by periods. Thus you will find all Chase Early English brackets, lanterns and ceiling fixtures in the Early English section, which is followed by sections showing Chase Early American fixtures, Federal, Georgian, Empire, Classic Modern and American Adaptations.

Preceding the fixture pages in each section is an interesting outline of the period, including its history, sponsorship; and characteristics of homes, furnishings and lighting fixtures of the era. Also on these introductory pages are beautiful paintings of rooms in typical homes of the period which serve to show the charm Chase Fixtures and Lamps contribute to such homes.

Complete indexes on pages 98 and 99 will enable you to quickly find any fixture in any period, by either its number, name or period.

FINISHES THAT ARE TRADITIONALLY CORRECT Chase Early English fixtures are finished in iron, bronze or both, as were the originals. Chase Early American fixtures include such old fashioned finishes as antique tin, brass and colorful painted finishes. Many fixtures in other periods were painted and Chase has faithfully reproduced these, such as the Chippendale bracket in the Georgian period, and the tole fixtures in the Empire group which are painted in correct colors. In the Classic Modern group, Chase Fixtures are made distinctive by their brilliant finish of non-tarnishing chromium.

On page 9 a complete color chart shows the various metal and painted finishes employed in each period in the Chase line.

"BETTER LIGHT BETTER SIGHT" That Chase believes in adequate diffused illumination in the home is seen in the drawings which appear by each fixture showing it in use, properly shaded to prevent glare.

As a service to its customers, Chase carries in stock suitable shades and shields for all Chase Fixtures, these being shown on page 92.

Many Chase brackets and chandeliers have been carefully designed to offer the charm of authentic design with the advantages of modern diffused light. Good illustrations are The Colebrook and The Brookfield, Early American ceiling fixtures, which successfully combine indirect lighting with the charm of pre-revolutionary chandeliers.

THE FIRST ENSEMBLE OF FIXTURES AND LAMPS Home owners and decorators will welcome the news that Chase Lighting includes beautiful table and floor lamps designed by Lurelle Guild.

Chase Lamps are offered in the same periods as Chase Fixtures, the designs being either identical to Chase Fixtures of the period or of related design.

Like Chase Fixtures, these lamps are not only of exquisite and authentic design but they are finely made of lasting Chase Brass, the prices being well below lamps of equal quality.

Attention is called to their use in the illustrations of period rooms in this catalog. Chase Lamp Catalogs are available to architects and decorators through Chase Lighting dealers.

11

As the concept of through-designed home lighting fixtures was a new one, Chase took care to explain in detail exactly what its 1934 Lighting Fixtures catalog had to offer.

CHASE FIXTURE AND LAMP COLOR CHART

ENGLISH BRONZE	FEDERAL BRASS	DEAD BLACK
HALF POLISHED IRON	FEDERAL BLACK	EMPIRE BRASS
BLACK IRON	GEORGIAN BRASS	POLISHED CHROMIUM
BARN RED	ADAM GREEN	SATIN CHROMIUM
LAUREL GREEN	REGENT RED	WHITE ENAMEL
CORN YELLOW	DIRECTOIRE WHITE	WEATHERED BRASS
COLONIAL BRASS	CORSICAN GREEN	IVORY
ANTIQUE TIN	REPUBLIC RED	ANTIQUE BRASS

93

Which color will work best? For easy reference, the 1934 Fixtures catalog provided a handy "Chase Fixture And Lamp Color Chart."

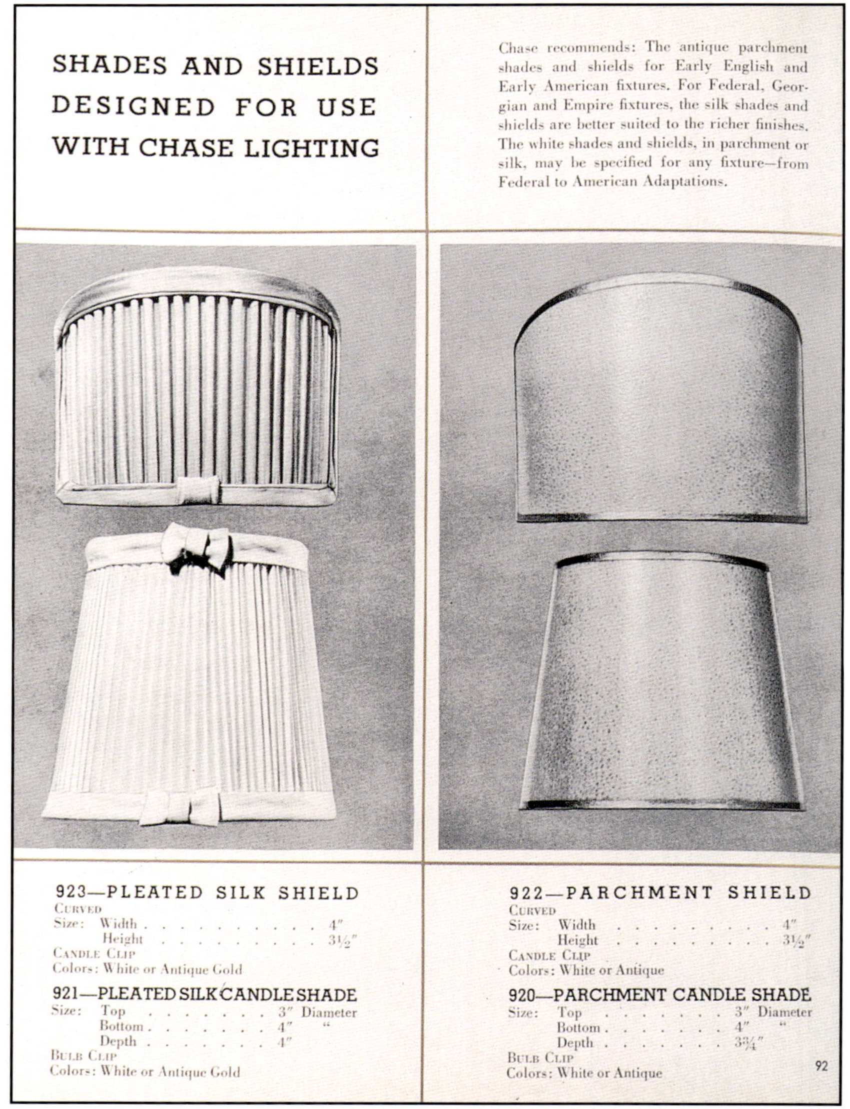

SHADES AND SHIELDS DESIGNED FOR USE WITH CHASE LIGHTING

Chase recommends: The antique parchment shades and shields for Early English and Early American fixtures. For Federal, Georgian and Empire fixtures, the silk shades and shields are better suited to the richer finishes. The white shades and shields, in parchment or silk, may be specified for any fixture—from Federal to American Adaptations.

923—PLEATED SILK SHIELD
CURVED
Size: Width . . . . 4″
Height . . . . 3½″
CANDLE CLIP
Colors: White or Antique Gold

921—PLEATED SILK CANDLE SHADE
Size: Top . . . . 3″ Diameter
Bottom . . . . 4″ "
Depth . . . . 4″
BULB CLIP
Colors: White or Antique Gold

922—PARCHMENT SHIELD
CURVED
Size: Width . . . . 4″
Height . . . . 3½″
CANDLE CLIP
Colors: White or Antique

920—PARCHMENT CANDLE SHADE
Size: Top . . . . 3″ Diameter
Bottom . . . . 4″ "
Depth . . . . 3¾″
BULB CLIP
Colors: White or Antique

92

Without the right shade, it's just another bare bulb. The 1934 catalog also provided a variety of fixture shade options. *1934 Lighting Fixtures catalog courtesy of John Myhre*

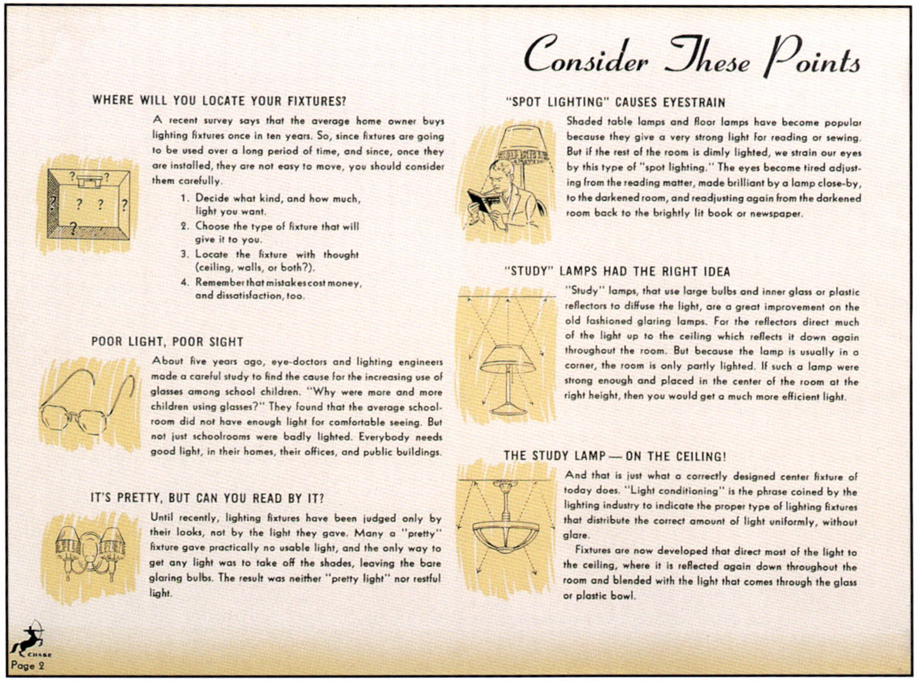

Consider These Points

WHERE WILL YOU LOCATE YOUR FIXTURES?

A recent survey says that the average home owner buys lighting fixtures once in ten years. So, since fixtures are going to be used over a long period of time, and since, once they are installed, they are not easy to move, you should consider them carefully.

1. Decide what kind, and how much, light you want.
2. Choose the type of fixture that will give it to you.
3. Locate the fixture with thought (ceiling, walls, or both?).
4. Remember that mistakes cost money, and dissatisfaction, too.

POOR LIGHT, POOR SIGHT

About five years ago, eye-doctors and lighting engineers made a careful study to find the cause for the increasing use of glasses among school children. "Why were more and more children using glasses?" They found that the average schoolroom did not have enough light for comfortable seeing. But not just schoolrooms were badly lighted. Everybody needs good light, in their homes, their offices, and public buildings.

IT'S PRETTY, BUT CAN YOU READ BY IT?

Until recently, lighting fixtures have been judged only by their looks, not by the light they gave. Many a "pretty" fixture gave practically no usable light, and the only way to get any light was to take off the shades, leaving the bare glaring bulbs. The result was neither "pretty light" nor restful light.

"SPOT LIGHTING" CAUSES EYESTRAIN

Shaded table lamps and floor lamps have become popular because they give a very strong light for reading or sewing. But if the rest of the room is dimly lighted, we strain our eyes by this type of "spot lighting." The eyes become tired adjusting from the reading matter, made brilliant by a lamp close-by, to the darkened room, and readjusting again from the darkened room back to the brightly lit book or newspaper.

"STUDY" LAMPS HAD THE RIGHT IDEA

"Study" lamps, that use large bulbs and inner glass or plastic reflectors to diffuse the light, are a great improvement on the old fashioned glaring lamps. For the reflectors direct much of the light up to the ceiling which reflects it down again throughout the room. But because the lamp is usually in a corner, the room is only partly lighted. If such a lamp were strong enough and placed in the center of the room at the right height, then you would get a much more efficient light.

THE STUDY LAMP — ON THE CEILING!

And that is just what a correctly designed center fixture of today does. "Light conditioning" is the phrase coined by the lighting industry to indicate the proper type of lighting fixtures that distribute the correct amount of light uniformly, without glare.

Fixtures are now developed that direct most of the light to the ceiling, where it is reflected again down throughout the room and blended with the light that comes through the glass or plastic bowl.

CHASE

Page 2

Before Lighting Your Home

MORE LIGHT BUT NO MORE CURRENT

Such re-directed, diffused lighting fixtures, because the light comes evenly from overhead, are close to the type of light that nature gives us. Because light comes from all directions, there are no harsh shadows, although there is plenty of pleasant, mellow light that is kind to the eyes.

Another advantage of modern "re-directed" lighting is that such fixtures usually use a large single bulb of 100 or 150 or 200 watts, instead of two, three, four or five small size bulbs. Curiously enough, mainly because of the design of the fixture, it is possible to get as much as 50% more light output from one such large bulb than can be obtained with the same wattage in smaller bulbs. And we obtain such an increase of light with no increase in current consumption!

WE USE ONLY 1% OF SUNLIGHT

The amount of light used in the average home is not even equal to one-hundredth percent of nature's light on an ordinary day. Our eyes are accustomed to nature's light. Yet when we use only one-hundredth, or even less, of this light with artificial lighting, it is only natural that the eyes are going to be over-worked in trying to see. Therefore, considerable thought should be given to the amount of light we should have in every room in our home. The higher the level of comfortable lighting, the more it meets the condition of the eyes as nature gave them to us.

CENTER FIXTURES MOST IMPORTANT

Remember that there are many different kinds of lighting fixtures to choose from. First of all, you should have good general illumination in your living room, for you will need it, for example, for bridge parties. You will need overhead light, too, in your dining room, and in the bedroom good overhead light is very useful in distinguishing colors and materials of clothes. So remember your center fixture!

TALK IT OVER WITH YOUR DEALER

If you are planning to build a home, to remodel your home, or merely to redecorate it, and this involves the lighting, we would suggest a visit to your electrical dealer who is competent to advise regarding lighting, and who can show you the various types of fixtures and the results that can be obtained from them.

MADE IN OUR OWN PLANTS

All these Chase fixtures are carefully and skillfully made by the Chase Brass & Copper Co. in their own Connecticut manufacturing plant, and all the brass and copper used in the fixtures comes from their own Chase brass mills. Brass and copper are used because it is only on these useful metals that beautiful and lasting finishes can be applied.

BOARD OF FIRE UNDERWRITERS' APPROVAL

All the Chase lighting fixtures shown in this catalog bear the Board of Fire Underwriters' label of approval. This means that these fixtures have been carefully checked for quality, construction and type of materials used, that they have passed the rigid specifications set up by the Board, and that each fixture has been tested before leaving our plant.

PRICES AND VALUES

The price that you pay for Chase fixtures is based entirely on the actual value built into the fixture. And comparative prices should be based on such values and not on comparative discounts. Each Chase fixture can be identified by a price tag. And when you buy, ask that the Chase price tag be supplied with the Chase fixture. It is your assurance of good quality at a reasonable price.

CHASE

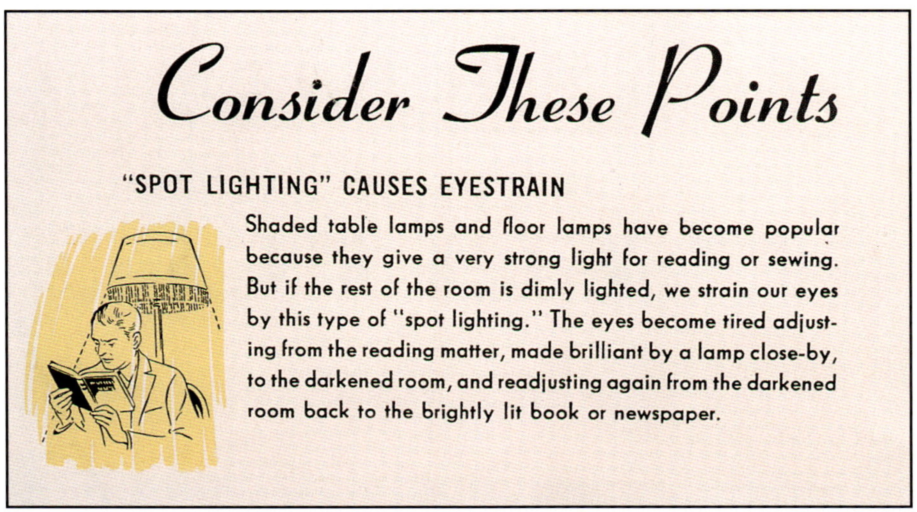

Consider These Points

"SPOT LIGHTING" CAUSES EYESTRAIN

Shaded table lamps and floor lamps have become popular because they give a very strong light for reading or sewing. But if the rest of the room is dimly lighted, we strain our eyes by this type of "spot lighting." The eyes become tired adjusting from the reading matter, made brilliant by a lamp close-by, to the darkened room, and readjusting again from the darkened room back to the brightly lit book or newspaper.

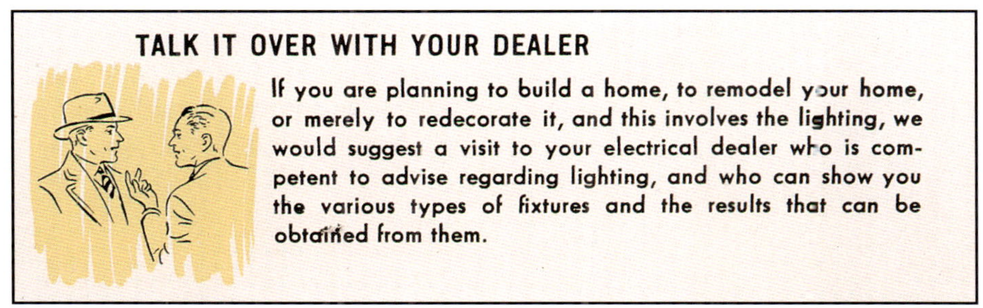

TALK IT OVER WITH YOUR DEALER

If you are planning to build a home, to remodel your home, or merely to redecorate it, and this involves the lighting, we would suggest a visit to your electrical dealer who is competent to advise regarding lighting, and who can show you the various types of fixtures and the results that can be obtained from them.

Top left and right: By 1940, the Chase Fixtures catalog found better luck employing the "hard sell." The whys and wherefores of selecting the right fixtures are outlined, complete with such cautionary warnings as "poor light, poor sight," and "spot lighting causes eyestrain." *1940 Lighting Fixtures catalog courtesy of Peter Linden and Eric Mendard*

Bottom left: Here, a victim of spot lighting reaps the consequences.

Bottom right: A visit to his Chase dealer, and all is well once more!

Early English Fixtures

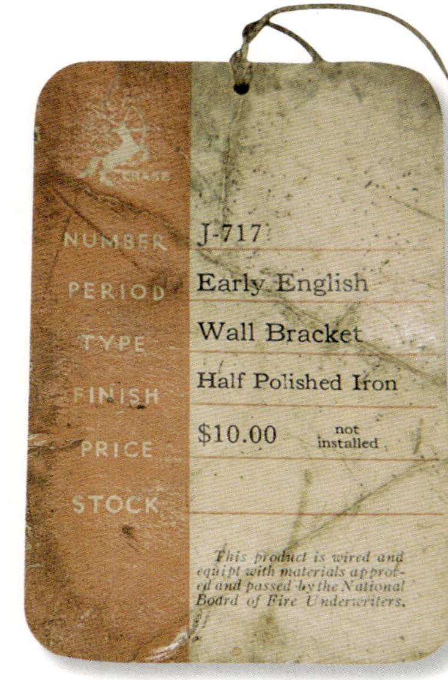

Above: Seeing is believing: April 1935's *House Beautiful* presents a dream house filled with Chase lighting fixtures, just right for the blushing (but well-lit) bride.

Top left: One such Chase fixture-filled residence was "Starkweather," home of Mr. and Mrs. Rodney Chase. Instrumental in the development of the Chase Specialty division, Mr. Chase also assisted in the design of the company's centaur trademark.

Bottom left: Early Jacobean in style is # J 717 "THE CLARENDON." The scrollwork is similar to decorations seen on Jacobean oak chests. 16-3/8" h.

Top center: Original hang tag for "THE CLARENDON."

Top right: Tag reverse. *"CLARENDON" photos courtesy of John and Donna Thorpe*

Bottom center: "Developed from authentic examples of Early English iron work, # J 719 "THE LANCASTER." The fixture is shown in the reading room of "Starkweather," former Watertown, Connecticut residence of the Rodney Chase family. 13" h.

Bottom right: From "Starkweather's" plant room, # J 736, "THE SOMERSET." Prospective purchasers were asked to imagine similar chandeliers "hanging from the dark hewn beams of Early English houses." 45" overall height; 14-3/4" fixture height. *"Starkweather" photos by Dale Endter*

Early American Fixtures

No. C 062

THE SALEM LANTERN

The Salem Lantern is an authentic reproduction of the earliest lantern used in America. The originals, in use before glass was made in this country, depended upon cow's horn, pounded thin and flat, to protect the flame. This model, a faithful copy of an old lantern, has an open bottom and comes finished either in Colonial brass or dead black. In this modern version, the cow's horn is replaced by an acid etched glass cylinder. This authentic example of Pilgrim handiwork is a useful lantern and will furnish a cheerful light in any Early American home whether used indoors or out.

Specifications: Basic material: Chase Brass. Finish: Colonial brass or black. Acid etched glass. Height over all, 11¼". Projection, 9½". Back plate, 5". Height of lantern, 10⅝". Width over all, 4⅜". Keyless porcelain socket. *Alternate:* No. C 012. Same as C 062, except fitted with chain hanger.

No. C 069

THE HADLEY LANTERN

This lantern is an exact copy of the Salem Lantern (C 062) except that it is slightly larger and the design of the supporting bracket is different. All Early American lanterns of this type were made of tin. As Chase reproduces this lantern in lasting brass, there is no danger of rust and its welcoming glow may well be used outdoors as well as indoors. This model—authentic in every detail, comes in Colonial brass—also in brass with a black finish. The Hadley Lantern may also be obtained with a chain hanger and both models have an open bottom so that there is no "blind" spot beneath.

Specifications: Basic material: Chase Brass. Finish: Colonial brass or black. Acid etched glass. Height over all, 16". Height of lantern, 12½". Width over all, 7¼". Projection, 10¾". Back plate, 4¾". Keyless porcelain socket. *Alternate:* No. C 013. Same as C 069 except with chain hanger.

27

Two Chase adaptations of Early American lanterns, # C 062 "THE SALEM LANTERN" and # C 069 "THE HADLEY LANTERN." As noted in the catalog descriptions, hanging chain versions of each were also available.

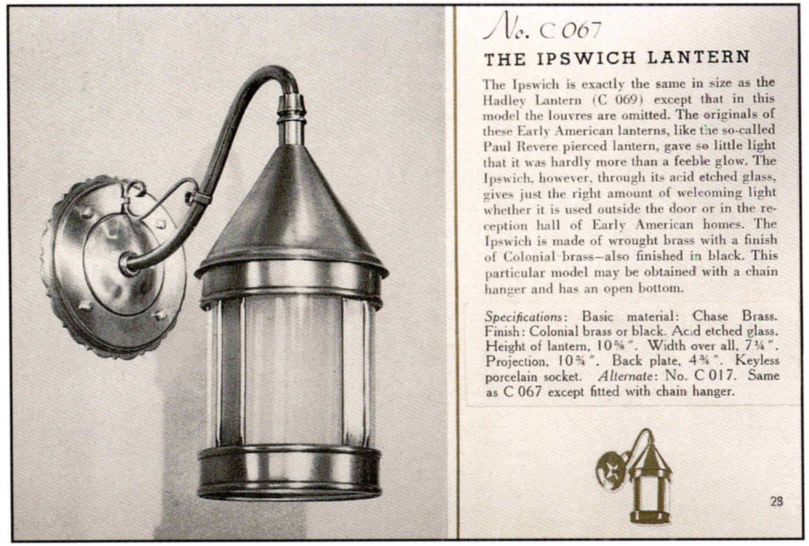

No. C 067

THE IPSWICH LANTERN

The Ipswich is exactly the same in size as the Hadley Lantern (C 069) except that in this model the louvres are omitted. The originals of these Early American lanterns, like the so-called Paul Revere pierced lantern, gave so little light that it was hardly more than a feeble glow. The Ipswich, however, through its acid etched glass, gives just the right amount of welcoming light whether it is used outside the door or in the reception hall of Early American homes. The Ipswich is made of wrought brass with a finish of Colonial brass—also finished in black. This particular model may be obtained with a chain hanger and has an open bottom.

Specifications: Basic material: Chase Brass. Finish: Colonial brass or black. Acid etched glass. Height of lantern, 10⅝". Width over all, 7¼". Projection, 10¾". Back plate, 4¾". Keyless porcelain socket. *Alternate:* No. C 017. Same as C 067 except fitted with chain hanger.

28

Another Early American lantern design, # C 067 "THE IPSWICH LANTERN." The "IPSWICH" was designed for either exterior or front hall use.

Colonial styles were still popular in the later years of the Chase Lighting Division, as evidenced by this ad for #11087, a "5-LIGHT COLONIAL FIXTURE," which appeared in the September 1940 issue of *The American Home*.

Federal Fixtures

Left: From the 1937 Lighting Fixtures catalog: #1601 "FIVE LIGHT CEILING FIXTURE WITH CUT GLASS CHIMNEYS." This Federal-inspired design is highlighted by a star-crossed central globe and eagle finial, reflective of the "gracious dignity and prosperity of the times. 36" overall length. *Courtesy of John and Donna Thorpe*

Above: From the front porch of "Starkweather:" # F 106 "THE JAMESTOWN." The lantern was reproduced from a vintage original found in Virginia. 17" h. *Photo by Dale Endter*

Empire Fixtures

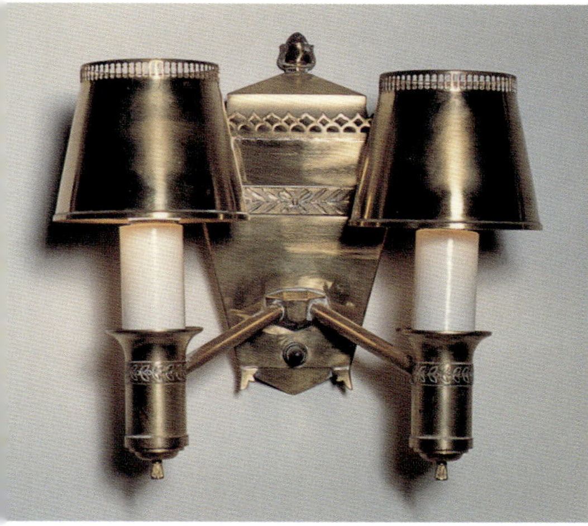

In the Empire style: # E 426 "THE RICHELIEU." "THE RICHELIEU" was modeled after the original painted tin fixtures of the French Empire period. This fixture is from the "Starkweather" dining room. 10" h.

Brightening a stair corner at "Starkweather," # E 422 "THE TEA TRADE LANTERN." Oriental figures are fired into the glass side panels. Available "TEA TRADE" finishes included "Republic Red" (shown), and "Empire Black." 13" h.

A "Starkweather" ceiling fixture, # E 441 "THE VENDOME." The laurel leaf decorations on the center body and candle cups are modeled in relief, and finished in Empire brass. 45" overall length; 13-1/4" fixture height.

From the "Starkweather" front foyer, an Empire "TWO-LIGHT BRACKET," #1651. 10" h.

Also from the foyer, and with similar design elements, #1600 "FIVE-LIGHT CEILING FIXTURE." 36" overall length. *"Starkweather" photos by Dale Endter*

Chase lighting fixtures often turned up as part of the decor in ads for Armstrong's Linoleum Floors. This June 1935 illustration from *Woman's Home Companion* includes, on the dining nook wall, Chase Empire fixture #E 321 "THE TALLEYRAND."

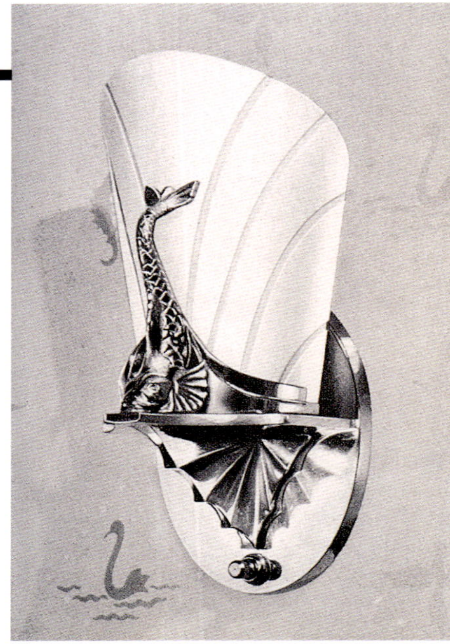

Left: Right at home in the bath at "Starkweather" is # M 531 "THE DOLPHIN." The dolphin's tail rested against a frosted glass shade with a shell motif. 8-1/2" h. *Photo by Dale Endter*

Right: 1934 catalog photo, "THE DOLPHIN."

Left: "Wouldn't you be proud to show your friends this bathroom?" This Carrara Structural Glass advertisement from the 1937 *Home Owners' Catalogs* also features two examples of Chase wall fixture # M 532 "THE OLYMPIA." The brackets could, if desired, be hung horizontally. 13" h. *Courtesy of Barbara Endter*

Right: 1934 catalog photo, "THE OLYMPIA."

Top left: "Radiant as an April morning," this *House Beautiful* advertisement from April 1935 was really designed to show off Celanese Decorative Fabrics. However, sharp eyes will also be drawn to the two Chase fixtures, # M 528 "THE COLONNADE," in the background. Light is thrown upward from lamps concealed in the crystal glass bowls. 16-1/2" h.

Top right: 1934 catalog photo, "THE COLONNADE."

Gleaming Spring in CELANESE

Radiant as an April morning, the guest room in "The Bride's House" extends a warm welcome. As with so rooms in the Contemporary manner, this decorative scheme centers around Celanese Decorative Fabrics. At ndows, warm colors of Celanese seem to melt into each other: *coral reef* Celanese Clairanese Taffeta blend th sheer Celanese Chifonese, in *romance*, softer in tone, and silvery *moonstone*. The mirror reflects a quilted read of Celanese Quixilver Satin which echoes this silvery shade, the bed canopy repeating the color harmo of the window setting. Three chairs designed by Modernage overed in *moonstone* and *coral reef* Celanese Moiranese.

CELANESE

Decorative Fabrics

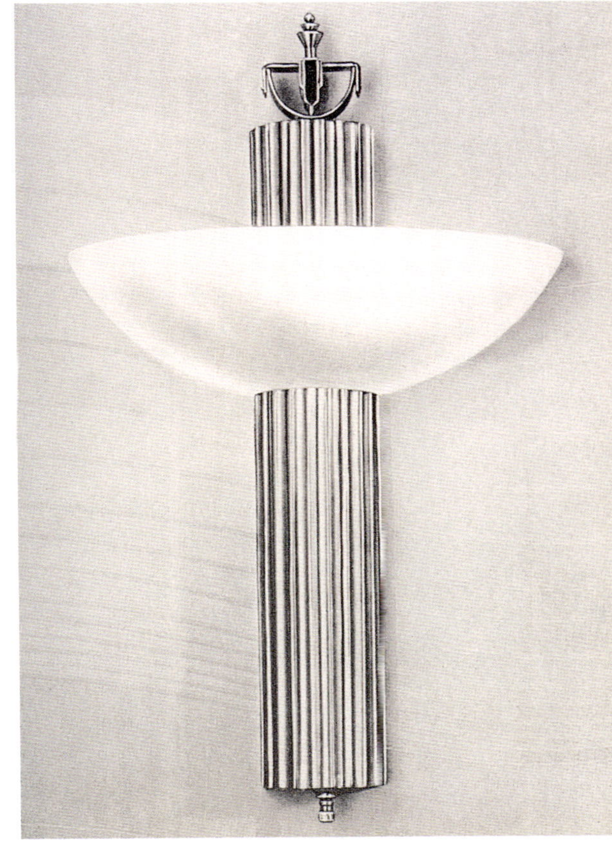

Kitchen by Rex Cole, General Electric equipment. Monel metal counters, sink, stove top, table, wall bands, International Nickel. Carrara glass walls by Pittsburgh Plate Glass. Excel Metal Cabinets. Aluminum blinds, J. G. Wilson. Linoleum floor, Armstrong. Utensils, small electric appliances, furniture, Lewis and Conger. Closidor, Hammacher Schlemmer; Seth Thomas clock. Chase Brass light

THE BRIDE'S KITCHEN

Bottom left: A thoroughly modern kitchen for the new bride, from the sleek metal counters and Carrara glass walls to Chase ceiling fixture # M 544, "THE APOLLO," overhead. 9" h. *House Beautiful*, April 1935.

Bottom right: 1934 catalog photo, "THE APOLLO."

American Adaptations

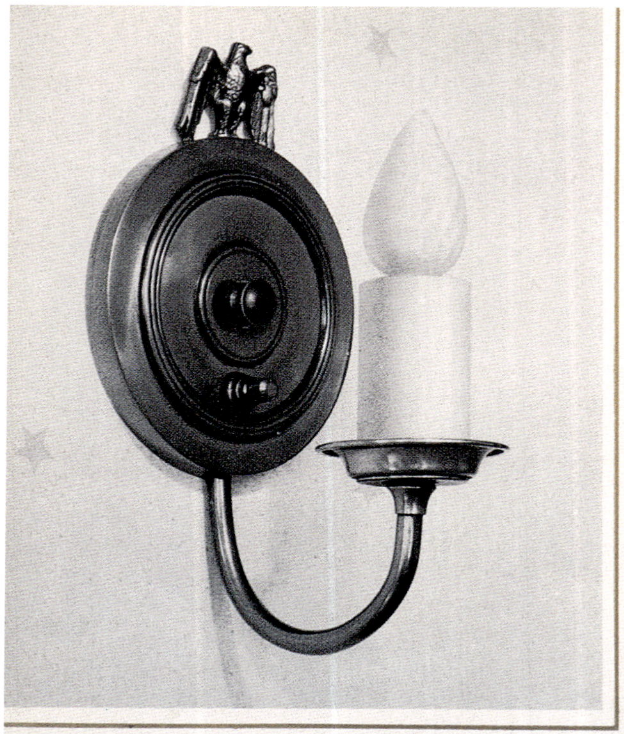

No. A 1104

THE FAIRFIELD

The simple dignity of this smartly designed bracket gives it appropriate charm for living room, dining room or bedroom. It is executed in a design reminiscent of the Colonial and Federal periods, but it can be used in many homes that are not of a definite period in their decoration. Finished either in satin chromium, antique brass or weathered brass.

Specifications: Basic material: Chase Brass. Finish: Satin chromium, antique brass or weathered brass. Height, 7⅞". Width, 4½". Projection, 4¼". Back plate: 4½" diameter. Keyless socket with pin switch.

#A 1104 "THE FAIRFIELD," in a design "reminiscent of the Colonial and Federal periods." 7-7/8" h.

"THE CLIPPER SHIP," # A 611, features, at top, a replica of the "Red Jacket," a famous old whaling ship. The ribbed Fresnal glass of "THE CLIPPER SHIP," modeled from an old whaling lantern, captures "all the salty tang and spirit of the sea." 13" h. *Photo courtesy of John and Donna Thorpe*

A 612, the two-light version of "THE CLIPPER SHIP." *Photo by Dale Endter. Courtesy of Barbara Endter*

Top: "THE JUPITER," # M 521.

Bottom: "THREE-LIGHT HANGING LANTERN" #1654, from the upstairs hall at "Starkweather." 36" overall length. *Photo by Dale Endter*

From the 1937 catalog, #1193 "ONE LIGHT BRACKET," specifically intended for bathroom walls. "THE JUPITER," is a more festively decorated version of this design. 7" projection. *Courtesy of H. James Pierce*

Another Armstrong ad, another lighting fixture by Chase. Among the furnishings in this vigorous red, white, and blue entry hall is #1720 "FOUR-LIGHT HANGING LANTERN." The patriotic setting is shown in the 1941 edition of the *Home Owners' Catalogs. Courtesy of Barbara Endter*

"Even-Glow" Fixtures

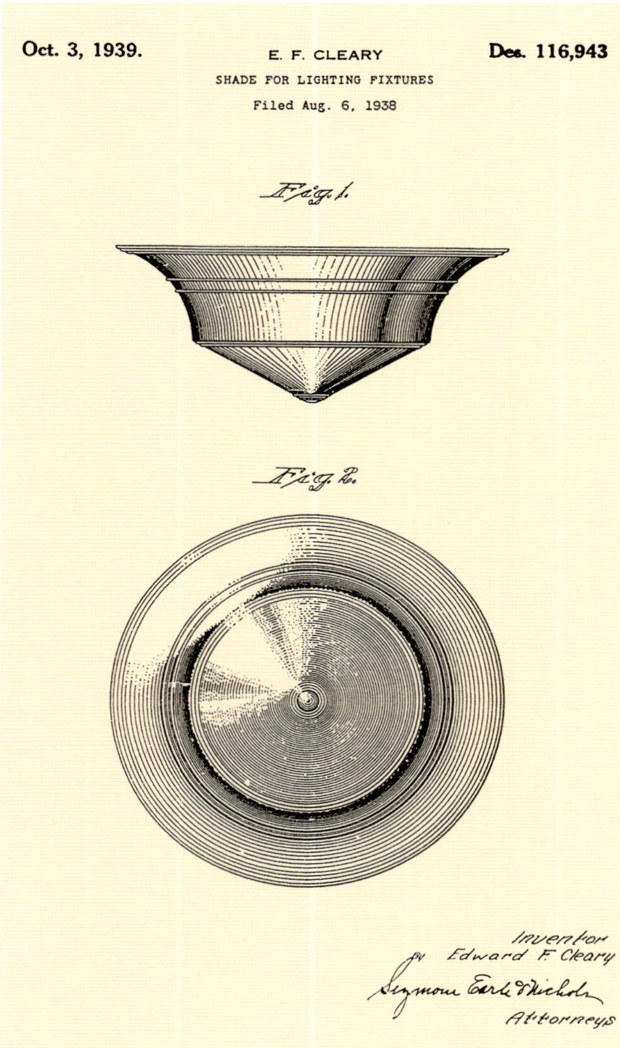

Patent for a Chase "Even-Glow" shade, granted to E. F. Cleary on October 3, 1939. The shade was used on "Even-Glow" fixture #1547.

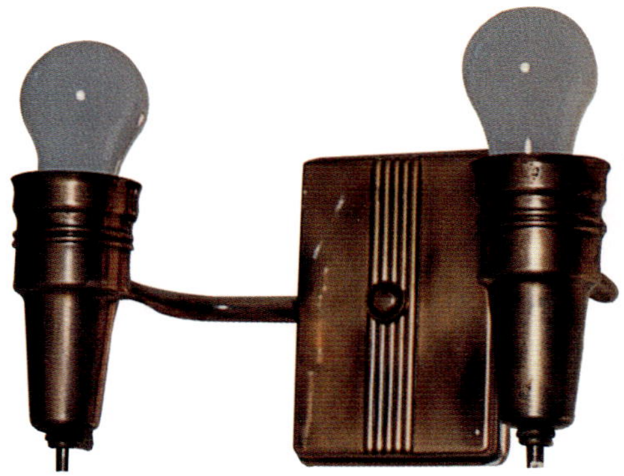

"EVEN-GLOW TWO-LIGHT BRACKET" #1562 (or at least the bracket portion). With translucent plastic bowls, the "Even-Glow" fixtures provided "modern Scientific Light"—glareless, and diffused. (All "Even-Glow" fixtures shown are from the Chase family home, "Starkweather.") 13-1/4" d.

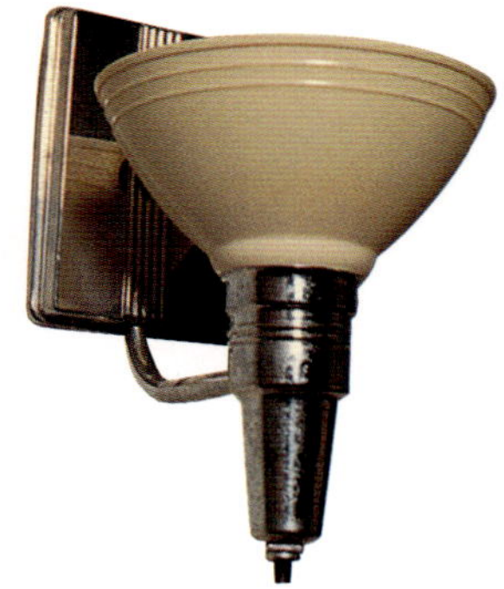

The "EVEN-GLOW ONE-LIGHT BRACKET," #1560. With "Even-Glow" fixtures, "there is no semi-darkness, no irritating bright spots to annoy the eyes." 7" extension.

#1559 "EVEN-GLOW ONE LIGHT CEILING FIXTURE," with decorative hanging ball. Chase marketed "Even-Glow" fixtures as providing "more light at no extra cost," using one large bulb rather than several smaller ones. #1559 could take up to 100 watts. 12" d., 10" l. *"Even-Glow" "Starkweather" photos by Dale Endter*

Uncataloged Chase Fixtures

One of three Chase fixtures at "Starkweather" that do not appear in the Chase fixtures catalog. This lantern, from the home's back porch, bears design similarities to the Early English-styled lantern # J 761 "THE HADDON HALL," shown in Chapter 9.

From the "Starkweather" plant room, a wall sconce with floral piece reminiscent of that appearing on # C 021 "THE CONNECTICUT SCONCE" (see Chapter 9).

A third mystery, but thoroughly Federal in style. Thi sconce, from a "Starkweather" bedroom, has elements in common with "THE JEFFERSON," # F 101, pictured in Chapter 3.

CHASE FIXTURES WITH *Colored Glassware* FOR LIVING ROOMS, DINING ROOMS, AND BED ROOMS

No. 1407
Three-light ceiling fixture with 14⅜″ satin crystal etched glass bowl. Length 30″. Finish: Colonial Brass.

No. 1400
Three-light ceiling fixture with 14⅜″ iridescent glass bowl, Gold lines. Length 18½″. Finishes: Ivory and Gold, Colonial Brass. Takes 3 bulbs up to 60 watts each.

No. 1408
Three-light ceiling fixture with 14⅜″ amber etched glass bowl. Length 30″. Crystal trim. Finish: Colonial Brass.

No. 1404
Two-light ceiling fixture with 10″ iridescent glass bowl with pastel nursery decoration. Length 7½″. Finishes: Ivory and Gold, Colonial Brass.

No. 1414
Two-light ceiling fixture with 10″ glass bowl with pastel floral decoration. Length 7½″. Finishes: Colonial Brass, Ivory and Gold.

No. 1406
Two-light ceiling fixture with 12″ iridescent bowl with pastel floral colors. Length 6¾″. Finishes: Ivory and Gold, Colonial Brass.

No. 1342
Three-light ceiling fixture with 14″ crystal luster glass bowl. Length 8″. Finishes: Ivory and Gold, Colonial Brass.
Order No. **1341** for two-light ceiling fixture with 12″ bowl, length 6½″.

No. 1416
Two-light ceiling fixture with 10″ iridescent glass bowl with pastel floral decoration. Length 7½″. Finishes: Colonial Brass, Ivory and Gold.

No. 1405
Two-light ceiling fixture with 10″ iridescent glass bowl with pastel floral colors. Length 7½″. Finishes: Ivory and Gold, Colonial Brass.

CHASE
Page 35

Elegant fixtures continued to join the Chase line in later years, as shown in this two-page spread from the 1940 Fixtures catalog, entitled "Chase Fixtures With Colored Glassware."
1940 Lighting Fixtures catalog courtesy of Peter Linden and Eric Menard

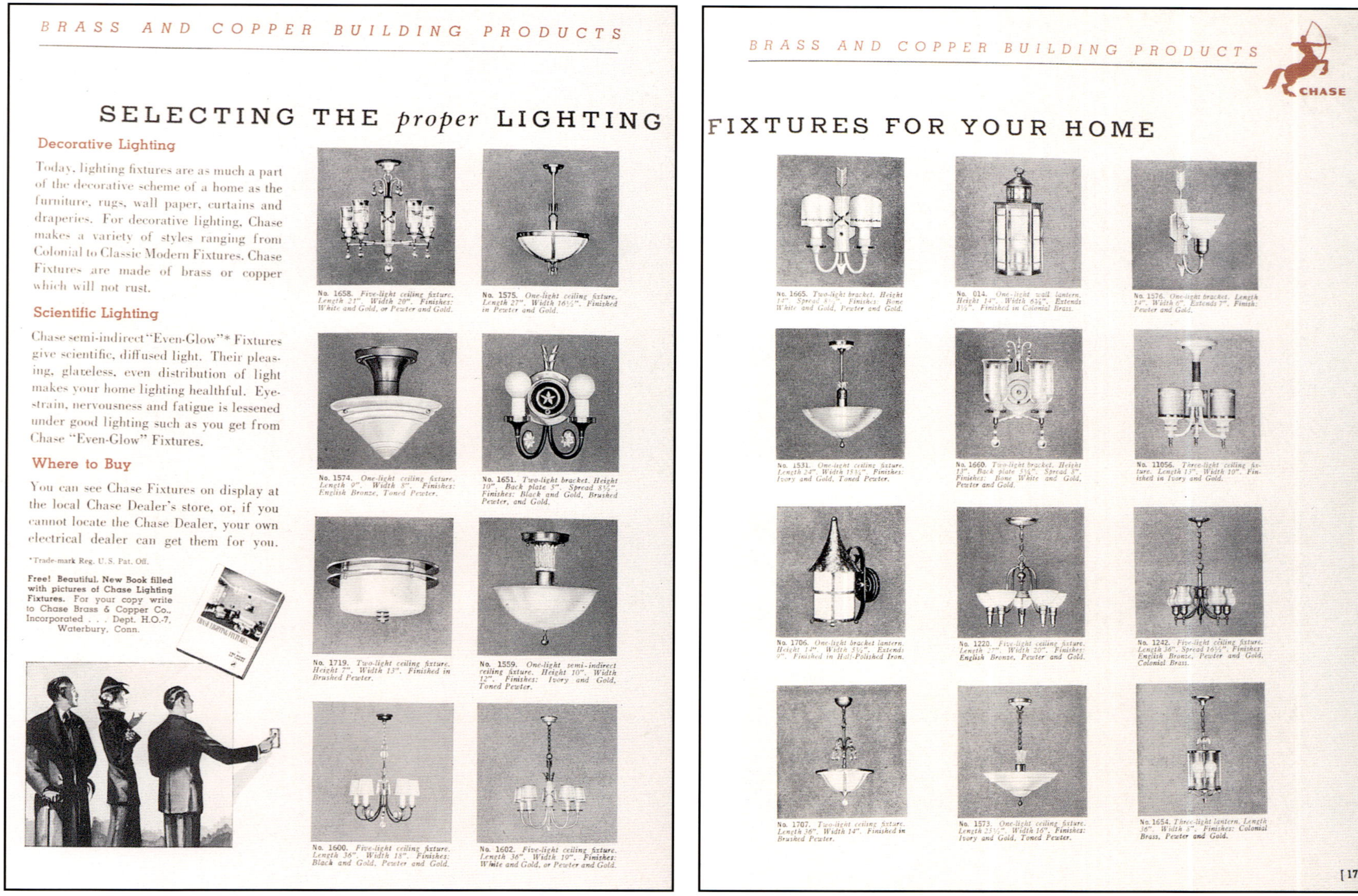

BRASS AND COPPER BUILDING PRODUCTS

SELECTING THE *proper* LIGHTING

Decorative Lighting

Today, lighting fixtures are as much a part of the decorative scheme of a home as the furniture, rugs, wall paper, curtains and draperies. For decorative lighting, Chase makes a variety of styles ranging from Colonial to Classic Modern Fixtures. Chase Fixtures are made of brass or copper which will not rust.

Scientific Lighting

Chase semi-indirect "Even-Glow"* Fixtures give scientific, diffused light. Their pleasing, glareless, even distribution of light makes your home lighting healthful. Eye-strain, nervousness and fatigue is lessened under good lighting such as you get from Chase "Even-Glow" Fixtures.

Where to Buy

You can see Chase Fixtures on display at the local Chase Dealer's store, or, if you cannot locate the Chase Dealer, your own electrical dealer can get them for you.

*Trade-mark Reg. U. S. Pat. Off.

Free! Beautiful, New Book filled with pictures of Chase Lighting Fixtures. For your copy write to Chase Brass & Copper Co., Incorporated . . . Dept. H.O.-7, Waterbury, Conn.

No. 1658. *Five-light ceiling fixture. Length 21". Width 20". Finishes: White and Gold, or Pewter and Gold.*

No. 1575. *One-light ceiling fixture. Length 27". Width 16½". Finished in Pewter and Gold.*

No. 1574. *One-light ceiling fixture. Length 9". Width 8". Finishes: English Bronze, Toned Pewter.*

No. 1651. *Two-light bracket. Height 10". Back plate 5". Spread 8½". Finishes: Black and Gold, Brushed Pewter, and Gold.*

No. 1719. *Two-light ceiling fixture. Height 7". Width 13". Finished in Brushed Pewter.*

No. 1559. *One-light semi-indirect ceiling fixture. Height 10". Width 12". Finishes: Ivory and Gold, Toned Pewter.*

No. 1600. *Five-light ceiling fixture. Length 36". Width 18". Finishes: Black and Gold, Pewter and Gold.*

No. 1602. *Five-light ceiling fixture. Length 36". Width 19". Finishes: White and Gold, or Pewter and Gold.*

BRASS AND COPPER BUILDING PRODUCTS

CHASE

FIXTURES FOR YOUR HOME

No. 1665. *Two-light bracket. Height 14". Spread 8½". Finishes: Bone White and Gold, Pewter and Gold.*

No. 014. *One-light wall lantern. Height 14". Width 6⅛". Extends 3½". Finished in Colonial Brass.*

No. 1576. *One-light bracket. Length 14". Width 6". Extends 7". Finish: Pewter and Gold.*

No. 1531. *One-light ceiling fixture. Length 24". Width 15¾". Finishes: Ivory and Gold, Toned Pewter.*

No. 1660. *Two-light bracket. Height 13". Back plate 5¼". Spread 8". Finishes: Bone White and Gold, Pewter and Gold.*

No. 11056. *Three-light ceiling fixture. Length 13". Width 10". Finished in Ivory and Gold.*

No. 1706. *One-light bracket lantern. Height 14". Width 5½". Extends 9". Finished in Half-Polished Iron.*

No. 1220. *Five-light ceiling fixture. Length 27". Width 20". Finishes: English Bronze, Pewter and Gold.*

No. 1242. *Five-light ceiling fixture. Length 36". Spread 16½". Finishes: English Bronze, Pewter and Gold, Colonial Brass.*

No. 1707. *Two-light ceiling fixture. Length 36". Width 14". Finished in Brushed Pewter.*

No. 1573. *One-light ceiling fixture. Length 25½". Width 16". Finishes: Ivory and Gold, Toned Pewter.*

No. 1654. *Three-light lantern. Length 36". Width 8". Finishes: Colonial Brass, Pewter and Gold.*

[17]

Let there be light! An assortment of popular Chase products takes center stage in "Selecting The Proper Lighting Fixtures For Your Home," a *Home Owners' Catalog* feature from 1937. *Courtesy of Barbara Endter*

Chapter 9

"The 1934 Chase Lighting Fixtures Brochures"

"If you are planning to redecorate, you will find these lovely Chase Lighting Fixtures different from any you have ever seen—and not at all expensive. But you must see them to appreciate how really lovely they are!"

Chase Lighting advertisement, 1935

And what better way to see them than in a free brochure from Chase? Folders illustrating each of the seven design periods for Chase fixtures were available upon request, with send-away coupons appearing in such publications as *House Beautiful* and *The American Home*.

Included in the pages that follow is every fixture from the Lurelle Guild-designed 1934 line, along with the original catalog descriptions. As the ads promised, "you'll find a Chase Fixture exactly suited for any room." *1934 Chase Lighting Fixtures brochures courtesy of Barbara Endter*

Covers of the 1934 Lighting Fixtures brochures. Chase commissioned prominent artists of the time to create the brochure illustrations, which were also featured in the 1934 Fixtures catalog.

CHASE LIGHTING
Federal Fixtures

CHASE LIGHTING
Georgian Fixtures

CHASE LIGHTING
Empire Fixtures

CHASE LIGHTING
CHASE
Classic Modern Fixtures

CHASE LIGHTING
CHASE
American Adaptation Fixtures

Early English Fixtures

The SUSSEX

nd materials are combined in the Sussex st advantage. Strongly fashioned of Chase is striking English lighting fixture is fin- half polished iron with the reflector-like ece in English bronze. The finely wrought on at the top is an authentic reproduction arly English design. Height, 13½ inches. inches. Projection, 5 inches. $13.50

The RISING SUN

The rollicking face of Old Sol gives a jovial personality to this authentically designed Early English fixture. The sun decoration, scalloped edge of the back plate and candle arms, are finished in English bronze; the inside of the back plate in half polished iron. An excellent choice for entrance hall, library or living room. Height, 11 inches. Width, 7½ inches. Projection, 5 inches. $12.00

The HAMPTON

Charmingly English in character, the Hampton is of authentic Jacobean design. Entirely made of Chase Brass, its shapely candle arms, cups and delicate top tracery are finished in half polished iron, with the center and lower body finished in English bronze. The two-color tone of this fixture is exceptionally effective. Height, 13 inches. Width, 10 inches. Projection, 4 inches. $12.00

The HATHAWAY

Rich in design and finish, the Hathaway is of authentic Jacobean origin. Chase makes this fixture of brass with an Elizabethan brass sun, symbol of light, silhouetted against a center plate finished in English bronze. The thoroughly English pierced border, candle arms and cups, are in traditional half polished iron. Height, 9½ inches. Width, 9 inches. Projection, 5 inches. $13.50

The LANCASTER

An authentic reproduction of Early English iron work, the back plate design and crudely fashioned deer are typical of 17th Century craftsmanship. The Lancaster comes either in half polished iron or black iron finish and the primitively drawn deer, in antique brass. This bracket is also equally suitable for Early American, Dutch Colonial or Spanish houses. Height, 13 inches. Width, 9 inches. Projection, 5 inches. $10.00

The CLARENDON

Eminently suited for simply furnished rooms, the Clarendon is an excellent choice for any early period home—English, American, Dutch, or even Spanish. Finished in half polished iron—also in black iron—it is exceptionally pleasing both in silhouette and primitively etched design. Height, 16½ inches. Width, 10¾ inches. Projection, 5 inches. $10.00

The LONDON TOWER

aracteristic of 17th Century London, this charm- g Jacobean lantern is reproduced of Chase Brass d finished in half polished iron—also in black n. The London Tower has an open bottom and furnished with a rough frosted glass cylinder ich spreads ample light in every direction. ight of lantern, 14⅝ inches. Width, 7⅝ inches. lf polished iron, $20.00. Black iron, $18.00

The LONDON TOWER

This is an exact duplicate of the London Tower bracket lantern except for the chain hanger. Made of wrought Chase Brass, it is impervious to the weather and will grace any Early English hall or doorway. Finished in half polished iron—also in black iron. Height over all, 45 inches. Lantern height, 14⅝ inches. Width, 7⅝ inches. Half polished iron, $16.50. Black iron, $15.00

The HADDON HALL

Duplicate of the Haddon Hall hanging lantern, this model, with a wall bracket attachment, will suit those spaces where a lantern is needed but cannot be hung. Appropriate for either Early American or English type homes. Finished in black iron or half polished iron. The glass cylinder is frosted. Height, 14¾ inches. Width, 7 inches. Half polished iron, $18.50. Black iron, $17.50

The HADDON HALL

Simplicity is the keynote of this sturdy English lantern and in this modern version Chase has cleverly caught and reproduced the fine iron work of Jacobean days. This lantern is made of wrought brass and finished in half polished iron—also in black iron. Height over all, 45 inches. Height of lantern, 14¾ inches. Width, 7 inches. Half polished iron, $15.50. Black iron, $14.00

The SOMERSET

Perfectly suited to the English type of house, the Somerset is a fine reproduction of typical Jacobean iron work. This type of lighting fixture was copied in America as early as 1628, hence it may also be used in very early Colonial homes. Black iron or half polished iron finish. Height overall, 45 inches. Height of fixture, 14¾ inches. Spread, 23 inches. Half polished iron, $30.00. Black iron, $27.00

The CROMWELL

Strength and grace are combined in thi chandelier of true Cromwellian design. in reproduction and made entirely of br fixture is authentically finished in half iron except for the large ball in the center one below it which are finished in English Height over all, 45 inches. Height of fixt inches. Spread, 18 inches. $28.00

Early American Fixtures

The GOODWILLIE SCONCE

The native ingenuity of Early American craftsmanship is seen in the cupped reflectors faithfully reproduced by Chase in this charming sconce, the back plate being an exact copy of an original decoration of the period. Chase makes this distinctive sconce of wrought brass, finishing it in antique tin, the center pine cone decoration being in Colonial brass. Height, 10 inches. Width, 10 inches. Projection, 4 inches. $7.50

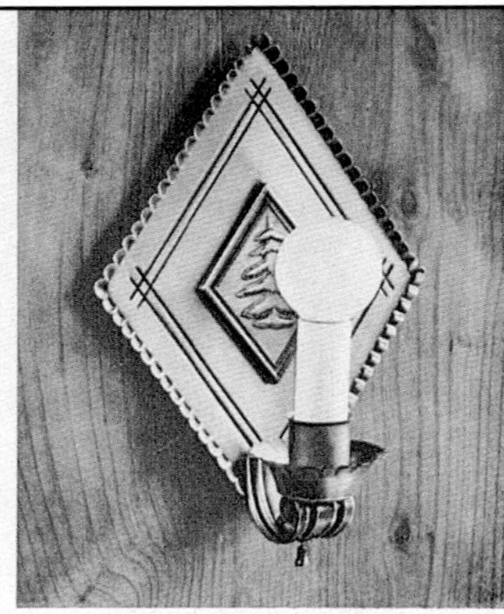

The PINE TREE SHILLING SCONCE

As an excellent example of Early American native art in fashioning lighting fixtures Chase presents the Pine Tree Shilling Sconce, which takes its name and center decoration from the famous Massachusetts coin of 1652. Its delightful scalloped edges, antique tin finish and authentic pine tree decoration of Colonial brass, are all evidence of its pre-revolutionary origin. Height, 11 inches. Width, 9 inches. Projection, 4 inches. $7.50

The PORTSMOUTH SCONCE

So faithfully has Chase copied the Portsmouth Sconce from an old candle holder found in New Hampshire that it might well be called an exact reproduction. In the shape of the pan, the reflector, the crimped edge top, it is intriguingly authentic. The reflector is finished in dull steel, the back plate in Colonial brass, making it most colorful against wood, plaster or wall paper. Height, 15½ inches. Width, 5½ inches. Projection, 3¼ inches. $7.50

The BULL'S EYE SCONCE

The bottle-green, glass bull's eye, scalloped edges and antique tin finish of this quaint sconce bespeak its Early American history in one glance. Made of lasting Chase brass it will contribute authentic charm to the lighting of any Early American or Early Colonial home. The back plate is sprayed dark green under the glass bull's eye. Height, 12 inches. Width, 8 inches. Projection, 4½ inches. $8.00

The CONNECTICUT SCONCE

The famous Connecticut sunflower decoration gives this stately Early American sconce added appeal and beauty. Authentically finished in antique tin, the character and size of this two-light sconce make it particularly well suited for Early American and Colonial libraries or living rooms. Staunchly made from fine, non-rusting Chase Brass. Height, 13 inches. Width, 7½ inches. Projection, 4 inches. $10.00

The WITCH LIGHT SCONCE

From its finely reproduced bull's eye glass reflector, called "Witch Light" in early Colonial days, to its scalloped edge back plate and crimped edge candle cup this sconce is authentically Early American, even to the cheerful colors in which it is finished—Barn Red, Corn Yellow or Laurel Green. The bull's eye glass is backed with a bright tin finish. Height, 12 inches. Width, 7 inches. Projection, 4 inches. $12.00

The GREEN MOUNTAIN SCONCE

Perfectly scaled from an early original, the stark simplicity of this sconce will make a lovely and authentic addition to any Early American home. The graceful hooded top and simply cut edges are accented by its finishes of either antique tin or Colonial brass. The spirit of early New England is perfectly expressed in its clean cut, severe lines. Height, 13 inches. Width, 4½ inches. Projection, 3¼ inches. Antique tin $7.50. Colonial brass, $7.00

The HARTFORD LANTERN

From the "Hartford", a famous fighter of our early Navy, comes this lantern of pleasing proportions and nautical air. Made entirely of Chase sheet brass, with a Colonial brass finish, the Hartford is fitted with clear glass panels and a white inside reflector to throw a goodly amount of light whether used in the hall or outside the front door. Height, 14 inches. Width, 6⅜ inches. Projection, 3½ inches. $15.00

The SAYBROOK LANTERN

As glass replaced the cow's horn originally used in the primitive Early American lanterns, the louvres or vents at the top were omitted, as in the Saybrook, shown above. The Chase reproduction, made of lasting brass, is finished in Colonial brass—also in black—with chain or bracket hanger. Its pleasing simplicity will lend an authentic touch to any Colonial home. Height, 10⅝ inches. Width, 4⅝ inches. Brass finish $12.00. Black finish $10.00

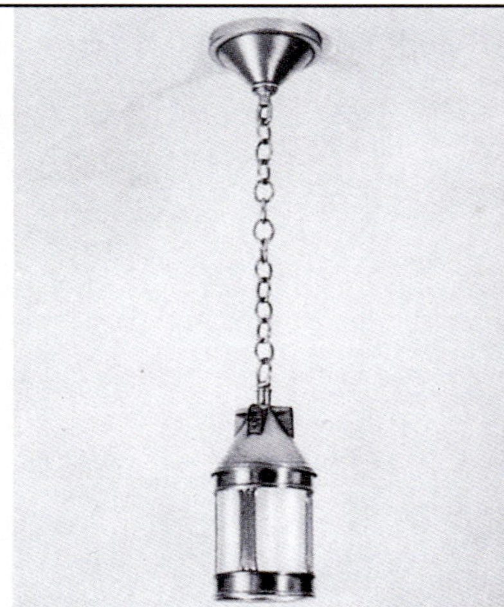

The SALEM LANTERN

Long before glass was made in this country, this quaintly styled Salem Lantern depended on cow's horn instead of glass to protect its feeble flame. As authentically reproduced by Chase, in lasting brass, the cow's horn is replaced by a sand-blasted glass cylinder which sheds welcome light over door or hall. Finished in Colonial brass—also in black. Lantern height, 10⅝ inches. Width, 4⅝ inches. Brass finish $10.00. Black finish $9.00

CHASE LIGHTING

Early American Fixtures

The NANTUCKET LANTERN

Accurately reproduced from an original whale oil lantern, the Nantucket is a true reproduction even to the irregular bottle glass found in the early originals. Made of sheet brass and finished in Colonial brass or black, it is the perfect light for a Colonial doorway, hall or nautical den. Also comes with bracket hanger. Height, 45 inches over all. Height of lantern, 11¼ inches. Width, 6¼ inches. Brass finish $9.00. Black finish $8.25

The WILLIAMSBURG LANTERN

This stately lantern is thoroughly characteristic of Colonial days when it lighted the streets and doorways of our forefathers. Of smaller scale than the Boston Lantern, it may be had either in Colonial brass or black finish with white interior. Admirably suited for either a Colonial porch or reception hall. Choice of chain or bracket hanger. Height of lantern, 13¼ inches. Width, 6½ inches. Colonial brass finish $21.00. Black finish $19.00

The BOSTON LANTERN

The original of this famous lantern, illuminated by whale oil, graced many homes during the American Revolution. Its beauty no less than its history make it ideal for foyer, hall or porch in Colonial or Federal homes of today. Reproduced by Chase in brass, it is finished in either Colonial brass or black, with white interior. Lantern height, 16¼ inches. Over all height, 45 inches. Width, 8 3/16 inches. Brass finish $25.00. Black finish $22.00

The BROOKFIELD

Graceful lines and lovely color distinguish this authentic reproduction of a Colonial chandelier found in Brookfield, Conn. Decorated in Corn Yellow and antique tin, it will lend colorful and authentic charm to Early American homes. A three-way switch makes the indirect lights in the top pan independent of the candle lights. Height of fixture, 15¼ inches. Height over all, 45 inches. Width, 22 inches. $37.50

The COLEBROOK

Colonial Barn Red is the color of this mellow, old chandelier, the relieving decorations being in antique tin. Faithfully copied from an old Connecticut fixture it is made of lasting Chase Brass, its one modern touch being an indirect light in the center cone. Old and quaintly appealing, it offers a rich touch of color to living room or dining room. Height of fixture, 19 inches. Overall height, 45 inches. Width, 20 inches. $35.00

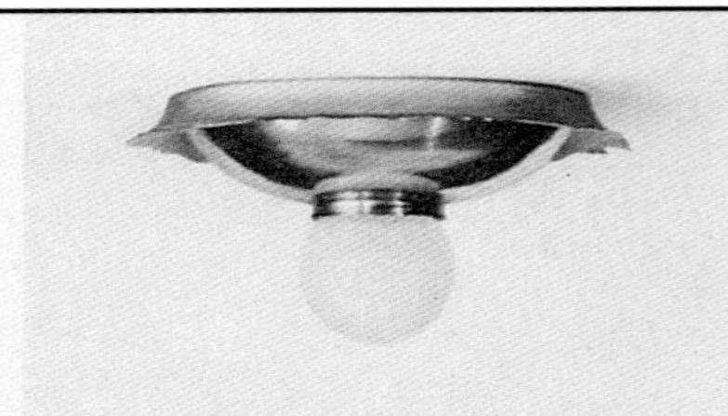

THE DEERFIELD The graceful design of this Early American beam light was inspired by an old Deerfield sconce. It is made of Chase Brass and finished in either Colonial brass or antique tin. Height, 2¼ inches. Width, 8¼ inches. $3.00

THE CAPE COD The charm of this Colonial ceiling fixture lies in its simple, authentic design which Chase has faithfully reproduced. Finished in Colonial brass or antique tin. Height, 2¼ inches. Width, 7¾ inches. $3.00

Federal Fixtures

The SALEM EAGLE

The eagle design which distinguishes this charming fixture is authentically reproduced from a Federal placque dated 1790. It is rendered in dull silver and framed in a circle of brass stars against a back plate of jet black. Finished in Federal brass, this bracket is recommended for the more formal Federal rooms. Height, 10 inches. Width, 12 inches. Projection, 4 inches. $14.00

The MONTICELLO

Rich in its color tones of black and gold, the Monticello lighting fixture is distinguished by a beautiful reproduction of Thomas Jefferson's famous tobacco leaf decoration. The Monticello is authentically Federal in design, decoration and finish of Federal brass and black. The back plate hides an indirect light. Height, 11 inches. Width, 10 inches. Projection, 4¾ inches. $20.00

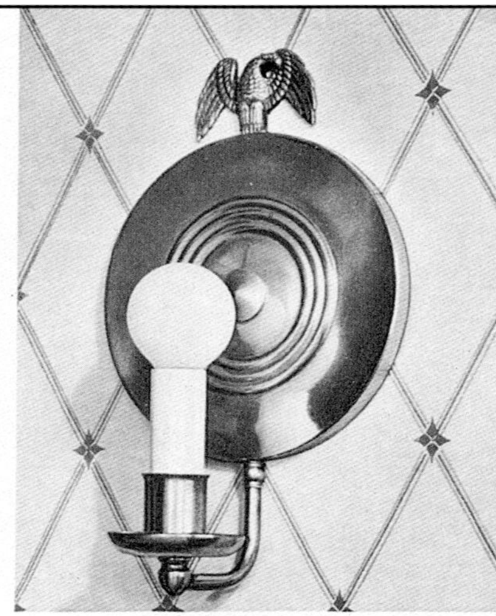

The JEFFERSON

Reflecting the dignity and simplicity of Federal times, the Jefferson is an authentic reproduction of period forms. The urn-shaped back plate with its row of stars and pineapple top finial is highly typical of Federal decoration. The Jefferson is finished entirely in Federal brass and also comes with one light. Height, 9½ inches. Width, 10 inches. Projection, 5 inches. $12.50

The CONCORD

Pleasing in its native simplicity, the Concord is an accurate reproduction of an early Federal lighting fixture design. Finished entirely in Federal brass with a forging of the American eagle at the top, the Concord is suitable for Early Colonial homes as well as Federal. It also comes with two lights. Height, 13½ inches. Width, 8 inches. Projection, 5 inches. $5.00

THE VICTORY the victory decoration of palms and swag gives this pleasing one-light bracket its name. Finished entirely in Federal brass, it also comes with two lights. Height, 10 inches. Width, 6 inches. Projection, 3¼ inches. $5.00

THE STAR a circle painted Federal black on the back plate emphasizes the center star of this wall bracket finished in Federal brass. Also obtainable with one light. Height, 8½ inches. Width, 7½ inches. Projection, 3½ inches. $4.00

The WHITE HOUSE

The eagle and torch design, so popular at the time of Washington's Presidency, forms the center design of this typically Federal lighting fixture. Taken directly from authentic designs and richly finished in Federal brass and toned black; this aristocratic bracket is completed by two exquisitely etched crystal chimneys. Height, 11 inches. Width, 9 inches. Projection, 4 inches. $17.50

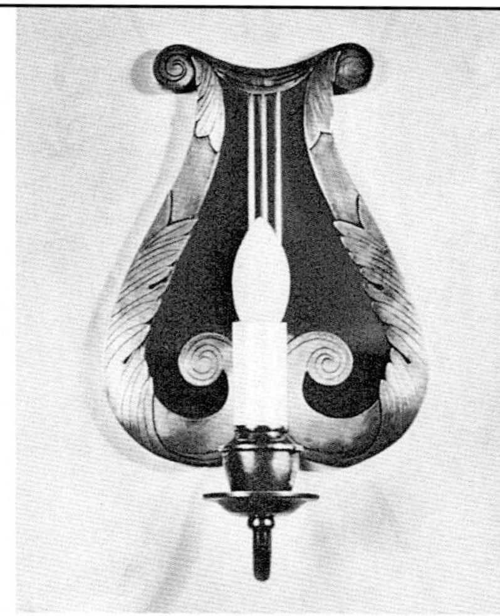

The PHYFE

Taking its name from the American designer who made the lyre design so popular, this lovely lighting fixture is an authentic addition to the Chase Federal group. A delicately incised acanthus leaf decorates the back plate which encloses a charming gun metal mirror reflector. Federal brass finish. Height, 12 inches. Width, 7½ inches. Projection, 5 inches. $15.00

The MONROE

Commemorating the founding of the new American nation, the authentic Federal design in the center of this exquisite lighting fixture is richly reproduced in burnished silver etched in dark ruby glass. This colorful effect is heightened by a Federal brass back plate and two very graceful candle arms, also of Federal brass. Height, 11 inches. Width, 10½ inches. Projection, 4 inches. $16.00

The BALTIMORE

Dominated by a many pointed variation of the Federal star, the Baltimore is an exceptional lighting fixture design. The star is a brass forging, silhouetted against a back plate of jet black. Finished in Federal brass, this bracket may also be used in Empire and Directoire interiors. Height, 10½ inches. Width, 7½ inches. Projection, 4½ inches. $12.50

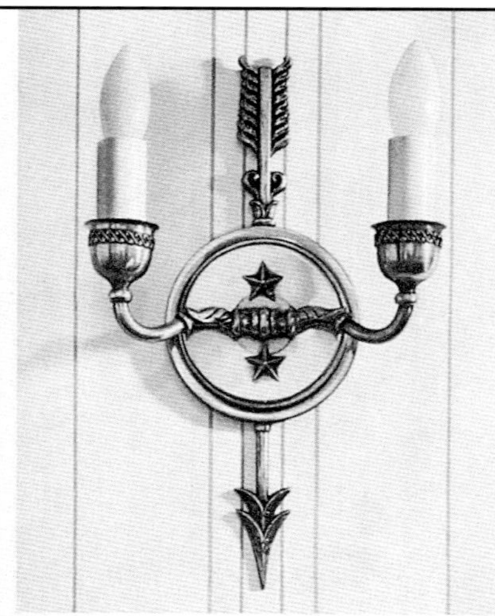

The FAIRFAX

Simple in conception, yet rich in its decorative details, the Fairfax is one of the most pleasing Federal lighting fixtures. A genuine reproduction of original Federal design, this bracket is entirely finished in Federal brass. Because of its decorations, the Fairfax is suitable to Empire and Directoire interiors as well as Federal. Height, 13 inches. Width, 9 inches. Projection, 3½ inches. $13.50

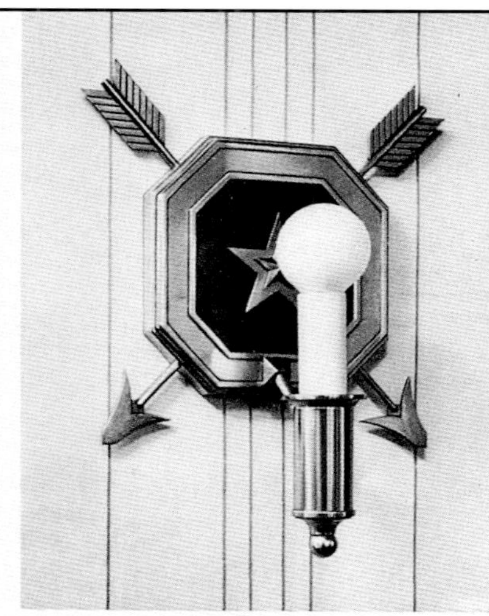

The MADISON

Boldly presented patriotic symbols and octagonal shape make the Madison an exceptionally brilliant Federal lighting fixture. The back plate, pierced by two shapely arrows, encloses a sheet of Bristol blue glass. Finished in Federal brass, this bracket harmonizes naturally with the Albemarle ceiling fixture. Height, 10½ inches. Width, 10½ inches. Projection, 4 inches. $12.50

The HAMILTON

An authentic example of the artistry of Federal designers, the Hamilton wall light is a distinguished addition to the Chase Federal group. Made of brass throughout and finished in Federal brass and toned black, this famous lantern, with its clear crystal globe, is equally suited to Federal or Georgian homes. Height, 16 inches. Width, 6 inches. Projection, 6½ inches. $12.00

The JAMESTOWN

Faithfully reproduced from an original of old Virginia, the Jamestown wall lantern is finished in Federal toned black with Federal brass decorations. Made entirely of Chase brass, and fitted with a quaint, crimp top chimney, it is sprayed scarlet inside with the light reflector executed in a dull steel finish. Height, 17 inches. Width, 8½ inches. Projection, 6½ inches. $30.00

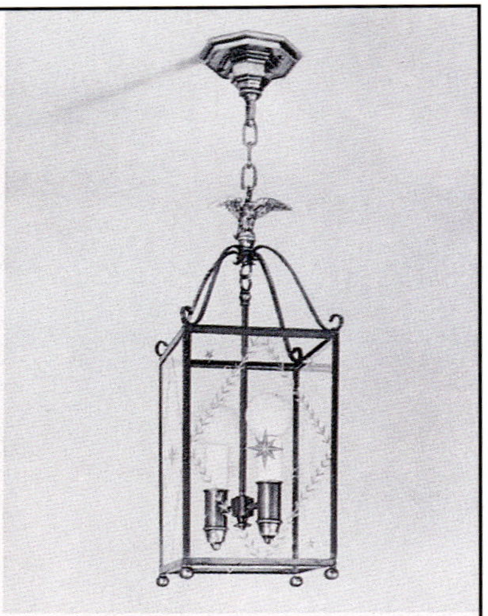

The CHARLESTON

Highly decorative, yet chastely simple in design, the Charleston graced "the" homes in Federal times. The exquisite glass decoration of burnished silver etched on the clear glass panels gives this lantern the distinctive touch needed for the staircase, hall or foyer. Chase finishes this lovely model entirely in Federal brass. Height, 45 inches. Width, 8 inches. $37.50

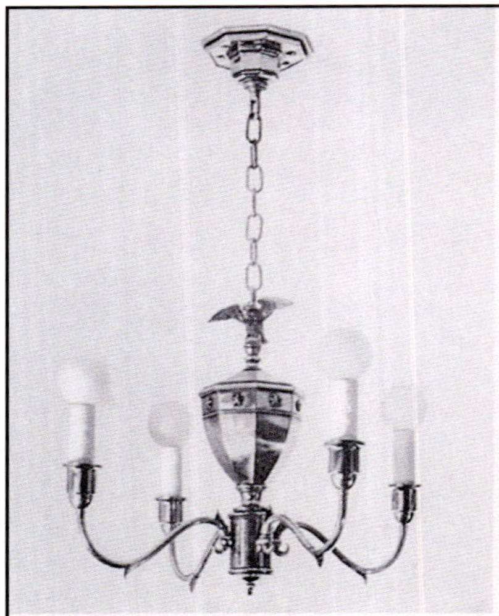

The RICHMOND

Thoroughly typical of the Federal fixtures of long ago, the Richmond is an authentic reproduction in design, in finish and in decoration. Finished entirely in Federal brass and employing for decoration both Federal stars and American eagle, this stately ceiling fixture is the same basic design as The Jefferson wall bracket. Height, 45 inches. Width, 17 inches. $35.00

The ALBEMARLE

Striking in its color tones of black and gold, its unusual octagonal shape and decorative stars and arrows, the Albemarle is thoroughly Federal. Finished in glossy Federal black and accented with Federal brass, this ceiling fixture holds two indirect lights in the center body and in basic design is in harmony with The Madison wall bracket. Height, 45 inches. Width, 21 inches. $42.00

CHASE LIGHTING
Federal Fixtures

Georgian Fixtures

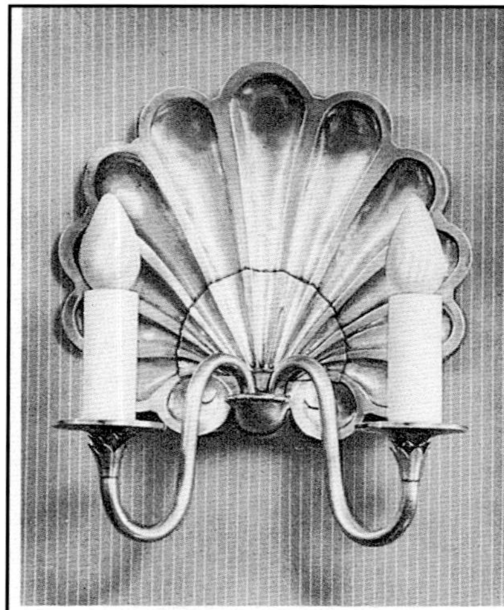

The GEORGIAN SHELL

Most popular of all Georgian decorative forms, the shell is adapted by Chase as a back plate in this charming two-light wall bracket. Richly finished in Georgian brass, this graceful fixture brilliantly reflects the light while its classic design brings unquestioned beauty to any room. It also comes with one light. Height, 12 inches. Width, 10 inches. Projection, 4 inches. $16.00

The PEMBROKE

In the Pembroke, Chase introduces the urn, swag drapery and crystal prisms so charmingly characteristic of Georgian design. Made entirely of brass in a Georgian brass finish, the elegance of this lighting fixture is suited to Georgian interiors, whether finely paneled or modestly painted. It also comes with one light. Height, 9 inches. Width, 9 inches. Projection, 4½ inches. $20.00

The BRIGHTON

Handsomely finished in tones of black and gold, the Brighton has for its main decorative features the urn, drapery and fluted column motifs of the Georgian period. In lustrous black and Georgian brass finish, this lovely wall bracket may be used in any type of room of the Georgian, Federal, Directoire or Empire periods. Height, 8 inches. Width, 9½ inches. Projection, 4¾ inches. $8.50

The HEPPLEWHITE

Illustrating the beauty of true simplicity, the Hepplewhite is a lovely example of the classic school of Georgian design. The shield shape was a favorite of Hepplewhite and appears here in the backplate, surmounted by a delicately forged urn and fitted with graceful forged handles. It is finished in Georgian brass. Height, 9½ inches. Width, 6 inches. Projection, 3½ inches. $7.00

The JAMESTOWN

Faithfully reproduced from an original of old Virginia, the Jamestown wall lantern is finished in toned black with Georgian brass decorations. Made entirely of Chase brass and fitted with a quaint, crimp-top chimney, this Georgian lantern is sprayed scarlet inside with the light reflector executed in a dull steel finish. Height, 17 inches. Width, 8½ inches. Projection, 6½ inches. $30.00

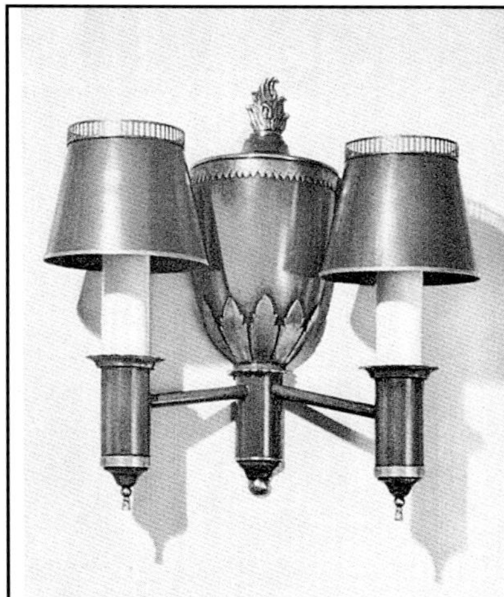

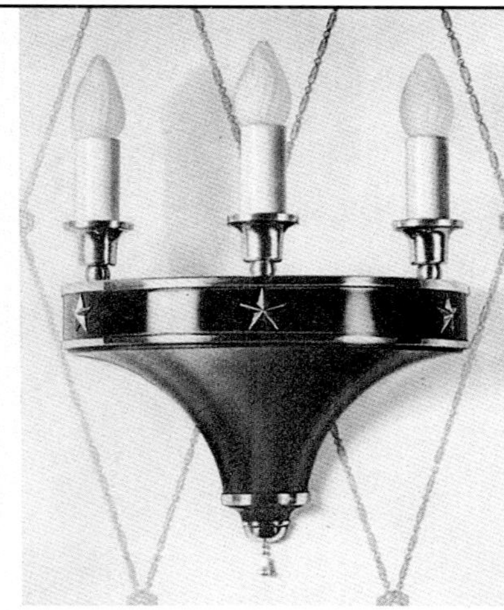

The SHERATON

Characteristic of the Late Georgian period, the classically designed Sheraton wall bracket is authentically reproduced by Chase either in Regent Red or Adam Green, richly trimmed with Georgian brass. Furnished with or without shades in the two light or one light model; the shades are metal, in colors to match. Height, 11 inches. Width, 9 inches. Projection, 3½ inches. $17.00

The CHIPPENDALE

Brilliant in either Regent Red or Adam Green, the Chippendale wall bracket is typical of the great English cabinet-maker's Chinese fretwork designs. Made entirely of Chase brass, this bracket has a gun metal mirror in the back plate and also comes with one light, if desired. It is an excellent choice for any Georgian interior. Height, 13 inches. Width, 7 inches. Projection, 5 inches. $13.00

The SHERWOOD

Distinguished by shapely lines and rich color tones, the Sherwood is a lovely Georgian wall bracket for living room, dining room or hallway. It comes in lustrous black, trimmed with Georgian brass. The back plate holds an indirect light which can be controlled separately from the rim lights. Height, 11 inches. Width, 10 inches. Projection, 4¾ inches. $15.00

The BROMPTON

The classic lines and simple richness of this Georgian lantern make it especially suitable for entrance halls or circular stair wells. Finished by Chase in Georgian brass, the beauty of the Brompton is heightened by a clear crystal cylinder. This fixture may be used wherever a rich but simple lantern is needed. Over all height, 45 inches. Height, 21¼ inches. Width, 9⅜ inches. $33.00

The SHAFTESBURY

Where lighting distinction is needed in a Georgian entrance hall, or stair well, the Shaftesbury has it in abundance. Reproduced by Chase from an authentic original, it has the familiar Georgian decoration of "S" shaped scrolls, drapery swag and urn. Made entirely of brass it has a Georgian brass finish which is accented by its clear glass. Height, 45 inches. Width, 10½ inches. $38.00

The MONMOUTH

The loveliness of this Georgian chandelier is emphasized by its etched crystal chimneys and the brilliant prisms suspended from each candle holder. Finished in Georgian brass, the urn and large open ring of the Monmouth are embellished with characteristic Georgian leaf designs. When lighted this chandelier glows with a myriad of lights. Height, 45 inches. Width, 18 inches. $50.00

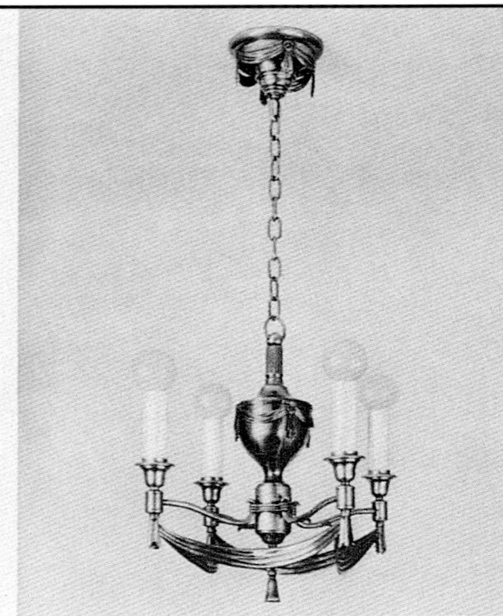

The GUILFORD

The sweeping lines of swag drapery make the Guilford an exceptionally pleasing Georgian ceiling fixture for the dining room or small hallway. Employing the characteristic Georgian urn, swag and tassel, the Guilford is made entirely of brass with Georgian brass finish. This ceiling fixture harmonizes with the Pembroke wall bracket. Height, 45 inches. Width, 15 inches. $35.00

The YORKTOWN

Exactly like the Guilford ceiling fixture, except for the center canopy with its Colonial crystal prisms, the Yorktown was designed for a later period of Georgian decoration. Made of brass, with a Georgian brass finish, the Yorktown is ideally suited for high Georgian ceilings and will also fit beautifully in a Victorian or late Empire setting. Height, 45 inches. Width, 15 inches. $42.00

The DUNBAR

Typically Georgian in decoration, the Dunbar is a modernization of Georgian design. The center glass cylinder encloses a light and is frosted to match the candle arm cylinders which are etched with the same swag decoration seen on the center cylinder in forged brass. Finished in Georgian brass, this ceiling fixture is for today's small house of modern or late Colonial design. Height, 45 inches. Width, 14 inches. $48.00

The WINDSOR

For homes that require a closed ceiling fixture far above the average in style, the Windsor, with its characteristic Georgian decoration, beautifully meets the need. Finished either in Georgian brass or satin chromium, this ceiling fixture supports a deep bowl of sandblasted glass and will meet the lighting requirements of any present-day homes. Height, 6¼ inches. Width, 11 inches. $12.00

Empire Fixtures

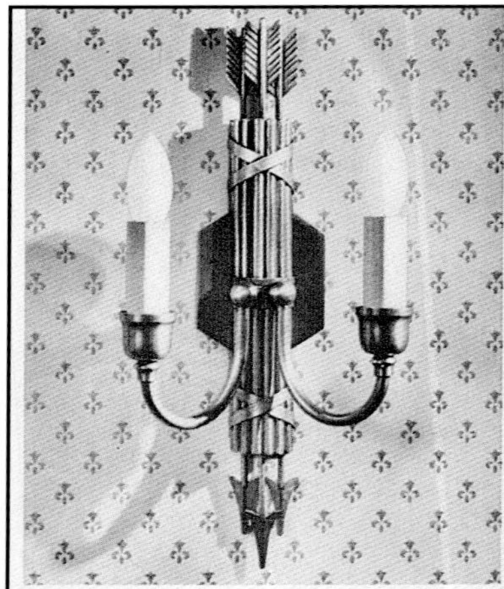

The INDEPENDENCE

Strongly expressive of the Republic, in its bold use of the traditional bound arrows and staves, The Independence is a distinguished Empire lighting fixture. Entirely finished in Empire brass, this two-light bracket harmonizes with either The Legionnaire or The Bastille ceiling fixture. It makes an excellent choice for Empire, Directoire and Federal interiors. Height, 16 inches. Width, 9½ inches. Projection, 4½ inches. $12.00

The ELBA

The symmetry and formal decoration of the Empire period are exquisitely expressed in the lovely Elba wall light. As reproduced by Chase, the Victor's Wreath of Laurel frames a gunmetal mirror in which the crystal etched chimney forms a charming reflection. Entirely finished in Empire brass, The Elba is admirable for Directoire or Empire interiors. Height, 11¾ inches. Width, 9 inches. Projection, 4½ inches. $15.00

The MURAT

Simple in conception, yet strikingly decorated with the crossed Torch of Freedom, The Murat is a charming wall light for Empire, Directoire or even Federal interiors. Made of lasting Chase brass and finished in Empire brass, this bracket has a black circle on the back plate to emphasize the center torch design. It may also be obtained with one light. Height, 8 inches. Width, 9½ inches. Projection, 4 inches. $5.00

The TALLEYRAND

Beautifully expressive of French classic design, the luxurious Talleyrand wall light, with its deeply etched crystal chimney, will bring charming illumination to Empire or Directoire interiors. Finished in Empire brass, the pierced laurel leaf decorations at the sides and the lacy gallery around the candle cup, serve as a lovely frame for the gunmetal mirror. Height, 11½ inches. Width, 6 inches. Projection, 4 inches. $12.50

The PHYFE

Taking its name from the designer who made the lyre design so popular in the American Empire period, this lovely lighting fixture is an authentic addition to the Chase Empire group. A delicately incised acanthus leaf decorates the back plate which encloses a charming gun metal mirror reflector. Empire brass finish. Height, 12 inches. Width, 7½ inches. Projection, 5 inches. $15.00

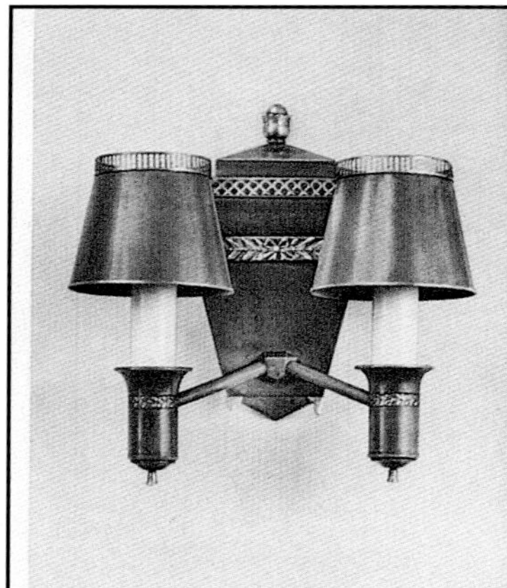

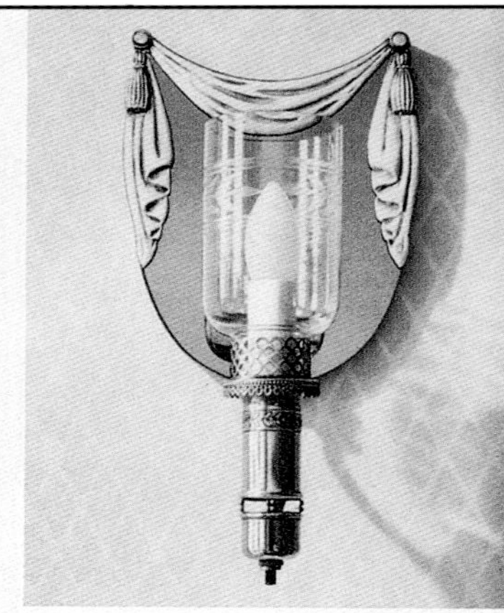

The RICHELIEU

Authentically reproduced from original French fixtures of painted tole, The Richelieu is beautifully finished in either Republic Red, Corsican Green or Directoire White and trimmed with Empire brass. The shades are of matching colors and are surmounted by an openwork gallery of Empire brass. Obtainable with or without shades, in one light or two light models. Height, 10 inches. Width, 5½ inches. Projection, 4¾ inches. $16.00

The RECAMIER

Thoroughly classic in design, The Recamier wall light is beautified by its top drapery swag which is painted white and relieved by touches of blue and gold. In this exquisite Chase reproduction, the candle holder and arm are finished in Empire brass, and in the gunmetal mirror, the crystal etched chimney, the candle and lacy gallery are pleasantly reflected. Height, 13 inches. Width, 7 inches. Projection, 4¼ inches. $15.00

The ORLEANS

Typical of a famous painted tole light of Empire origin, the lovely Orleans is made entirely of Chase brass and glazed in Republic Red, Directoire White or Corsican Green. Relieved by trimmings of Empire brass, this bracket pairs beautifully with the Beauvais ceiling fixture and comes with or without shades in one-light or two-light models. Height, 13 inches. Width, 9 inches. Projection, 3¾ inches. $16.00

The TEA TRADE LANTERN

Commemorating the great trade that existed between Europe and China in the 18th Century, this lovely wall lantern is an authentic reproduction in either Republic Red or Empire black, with trimmings of Empire brass. The inside is sprayed white and on the side panels, two silver etched Chinese figures are fired into the glass and burnished. Height, 13 inches. Width, 6 inches. Projection, 4½ inches. $17.50

The VENDOME

Colorful in Directoire White, Republic Red or Corsican Green, The Vendome, as reproduced by Chase, is authentic in every detail. This delightful ceiling fixture is especially suited to halls, living rooms or dining rooms in the Directoire or Empire styles. Trimmed with Empire brass it harmonizes with The Richelieu bracket and may be had without shades. Height, 45 inches. Spread, 14 inches. $45.00

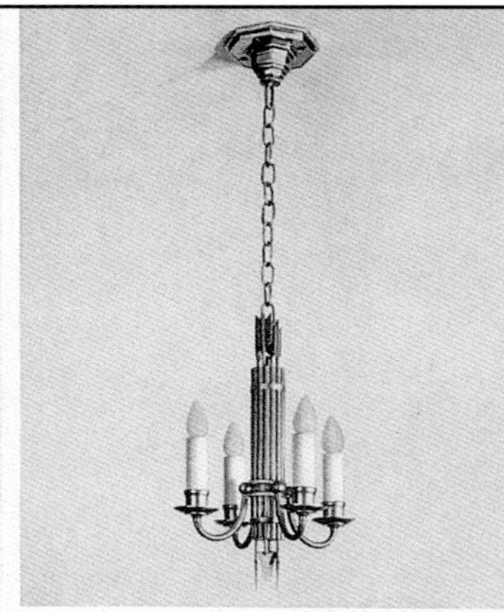

The LEGIONNAIRE

Decorated with the symbols of the early Republic this pleasing Chase ceiling fixture is authentically reproduced from an original and historical design. The smartness of repeating lines makes the lustrous Empire brass finish exceptionally attractive and highly decorative. This ceiling fixture is an excellent choice for Federal, Directoire and Empire interiors. Height over all, 45 inches. Height of fixture, 16 inches. Width, 12 inches. $25.00

The ST. CLOUD

Styled for present day needs, yet employing decorative features that are typically Empire, The St. Cloud is a ceiling light for rooms of many types. The delicately pierced gallery around the white, sandblasted glass bowl is extremely decorative in an Empire brass finish. Made entirely of Chase brass, the St. Cloud has a special metal disc to prevent light leakage on the ceiling line. Height, 6½ inches. Width, 12 inches. $15.00

The ELYSEE

Employing decorations typical of the Empire period, The Elysee is beautifully adapted for low ceilings or rooms where chandeliers are impractical. Finished either in Empire brass or polished chromium, this lovely ceiling light is decorated with the traditional Imperial stars and laurel spray. It will grace either formal or simple interiors. Height, 2¾ inches. Width, 6¾ inches. Brass finish, $[illegible].00. Chromium finish, $5.00

The FONTAINEBLEAU

The graceful design of The Fontainebleau is greatly enhanced by its color tones of black and gold and two exquisite crystal decorations. Although a large chandelier, its delicacy and smart styling are characteristic of Empire design at its best. An exceptional fixture for Empire, Federal or Directoire interiors, The Fontainebleau is finished in Empire brass and black. Height, 45 inches. Height of fixture, 28¾ inches. Width, 26¼ inches. $48.00

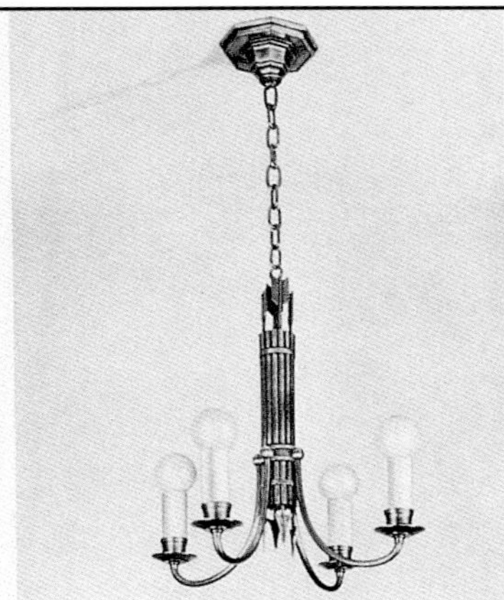

The BASTILLE

This ceiling fixture is exactly like The Legionnaire except that the candle arms have a wider sweep. Like its twin, The Bastille is finished entirely in Empire brass with the arrow heads and feathers carefully forged and the body of heavy cast brass. An admirable choice for the larger rooms of Federal, Directoire or Empire homes. Height over all, 45 inches. Height of fixture, 16 inches. Width, 14 inches. $26.00

The BEAUVAIS

True to the decorative tradition of the Empire period, The Beauvais ceiling fixture has the necessary color and authenticity for American or French homes furnished in the Directoire or Empire styles. Chase glazes The Beauvais in Republic Red, Directoire White and Corsican Green with contrasting trimmings of Empire brass. The Orleans is the matching wall bracket. Height, 45 inches. Spread, 14 inches. $37.50

Classic Modern Fixtures

The ATHENA

In this exquisite adaptation of classical decorative forms, Chase has created a bracket that embodies the very essence of Classic Modern design. The stately, frosted-glass column is relieved with clear glass flutings—the swag, urn and laurel decorations being finished in polished chromium. A tubular lamp contributes the mellow light so sought in modern decoration. Height, 23 inches. Width, 10 inches. Projection, 2½ inches. $17.50

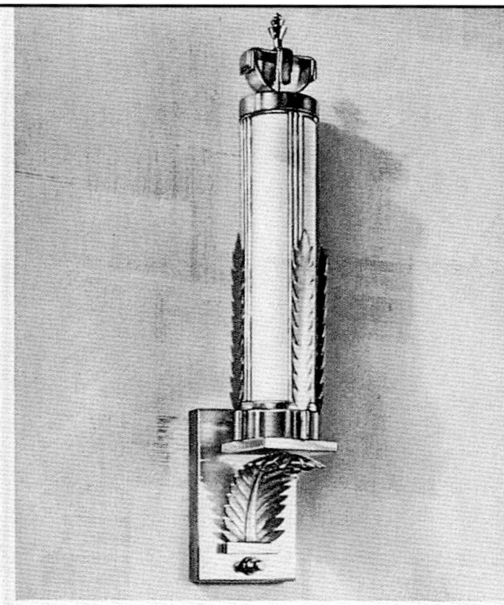

The IMPERATOR

The happy conjunction of classic and modern influence is perfectly illustrated in the beauty of this impressive bracket, with its polished chromium back plate and etched glass column accented by modern adaptations of leaf, crown and reed motifs. A truly superb fixture for the more formal rooms of homes done in the Classic Modern manner. Height, 13½ inches. Width, 3¾ inches. Projection, 3¼ inches. $10.00

The TROY

The versatility of Chase Lighting is well illustrated by this superbly designed bracket scaled for smaller rooms, in the Classic Modern manner. Truly modern in its finish of polished chromium, the classic influence is seen in the reeded pattern of the metal and in the imperial leaf design of frosted glass which insures generous but glareless light. Height, 11½ inches. Width, 3¾ inches. Projection, 3 inches. $12.00

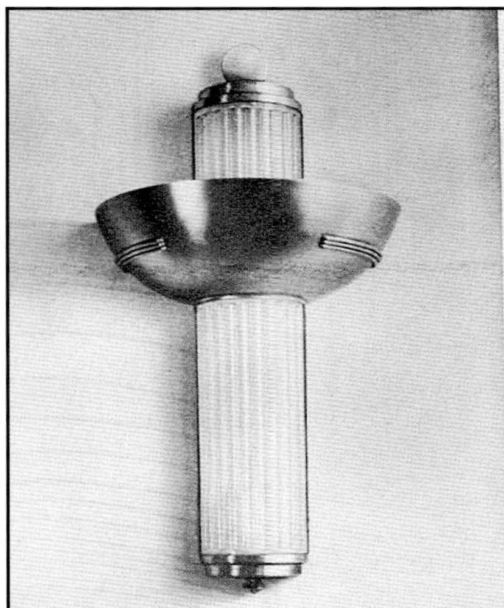

The MINERVA

The spirit and purity of Greek forms are revived in this graceful wall light which contains two light-sources—one within the classic column of frosted glass to give softly diffused illumination, the other shielded by the polished chromium bowl to cast indirect light against the wall and ceiling. Both lights can be used independently, or together. Height, 17 inches. Width, 10 inches. Projection, 5½ inches. $18.50

The COLONNADE

Classic in design, modern in its method of illumination, The Colonade's indirect light is thrown upward from the crystal glass bowl of this brilliantly designed bracket, the eye-level light being diffused to scientifically shaded softness. The classic influence is evident in the stately, fluted column and graceful finial in lustrous polished chromium. Height, 16½ inches. Width, 10 inches. Projection, 5½ inches. $15.00

The DIANA

An effect altogether unique is created in this Classic Modern fixture by the polished chromium arrow bisecting a graceful laurel spray which is etched in burnished silver on the crystal frosted glass. The light, properly diffused outward into the room, is also thrown boldly upward to give an effect as dramatic as the design of the bracket itself. Height, 12 inches. Width, 10 inches. Projection, 3½ inches. $10.00

The THOR

As interesting as its decorations of cross-ribboned bands, imprisoned lighting and stars, is the half-disc and circle form of this effective bracket. The light, diffused through frosted glass, is reflected by the chromium circular back plate insuring correct diffused lighting. Whether hung vertically or horizontally it is a truly individual fixture. Height, 7¼ inches. Width, 7¼ inches. Projection, 4½ inches. $15.00

The DOLPHIN

The dolphin, fantastic creature of the sea, gave inspiration for many an ancient maritime design. One such design, on an old sea chart, in turn gave inspiration for this bracket, wherein the shell-and-dolphin motif is handled with all the simplicity and grace of the classic-modern manner. Chromium finished with frosted glass, The Dolphin makes an ideal bathroom light. Height, 8½ inches. Width, 4¼ inches. Projection, 4¼ inches. $7.50

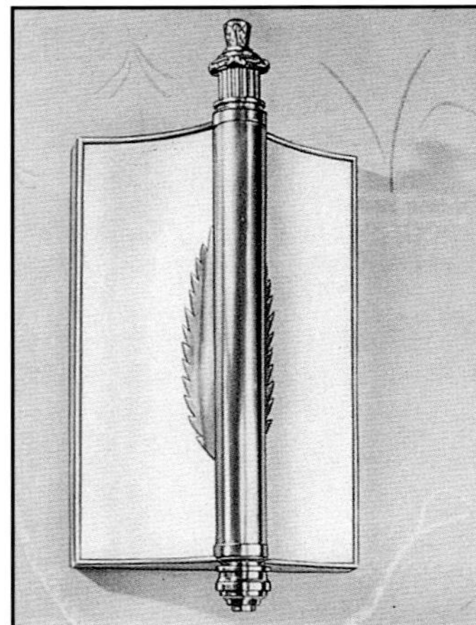

The VESTA

The simple dignity of this bracket is due to its design being influenced by the classic column-and-capital and executed in the rich lustre of polished chromium. The beauty of its classical treatment is enhanced by silhouetting a modernized leaf decoration against its two frosted glass panels which insure a maximum of even and properly diffused light. Height, 9 inches. Width, 6 inches. Projection, 3¼ inches. $13.50

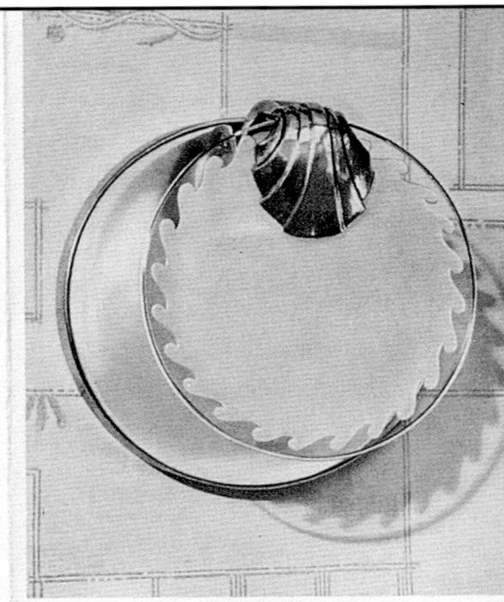

The THESSALY

The merit of adapting classical decorations to dynamic modern design is notably apparent in this distinctive bracket, with its utilization of the Greek wave design etched on the circular disc of plate glass, and the "shell", forged of Chase Brass and finished in polished chromium. These sea symbols render The Thessaly particularly harmonious for use in the bath. Height, 7 inches. Width, 7 inches. Projection, 3¾ inches. $12.00

The ROMA

In this pleasing bracket, the circular reflector plate and convex crystal-glass disc are given classical significance by conventionalized laurel leaves. The metal parts are of Chase Brass, finished in polished chromium and the glass is frosted. In rooms of Classic Modern influence the Roma is admirably suited in its design no less than its modern illumination. Height, 8½ inches. Width, 8½ inches. Projection, 3½ inches. $10.00

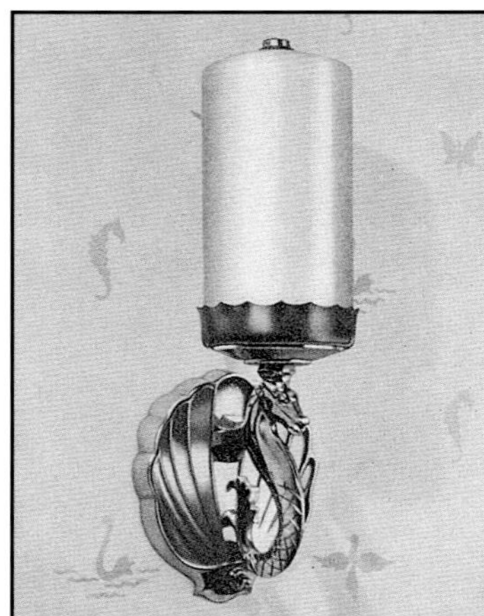

The SEA HORSE

This interesting yet highly efficient and decorative bracket is, in its design, a modern adaptation of the sea-symbols of classic antiquity. Carefully cast in Chase brass and finished in satin chromium, this lovely wall light is altogether in harmony with the fittings of the modern bath and thus is perfectly suited to such use in homes of all periods. Height, 11 inches. Width, 4½ inches. Projection, 4 inches. $7.50

The JUPITER

While it may be used with excellent taste in hallways, closets and bedrooms, this simple bracket was created as an ideal bath and dressing room light. The frosted glass shade, decorated with a reeded band of polished chromium and sprays of burnished silver, slips into the chromium back plate. A fine example of a utility light made beautiful by intelligent designing. Height, 3½ inches. Width, 3½ inches. Projection, 5½ inches. $5.50

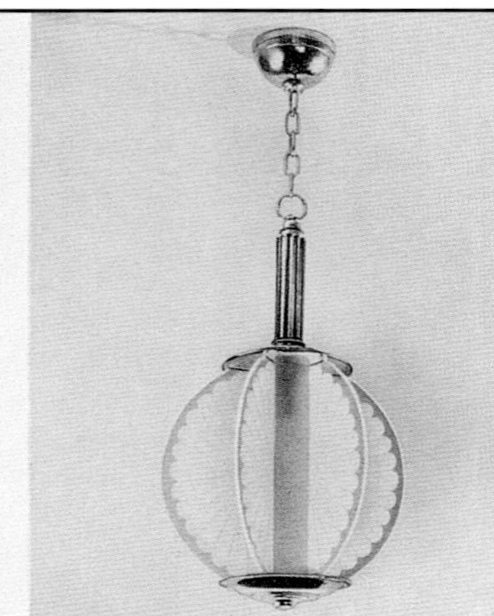

The AURORA

While dynamically modern in its execution, the exquisite decorative beauty of this classical ceiling fixture, is reminiscent of the gracious forms of Georgian design. Six half circles of plate glass etched with a modernized version of the lotus design are arranged around a center column of illumination producing a lighting effect that must be seen to be appreciated. Height, 45 inches. Width, 14 inches. $40.00

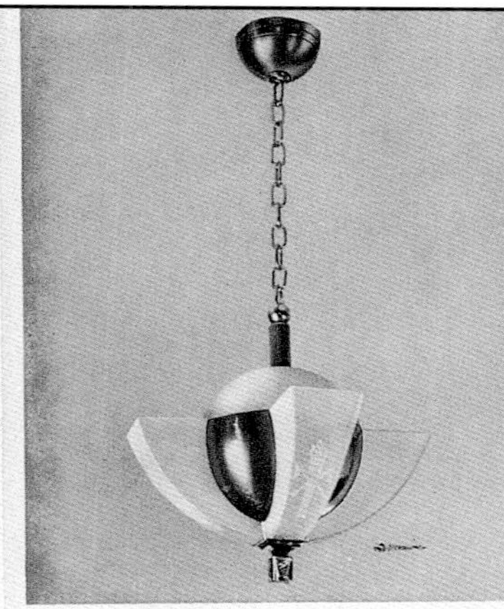

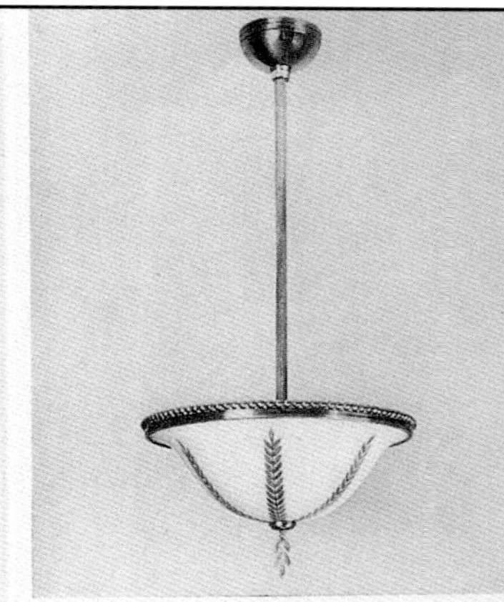

The PLANETARIUM

While modern in its design this beautiful and symbolic fixture is thoroughly appropriate for Empire, Federal and even Colonial homes, if antique brass finish is chosen. For modern homes it comes in polished chromium. The idea and design were inspired by an old astrolabe of about 1750. The globe is of frosted glass sprinkled with clear glass stars. Height, 45 inches. Width, 13 inches. Chromium finish, $32.00. Brass finish, $27.50

The ZEUS

While the classic decorations of this unusual fixture are 18th Century in origin, only the 20th Century could have produced its dynamic design and scientific illumination. Providing indirect light from the glass top of the polished chromium sphere and diffused light from the four frosted glass pockets surrounding its base, it casts the glareless illumination that is the triumph of modern lighting. Height, 45 inches. Width, 16 inches. $37.50

The SYBIL

The grace apparent in this fixture is illustrative of the way in which Classic Modern design can achieve pure beauty without sacrificing scientific illumination. The symmetrical curve of the bowl, the burnished silver laurel sprays, the slender satin chromium stem—all contribute great charm to a ceiling fixture that gives the shadowless glow of perfect indirect lighting. Height, 45 inches. Width, 14 inches. $20.00

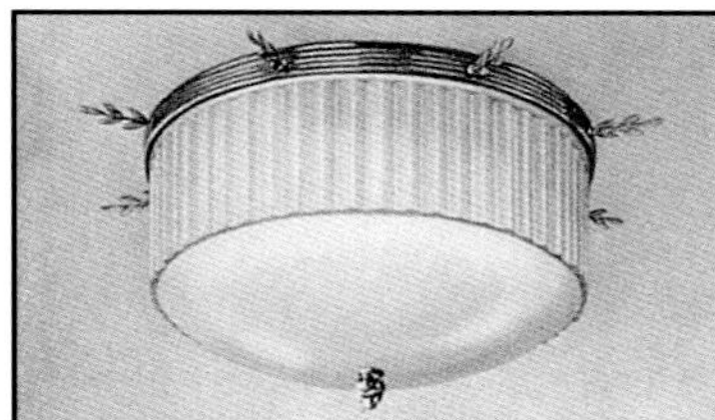

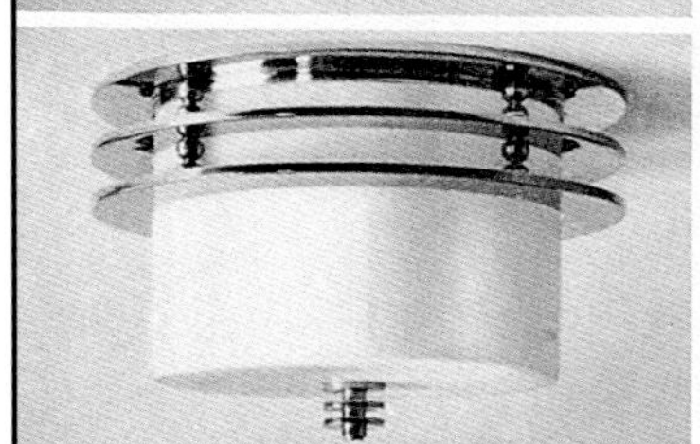

THE PARIS Inspired by the glittering splendor of the crystal chandeliers of the Empire Era. The Paris, with polished chromium top-plate, interspersed with laurel sprays, is thoroughly Classic Modern. Height, 12 inches. Width, 18 inches. $25.00

THE APOLLO With its repetition of polished chromium rings and its severely simple frosted glass bowl, this fixture verges toward the pure modern. Made of lasting Chase Brass, it is finished in polished chromium. Height, 9 inches. Width, 13 inches. $22.50

THE CYPRUS Exceptional decorative value is achieved in the Cyprus by a star design carried out either in polished chromium or antique brass at the top and in clear glass star-shapes on the frosted glass. Height, 5½ inches. Width, 11 inches. Chromium, $12.50. Brass, $10.00

THE AUGUSTA Because of the simplicity of its decoration The Augusta can be properly used in rooms and periods other than Classic Modern. Height, ¾ inch. Width, 6½ inches. Polished chromium, $3.25. Antique brass, $2.75

American Adaptations

The PORT HOLE SCONCE

Anyone who has longed for a room that smacks of taut ropes and white-crested water will delight in this sea-going sconce. Even an exacting seaman could find no fault with the accurate details of anchor and rope decorations modeled against a back plate of dark sea-green etched with a wave motif. Finished in Colonial brass and also available with two lights. Height, 10 inches. Width, $7\frac{1}{2}$ inches. Projection, $3\frac{1}{2}$ inches. $8.00

The BENNINGTON

Like the Woodbury, the Bennington has distinctive Colonial character in its graceful curving design. Excellently suited for living and dining rooms, it is finished in either satin chromium, Colonial brass or weathered brass and is fitted with clear glass chimneys attractively decorated with frosted bands. Also comes without chimneys. Height, 13 inches. Spread, 7 inches. Projection, $6\frac{1}{8}$ inches. $10.50

The FRAMINGHAM

This bracket has all the quaint grace and charm of Colonial and Federal design. It is wrought of lasting Chase Brass, with a beautifully modeled Colonial eagle surmounting its simply designed back plate. To harmonize with individual furnishings of dining or living rooms, it is finished in satin chromium, Colonial brass or weathered brass. Height, 8 inches. Width, $4\frac{1}{2}$ inches. Projection, $2\frac{7}{8}$ inches. $3.25

The NASHUA

Exactly suited to the frequent need for a single and inexpensive wall bracket in attic, basement or kitchen, the simple design and modest price of The Nashua will recommend it for many uses. Made of lasting Chase brass, it is finished either in white enamel or in polished chromium and is also available without the frosted glass shade. Height, $11\frac{1}{2}$ inches. Width, 5 inches. Projection, $9\frac{3}{4}$ inches. Polished chromium, $1.95. White enamel, $1.70

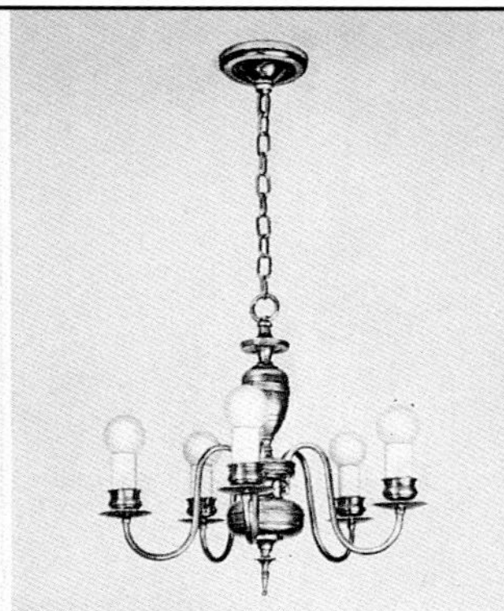

The LENOX

This attractive five-light ceiling fixture suggests the Colonial in the design of its nicely proportioned body and the graceful curve of the arms. An ideal central fixture for living or dining rooms, it is finished in satin chromium, Colonial or weathered brass, to harmonize with furnishings of various character. Height, 45 inches. Width, 18 inches. Spread, 18 inches. $17.50

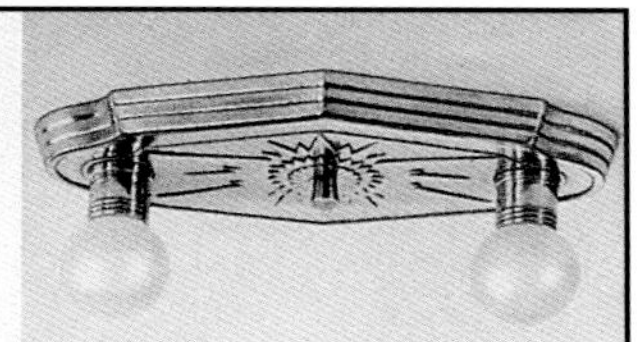

THE DARIEN This modern, close-fitting ceiling fixture is finished either in polished chromium, weathered brass or ivory and is wrought of lasting brass. Height, $2\frac{3}{4}$ inches. Width, $6\frac{3}{4}$ inches. $4.50

THE RICHFIELD Smartly modern in design, this close ceiling fixture is fitted for a variety of uses by the alternative finishes of antique brass, ivory, or polished chromium. Height, $2\frac{1}{4}$ inches. Width, 12 inches. $6.00

The WOODBURY

While the lines of this interesting wall bracket are Colonial in character, it can be used with excellent taste in any home of average American style. Wrought of durable Chase brass, the bracket is finished in either satin chromium, weathered brass or Colonial brass. It also comes fitted with a clear glass chimney with frosted band decoration. Height, 13 inches. Spread, $4\frac{1}{2}$ inches. Projection, $7\frac{1}{2}$ inches. $6.00

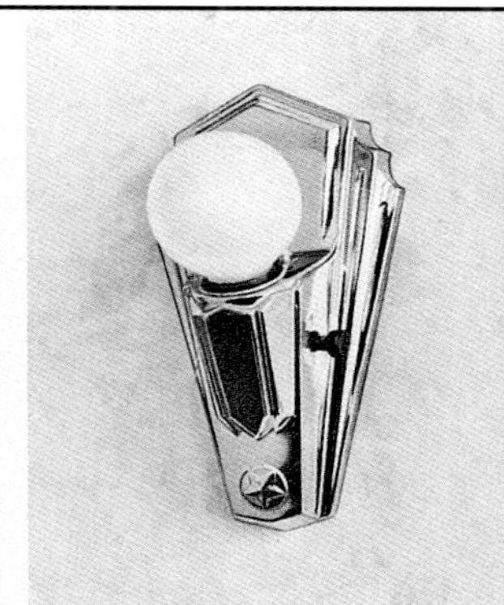

The NEWPORT

Finished in non-tarnishing polished chromium and definitely modern in design, this bracket combines smart beauty with unusual usefulness in kitchen or bath. Wrought of lasting Chase Brass, it is both a serviceable and decorative fixture for the modern home or apartment. Also made with a convenience outlet below the lamp. Height, $7\frac{1}{2}$ inches. Width, $4\frac{1}{4}$ inches. Projection, $2\frac{3}{4}$ inches. $2.10

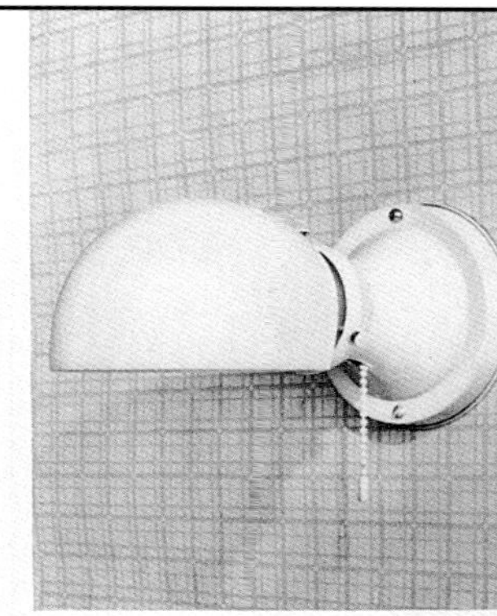

The SOUTHPORT

In service halls, maid's rooms, closets and pantries, a simple, inexpensive bracket serves a useful purpose in proper illumination. The Southport is such a bracket, excellently proportioned and finished either in white enamel or highly polished non-tarnishing chromium. Also made without the frosted glass half-shade. Back plate, $4\frac{1}{2}$ inches diameter. $2\frac{1}{2}$ inch fitter. Projection to glass holder, 3 inches. Chromium, $1.75. White enamel, $1.65

The BRIDGETOWN

Ample illumination from a simple, dignified ceiling fixture characterizes the Bridgetown, with its attractive parchment shade finished in white and silver to harmonize with the satin chromium finish of the metal, or in brown and beige to go with the alternative finishes of weathered or antique brass. For dining rooms, the Bridgetown also comes with an appliance receptacle at the bottom. Height, 45 inches. Diameter of shade, 17 inches. $12.75

The DRAKE

Like the Trenton except that it is fitted with three lights instead of five, this close ceiling fixture is equally well adapted for use in smaller rooms where the illumination from three lamps will be found adequate. Finished to suit individual taste and appointments, in satin chromium, Colonial brass or weathered brass. Height, 10 inches, Width, 10 inches. $5.50

The SHELDON

The five lights clustered close to the ceiling in this graceful fixture will provide ample central illumination for living room or dining room. Reflecting the simplicity of Colonial design, the Sheldon is finished in either satin chromium, weathered brass or Colonial brass and is made entirely of lasting Chase Brass. Height, 18 inches. Spread, 18 inches. $14.00

The NORFOLK

Typically American is this attractive three-light ceiling fixture, with the influence of Colonial design evident in its harmonious proportions. Typical of Chase quality is the durable brass of which it is wrought, the fine character of its workmanship. Finished in either satin chromium, Colonial brass or weathered brass. Height, 45 inches. Spread, 10 inches. $8.50

The ENFIELD

While Colonial influence is apparent in the graceful design of this three-light ceiling fixture, its use is by no means limited to homes of that period. Like all fixtures in the Chase American Adaptations group, it will be found in harmony with a wide variety of interior furnishings. Wrought of Chase Brass in satin chromium, Colonial brass or weathered brass finish. Available with or without the glass chimneys. Height, 45 inches. Spread, 14 inches. $16.25

The CORNWALL

Modestly priced yet beautifully made and finished, this five-light ceiling fixture will give pleasing illumination to living room or dining room. It is made entirely of durable Chase brass and is available in any one of three finishes: satin chromium, Colonial brass or weathered brass. Height over all 45 inches. Height of fixture, 17 inches. Spread, 15 inches. $11.50

The TRENTON

As a central source of illumination in living or dining room, this five-light ceiling fixture is simple and graceful. Like all Chase American Adaptations, it will harmonize excellently with the interior decoration of homes or apartments which are not definitely period in character. Made of lasting Chase Brass and finished in satin chromium, weathered brass or Colonial brass. Height, 12 inches. Width, 16 inches. $8.50

THE SARATOGA This simple ceiling fixture comes with either pull chain or keyless socket. Height, 3⅝ inches. Width, 5½ inches. Chromium, $1.20. Brass or Ivory, $.90

THE KEENE A simple beam-light, designed to provide adequate light for closets and similar locations. Height, 2 inches. Width, 4½ inches. Chromium, $.90. White enamel, $.80

THE BURLINGTON A beautifully proportioned beam light. Finished in satin chromium, weathered or antique brass. Height, 5 inches. Width, 4⅞ inches. $1.80

The MILFORD

Extremely simple yet pleasing in its proportions, this pendant ceiling fixture is admirably adapted for service where a single light-source is desired for utility. It is finished in polished chromium, white enamel or brushed brass and is also available without the frosted glass shade. Height, 45 inches. Canopy, 4½ inch diameter, 2¼ inch fitter. Chromium, $2.60. White enamel, $2.25

The BERKELEY

With its frosted glass for scientific light diffusion and its pendant switch with convenient electrical outlet this practical ceiling fixture will be found useful in bathroms, kitchens, laundries and pantries. Finished in polished chromium or white enamel, it is available either with or without the glass bowl and with or without the pendant switch and receptacle. Canopy, 5½-inch diameter, 4-inch fitter. Polished chromium, $3.85. White enamel, $3.55

Chapter 10

"The 1937 Chase Lighting Fixtures Catalog"

"Chase offers in this Catalog a Complete Line of Correctly Designed and Properly Constructed Fixtures."

Chase Lighting Fixtures catalog, 1937

Or, "what you see is what you get." The colorful hyperbole of the 1934 Fixtures catalog had, by 1937, made its way back down to earth. While many of the original Lurelle Guild designs were still part of the Chase inventory, numbers, rather than names, now served as their sole identification. Categorization by function began to take the lead over categorization by decor period.

Joining the Chase line in 1937 were over 100 new fixtures. Many were adaptations of existing designs; others were purely functional, or part of the "Even-Glow" series. Each and every one, however, was touted as an example of "scientific illumination, of adequate lighting that will put an end to eyestrain, headaches, and other evils of gloom and glare in the home." *1937 Lighting Fixtures catalog courtesy of Olga Laylon and the late Harry Laylon*

In this plant, one of the largest of its kind, all Chase lighting fixture metal parts are fabricated

This plant, almost a mile in length, is one of three large Chase brass and copper mills

Here is a view of the Chase rolling mills, where brass and copper are rolled and annealed

Factories and Facilities

Ever since the year 1837, that is 100 years ago, the manufacturing plant of the Chase Brass & Copper Co. has maintained a keen interest in the progress and advancement of lighting equipment. Starting with candlestick holders, then to kerosene lamps, Bunsen burners and finally to the manufacturing of a complete line of Residential and Commercial Lighting Fixtures.

Chase Lighting Fixture metal parts are made of rust-proof Brass or Copper, and the fabrication of metal parts used in the construction of Chase Fixtures is all done in our own plant under our own supervision.

The designing and manufacturing of Chase Fixtures is managed by a competent staff, many of whom have devoted their entire business lives to lighting. We have been fortunate in securing the services of designers, mechanics and supervisors who have an intimate and thorough knowledge of Lighting Fixtures.

You may feel sure that in selecting Chase Fixtures you have correct designs, proper mechanical construction and the assurance that, with the exception of brackets that have French hooks, which are not considered an approved style of construction by the National Board of Fire Underwriters, *Chase Fixtures bear the label of approval of the National Board of Fire Underwriters.*

Chase Fixtures are sold only through qualified Electrical Dealers and Contractors.

Chase Tower →

A complete and permanent display of Chase Lighting Fixtures is maintained on the entire 48th floor at Chase Tower — 10 East 40th St., New York City.

Here most of the Chase Fixtures are separated into various period designs and appropriately displayed in alcoves which are decorated in the same style as the fixture.

To all distributors of lighting fixtures and to your prospects and customers, we extend a cordial invitation to see this beautiful display of ceiling fixtures, wall brackets and lanterns.

THE ADVANTAGES OF SCIENTIFIC LIGHTING

BEFORE:
This is a room improperly lighted with ordinary lighting fixtures.

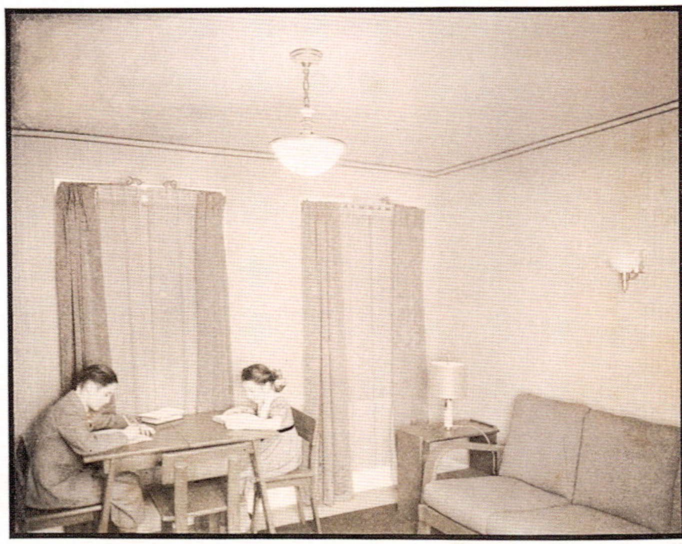

AFTER:
This is the same room lighted with Chase "Even-Glow" fixtures that give scientific diffused light.

Glare Blinds and Darkness Strains the Eyes

The wrong kind of light is injurious to the eyes and is just as bad as not having enough light.

For example, too bright a light concentrated in a small spot with the rest of the room improperly lighted or in darkness, is harmful to the eyes because of the extreme contrasts between the intense light and dark areas, and causes nervousness and fatigue.

Ceiling Fixtures Give Best Results

The importance of not only adequate lighting throughout a room, but an adequate amount of light properly distributed for eye protection, can be accomplished best with the use of a ceiling fixture.

Scientific Light Saves Eyesight

Scientific light is diffused, glareless light, light that is evenly distributed throughout a room, so that there are no areas of semi-darkness. A large percentage of defective eyesight is caused by improper light, and is a reason for many a backward school child. And that tired feeling brought on by reading or playing cards under inadequate light, or glaring light, can be avoided by properly lighting the room with scientific, diffused light.

Diffused Light is Restful to the Eyes

Tired feet make a tired body, but tired eyes make one mentally and physically weary. Under the right kind of light, the eyes are relaxed, and can see without effort. Diffused light is science's best approach to daylight. It is so natural to the eyes that it makes reading and working indoors easy on the eyes and restful.

5

CHASE "EVEN-GLOW"* LIGHTING FIXTURES

Give Scientific Illumination

BEFORE: *Excessive glare from the fixtures in this room causes uncomfortable seeing conditions; it also causes headaches, nervousness and fatigue.*

AFTER: *Here's the same room properly lighted with Chase "Even-Glow" fixtures. There is no semi-darkness, no irritating bright spots to annoy the eyes.*

Scientifically Designed

Chase "Even-Glow" Fixtures were one of the first complete residential lines designed to give Scientific Light. They were designed by an outstanding illuminating engineer and experienced lighting fixture designers after much study and research, to give better light in the homes of today.

Diffused Light

Chase "Even-Glow" Fixtures give correct light because they direct the light to the ceiling from where it is reflected evenly throughout the room.

More Light at Same Cost

Chase "Even-Glow" Fixtures give more light at no extra current cost. How? By using one large bulb rather than several small bulbs. A single 200 watt bulb in a Chase "Even-Glow" fixture gives 3,400 units of light or 1,240 units of light more than do five 40 watt bulbs in an ordinary fixture using the same amount of current. That is, you get 57% more light from a large bulb in a Chase "Even-Glow" Fixture — plus modern Scientific Light.

New Bowls

The bowls of Chase "Even-Glow" Fixtures are moulded of translucent plastic. These plastic bowls give a pleasing, soft, glareless light. They are extremely durable — practically shatterproof — light in weight, and easier and safer to handle.

Finishes

There are beautiful, lasting finishes applied to these Chase "Even-Glow" Fixtures and the prices are within reach of the purse of the average home owner and builder.

*Trade Mark

Do not use a larger bulb than the size recommended for each Chase "Even-Glow" Fixture. Use only inside frosted bulbs for even illumination.

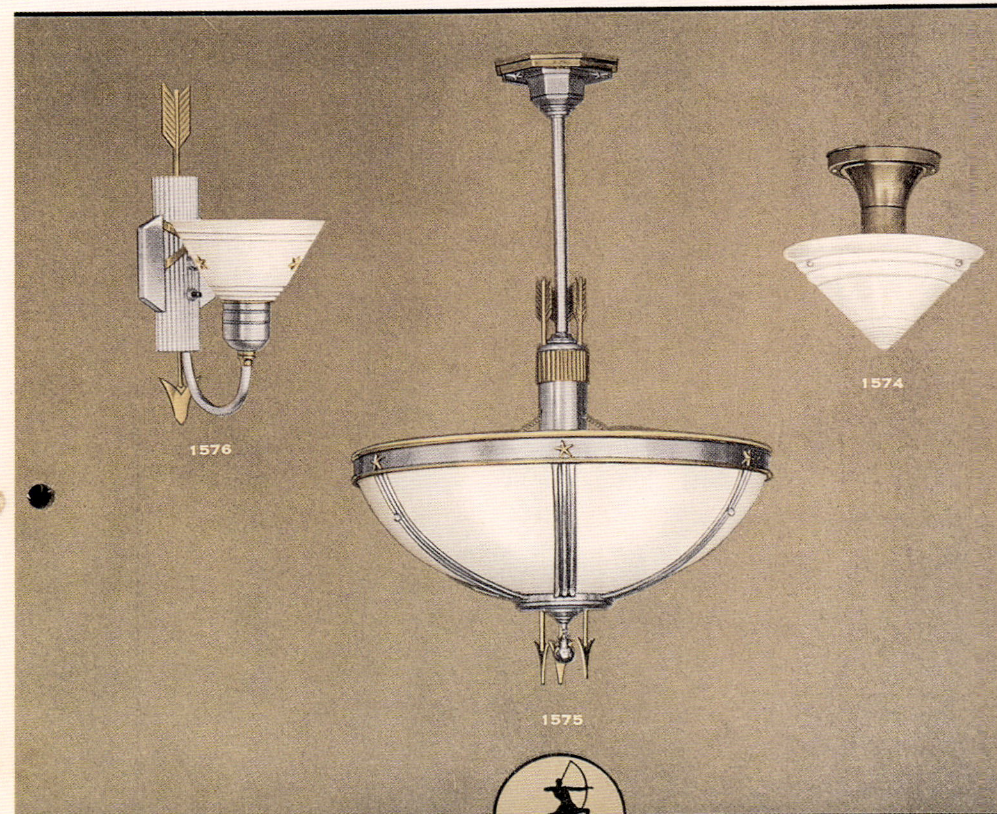

No. 1576
One-light bracket with a 5⅞" Plastic reflector. Metal star decorations are in the shade. Over-all length 14". Extends 7". Has switch. Finish: Pewter and Gold.

No. 1575
One-light ceiling fixture with a 16½" Plastic reflector metal trimmed. Over-all length 27". Takes up to and including a 200 watt bulb. Finish: Pewter and Gold.

No. 1.
One-light ceiling fixture with an 8" Plastic refect Over-all length 9". Takes up to and including a watt bulb. Finishes: English Bronze, Toned Pewt Polished Gold, Polished Chromium, Ivory, Color Brass.

6

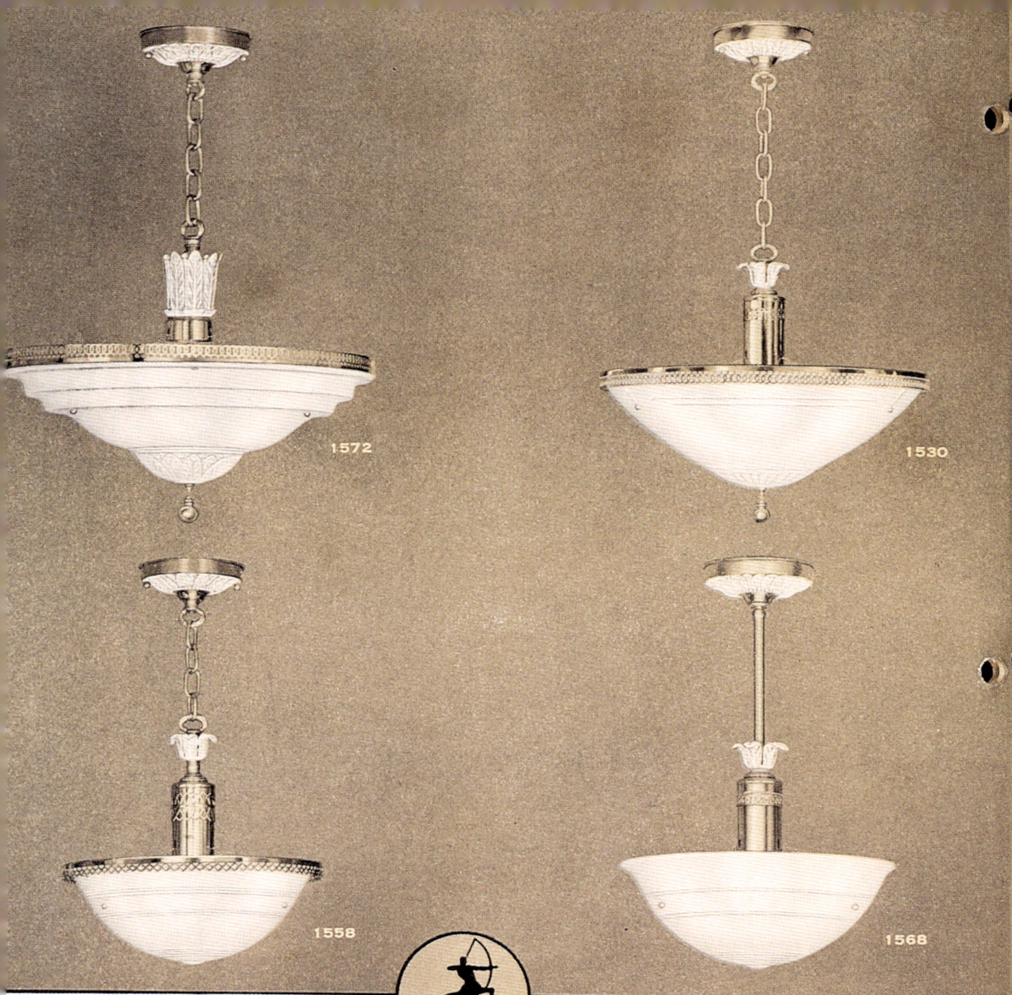

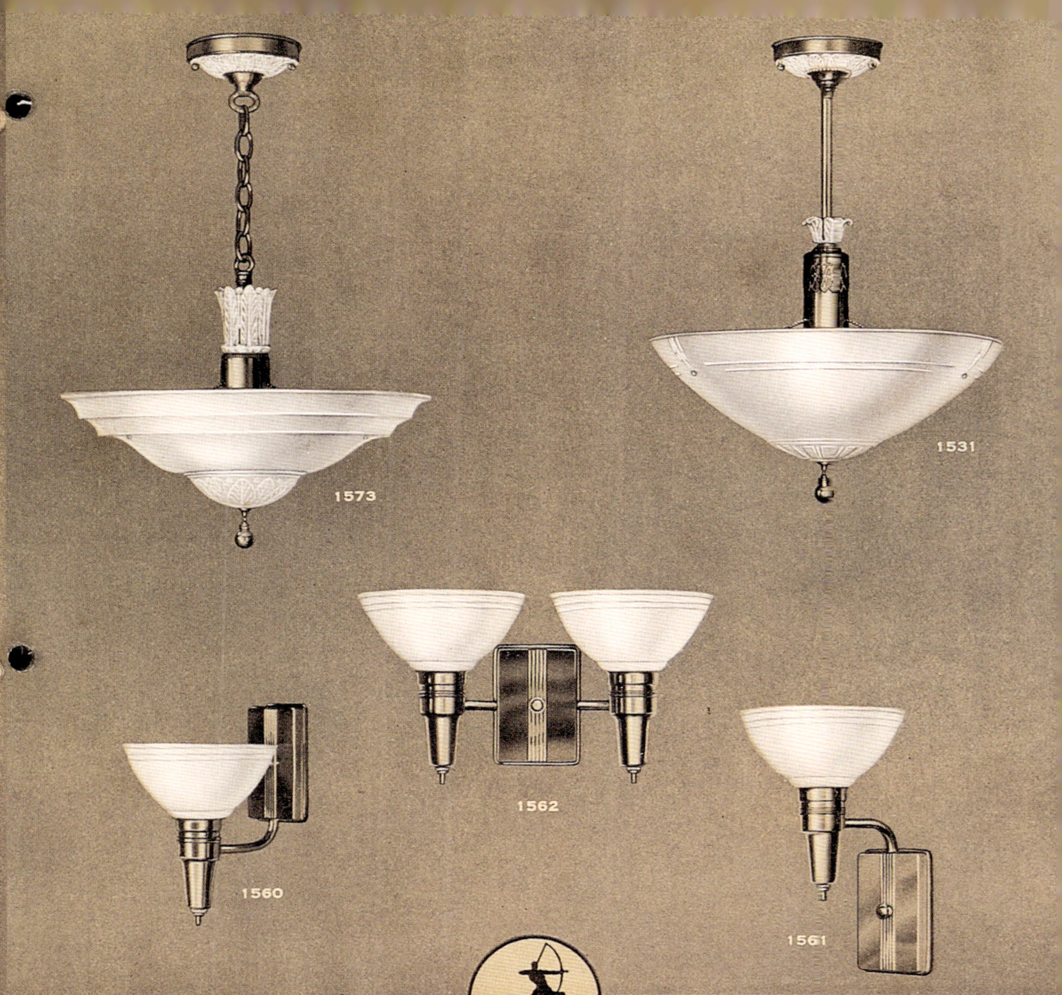

o. 1572
ne-light ceiling fixture with a 16″ Plastic reflector mmed with a metal gallery. Over-all length 25½″. kes up to and including a 200 watt bulb. Finies: Ivory and Gold or Toned Pewter.

o. 1558
ne-light ceiling fixture with a 12″ Plastic reflector etal trimmed. Over-all length 19″. Takes up to d including a 100 watt bulb. Finishes: Ivory and old or Toned Pewter.

No. 1530
One-light ceiling fixture with a 15¾″ Plastic reflector metal trimmed. Over-all length 24½″. Takes up to and including a 200 watt bulb. Finishes: Ivory and Gold or Toned Pewter.

No. 1568
One-light ceiling fixture with a 12″ Plastic reflector. Over-all length 19″. Takes up to and including a 100 watt bulb. Finishes: Ivory and Gold or Toned Pewter.

No. 1573
One-light ceiling fixture with a 16″ Plastic reflector. Over-all length 25½″. Takes up to and including a 200 watt bulb. Finishes: Ivory and Gold or Toned Pewter.

No. 1560
One-light bracket with a 5½″ Plastic reflector. Back plate 5″ x 3¼″. Extends 7″ from wall. Suitable for 25 or 40 watt bulbs. Has switch. Finishes: Polished Gold, Polished Chromium, Toned Pewter, English Bronze or Ivory and Gold.

No. 1562
Two-light bracket with 5½″ Plastic reflectors. Back Plate 5″ x 3¼″. Over-all spread 13¼″. Suitable for 25 or 40 watt bulbs. Has switch. Finishes: Polished Gold, Polished Chromium, Toned Pewter, English Bronze or Ivory and Gold.

No. 1531
One-light ceiling fixture with a 15¾″ Plastic reflector. Over-all length 25½″. Takes up to and including a 200 watt bulb. Finishes: Ivory and Gold or Toned Pewter.

No. 1561
One-light bracket with a 5½″ Plastic reflector. Back plate 5″ x 3¼″. Extends 7″. Suitable for 25 or 40 watt bulbs. Has switch. Finishes: Polished Gold, Polished Chromium, English Bronze, Toned Pewter or Ivory and Gold.

9

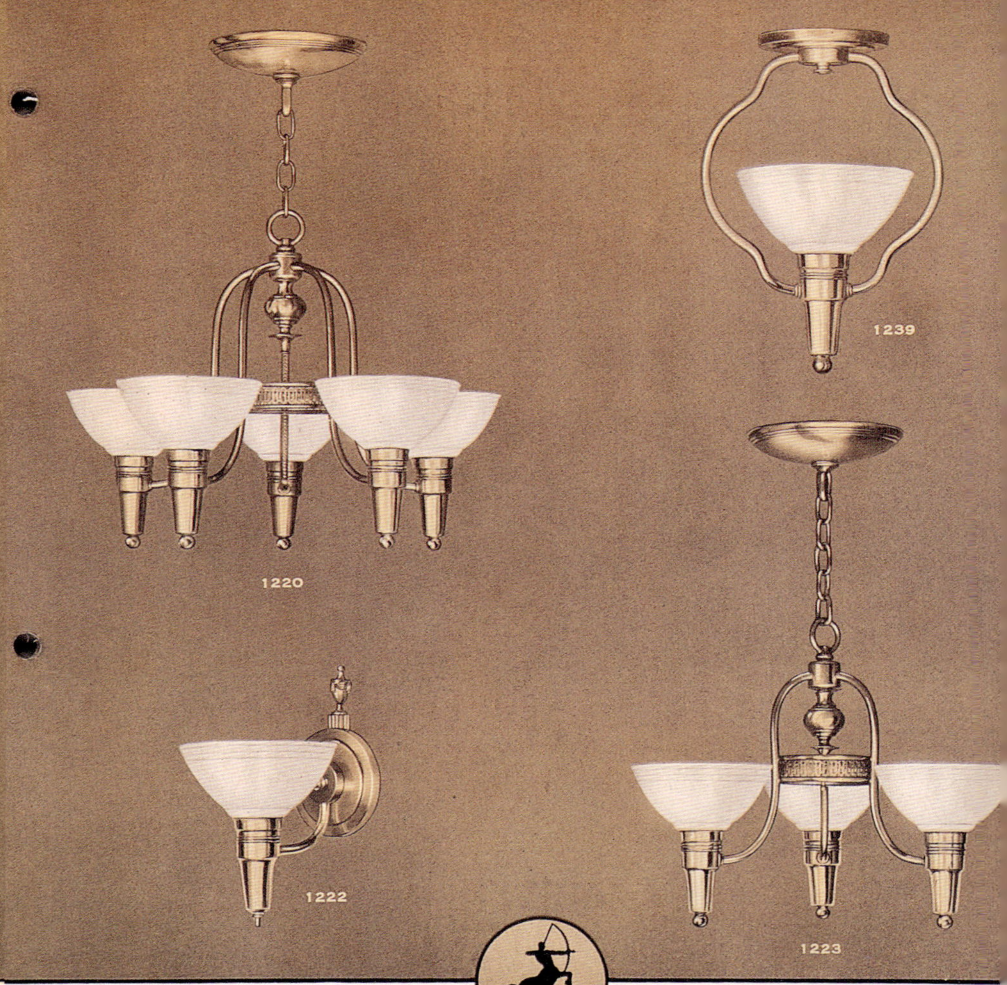

No. 1218
One-light ceiling fixture with a 6″ Plastic reflector. Over-all length 20″. Width 9½″. Suitable for 25 or 40 watt bulbs. Finishes: Polished Gold, Toned Pewter.

No. 1219
One-light bracket with a 5½″ Plastic reflector. Back plate 5¼″ x 4″. Extends 6″. Suitable for 25 or 40 watt bulbs. Has switch. Finishes: Polished Gold, Toned Pewter.

No. 1217
Five-light ceiling fixtures with 6″ Plastic reflectors. Over-all length 27½″. Spread 22″. Suitable for 25 or 40 watt bulbs. Has 3 way switch. Finishes: Polished Gold, Toned Pewter.

No. 1220
Five-light ceiling fixture with 6″ Plastic reflectors. Over-all length 27″. Spread 20″. Suitable for 25 or 40 watt bulbs. Has 3 way switch. Finishes: English Bronze or Pewter and Gold.

No. 12
One-light ceiling fixture with a 6″ Plastic reflecto Over-all length 12½″. Width 8¼″. Suitable fo 25 or 40 watt bulbs. Finishes: English Bronze, Pew- ter and Gold, Colonial Brass, Polished Gold.

No. 1222
One-light bracket with 5½″ Plastic reflector. Back plate 4½″. Extends 7″. Suitable for 25 or 40 watt bulbs. Has switch. Finishes: English Bronze or Pewter and Gold.

No. 12
Three-light ceiling fixture with 6″ Plastic reflectors Over-all length 27″. Spread 18″. Suitable for 2 or 40 watt bulbs. Finishes: English Bronze or Pew- ter and Gold.

o. 1251
hree-light ceiling fixture with 5⅞″ Plastic reflectors. ver-all length 14″. Spread 14″. Suitable for 25 40 watt bulbs. Finishes: Colonial Brass or Pew- r and Gold.

No. 1224
One-light wall bracket with a 5⅞″ Plastic reflector. Back plate 4½″. Extends 6″. Suitable for 25 or 40 watt bulb. Has switch. Finishes: Colonial Brass or Pewter and Gold.

No. 1237
Five-light ceiling fixture with 5⅞″ Plastic reflectors. Over-all length 36″. Spread 18½″. Suitable for 25 or 40 watt bulbs. Finishes: Colonial Brass or Pewter and Gold.

No. 1559
One-light ceiling fixture with a 12″ Plastic reflector. Over-all length 10″. Takes up to and including a 100 watt bulb. Finishes: Ivory and Gold or Toned Pewter.

No. 1569
One-light ceiling fixture with a 12″ Plastic reflector. Over-all length 11″. Takes up to and including a 100 watt bulb. Finishes: Satin Chromium, English Bronze, toned Pewter, Ivory and Gold, Polished Gold.

No. 1570
One-light ceiling fixture with a 12″ Plastic reflector. Over-all length 10½″. Takes up to and including a 100 watt bulb. Finish: Polished Chromium.

CHASE LIGHTING FIXTURES

This dining room is lighted with the No. 1261 Chase ceiling fixture and two No. 1262 Chase brackets.

Suitable for
Early American and Colonial Interiors

The Chase Lighting Fixtures in this group have been designed to meet the growing demand for fixtures for the Colonial and Early American type homes of today that are being built throughout the country.

We have developed a wide range of designs, including wall brackets, ceiling fixtures, hall and porch lanterns and beam lights which are suitable in both design and finish for interiors of this type.

These fixtures range from authentic Early Colonists' designs to the more modernized Colonial that is so popular today.

Chase Lighting Fixtures are made of Chase Brass or Copper which will not rust or deteriorate, and assuring the owner a long life for his fixtures. The beautiful finishes applied to Chase Fixtures are also lasting because of the rustproof basic metal on which they are applied.

1249

1247

1240

No. 1249
Two-light bracket with etched glass chimneys. Back plate 4½″. Spread 8″. Has switch. Finishes: English Bronze, Colonial Brass.

No. 124
One-light bracket with etched glass chimneys. Bac plate 4½″. Height 9″. Extends 5½″. Has switc Finishes: English Bronze, Colonial Brass.

No. 1240
Five-light ceiling fixture with etched glass chimneys. Over-all length 36″. Spread 16½″. Finishes: English Bronze, Colonial Brass.

No. 1238
Five-light ceiling fixture with cut glass chimneys. Over-all length 18½″. Spread 18″. Finishes: English Bronze or Pewter and Gold.

No. 1233
Five-light ceiling fixture with cut glass chimneys. Over-all length 36″. Spread 26″. Finishes: Pewter and Gold or English Bronze.

No. 1248
One-light bracket with cut glass chimneys. Back plate 4½″. Extends 6″. Has switch. Finishes: English Bronze or Pewter and Gold.

No. 1241
One-light ceiling fixture with cut glass chimney. Over-all length 12″. Width 8¼″. Finishes: English Bronze, Pewter and Gold, Colonial Brass.

No. 1250
Three-light ceiling fixture with cut glass chimneys. Length 14″. Spread 12″. Finishes: English Bronze, Pewter and Gold, Colonial Brass.

No. 1243
One-light bracket with cut glass chimney. Back plate 4½″. Extends 5″. Has switch. Finishes: English Bronze, Pewter and Gold, Colonial Brass.

No. 1244
Two-light wall bracket with cut glass chimneys. Back plate 4½″. Spread 9″. Has switch. Finishes: English Bronze, Pewter and Gold, Colonial Brass.

No. 1242
Five-light ceiling fixture with cut glass chimneys. Over-all length 36″. Spread 16½″. Finishes: English Bronze, Pewter and Gold, Colonial Brass.

1104

1101

1106

1236

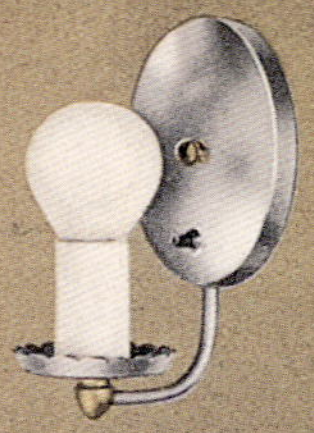

1202

1266

1099

1265

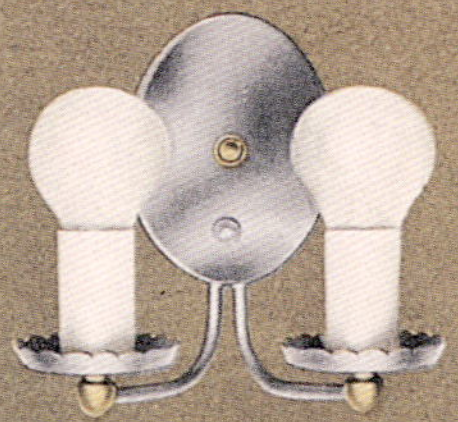

1198

1245

CHASE

No. 1104
One-light bracket. Back plate 4½″. Extends 4¼″. Has switch. Finishes: English Bronze, Colonial Brass, Ivory and Gold.

No. 1266
One-light bracket. Back plate 4½″. Height 8″. Extends 5″. Has switch. Finishes: English Bronze, Colonial Brass, Ivory and Gold, Pewter and Gold.

No. 1101
Five-light ceiling fixture. Over-all length 12″. Spread 16″. Finishes: English Bronze or Colonial Brass.

No. 1099
Three-light ceiling fixture. Over-all length 10″. Spread 10″. Finishes: English Bronze, Colonial Brass, or Ivory and Gold.

No. 1106
Two-light bracket. Back plate 4½″. Spread 7½″. Extends 3″. Has switch. Finishes: English Bronze, Colonial Brass or Ivory and Gold.

No. 1265
Two-light bracket. Back plate 4½″. Height 8″. Spread 7½″. Extends 4″. Has switch. Finishes: English Bronze, Pewter and Gold, Ivory and Gold, Colonial Brass.

CHASE

No. 1236
Five-light ceiling fixture. Over-all length 36″. Spread 20″. Shades not included. Finishes: Copper and Weathered Brass or Pewter and Gold.

No. 1198
Two-light wall bracket. Back plate 5¼″ x 3⅞″. Spread 7½″. Has switch. Finishes: Pewter and Gold, Ivory and Gold, English Bronze or Copper and Weathered Brass.

No. 120
One-light wall bracket. Back plate 5¼″ x 3⅞″ Extends 4¾″. Has switch. Finishes: Pewter an Gold, Ivory and Gold, English Bronze or Coppe and Weathered Brass.

No. 124
Three-light ceiling fixture. Over-all length 36′ Spread 16″. Shades not included. Finishes: Cop per and Weathered Brass or Pewter and Gold.

No. 1263
One-light bracket with a cast-back and etched glass chimney. Length 13″. Extends 7½″. Has switch. Finishes: Weathered Brass or Colonial Brass.

No. 1262
Two-light bracket with a cast back and etched glass chimneys. Height 13″. Spread 7½″. Extends 5″. Has switch. Finishes: Weathered Brass or Colonial Brass.

No. 1261
Five-light ceiling fixture with etched glass chimneys. Over-all length 36″. Spread 19″. Finishes: Weathered Brass of Colonial Brass.

No. 1150
One-light bracket with a cast back. Height 13″. Extends 7½″. Has switch. Shield not included. Finishes: Weathered Brass or Colonial Brass.

No. 1151
Two-light bracket with a cast back. Height 13″. Spread 7½″. Extends 5″. Has switch. Shields not included. Finishes: Weathered Brass or Colonial Brass.

No. 1142
Five-light ceiling fixture. Over-all length 36″. Spread 18″. Shades not included. Finishes: Weathered Brass or Colonial Brass.

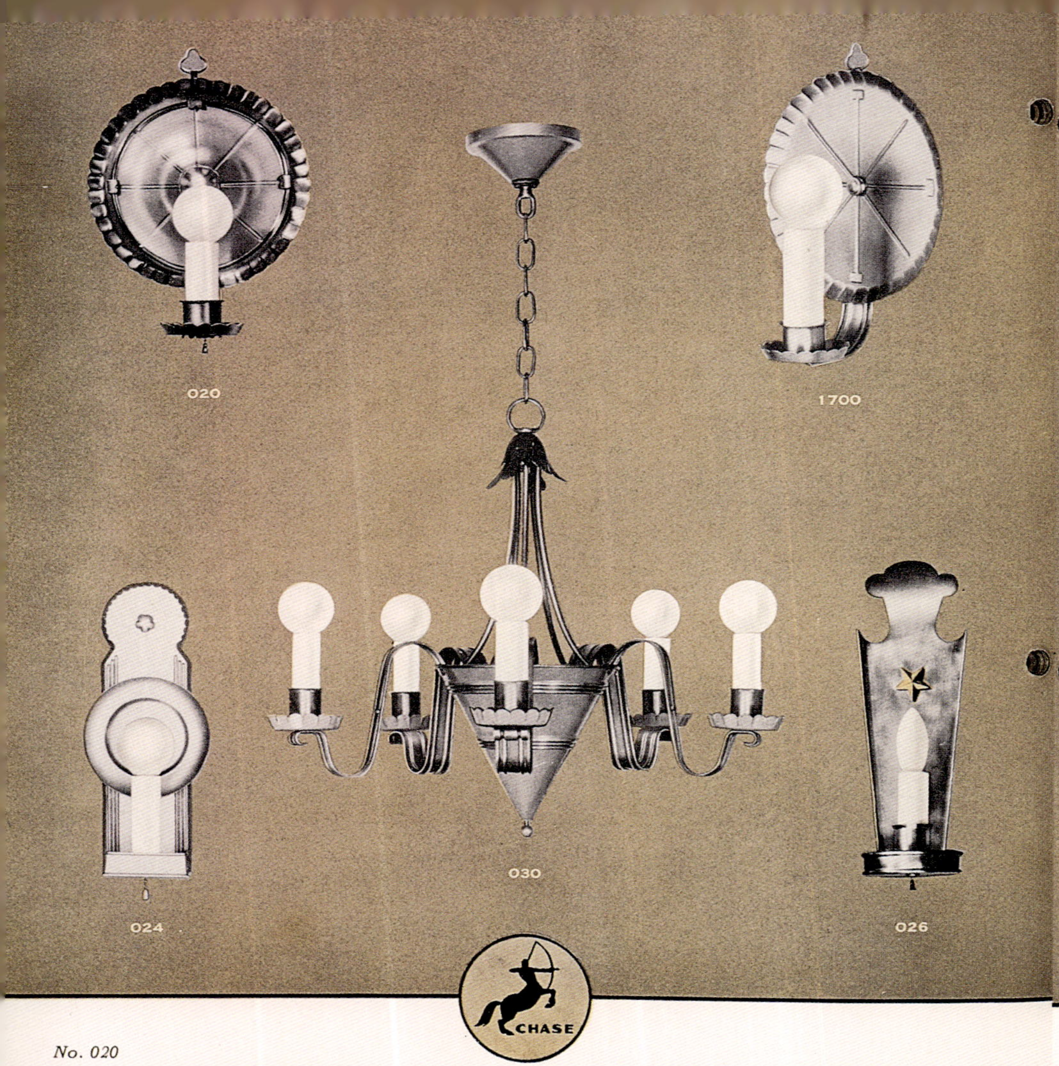

No. 020
One-light bracket. Height 10½″. Extends 4″. Width 8″. Has pull chain socket. Fitted with sea-green bull's eye glass disc. Finish: Toned Pewter.

No. 024
One-light bracket. Height 12½″. Extends 3¾″. Width 5½″. Has pull chain socket. Finish: Toned Pewter.

No. 030
Five-light ceiling fixture. Over-all length 36″. Spread. 20″. Finish: Combination of Colonial Red and Pewter.

No. 1700
One-light bracket. Height 10½″. Extends 4½″. Width 8″. Same design as No. 020 except it has no glass center. Has pull chain socket. Finish: Toned Pewter.

No. 026
One-light bracket. Height 10½″. Extends 3¾″. Width 4½″. Has pull chain socket. Finish: Toned Pewter with Brass star.

No. 031
Five-light ceiling fixture. Over-all length 36″. Spread 22″. Finish: Combination of Corn Yellow and Toned Pewter.

No. 023
One-light bracket. Height over-all 11″. Extends 4″. Width 9″. Has pull chain socket. Finish: Toned Pewter with Brass center.

No. 02
Two-light bracket. Height over-all 13″. Extends 4″ Width 7½″. Has pull chain socket. Finish: Tone Pewter.

No. 02
One-light bracket. Height 12″. Extends 4″. Widt 7″. Has pull chain socket. Fitted with green bull' eye glass panel. Finish: Toned Pewter.

CHASE
LIGHTING
FIXTURES

This dining room is lighted with the Chase No. 1601 ceiling fixture and No. 1653 wall brackets. Larger illustrations of these fixtures are shown on opposite page.

Suitable for

ederal Interiors

cause of the close relation of Directoire, Empire, lonial, Adam, Hepplewhite, Sheraton and Duncan yfe designs, the Chase Fixtures in this Federal oup may be used satisfactorily with any of these riods. They are shown on pages 25, 26, 27 and 28.

e interiors of the Federal era were generally ite, high ceilinged, and the doors beautifully neled. This reflected the gracious dignity and osperity of the times. Lighting Fixtures of this era became beautiful examples of the decorative arts.

In reproducing fixtures for the Federal era, we have sought to make use of symbols such as the American Eagle, and the stars and flags which were symbolic of the young republic.

Home owners so frequently ask for ceiling fixtures and wall brackets of matching design that we have shown ensembles on these catalog pages.

No. 1652
One-light bracket with cut glass chimneys. Height 10″. Extends 5½″. Suitable for 25 watt flame type bulb. Has switch. Finishes: Weathered Brass or Pewter and Gold.

No. 1653
Two-light bracket with cut glass chimneys. Height 10″. Spread 9″. Suitable for 25 watt flame type bulb. Has switch. Finishes: Weathered Brass or Pewter and Gold.

No. 1601
Five-light ceiling fixture with cut glass chimneys. Over-all length 36″. Spread 18″. Suitable for 25 watt flame type bulbs. Finishes: Weathered Brass or Pewter and Gold.

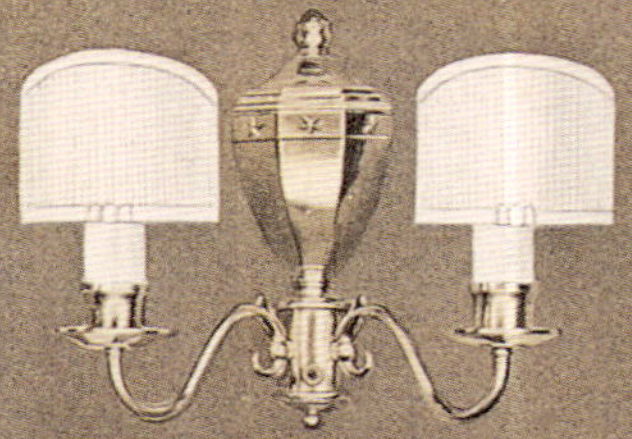

101

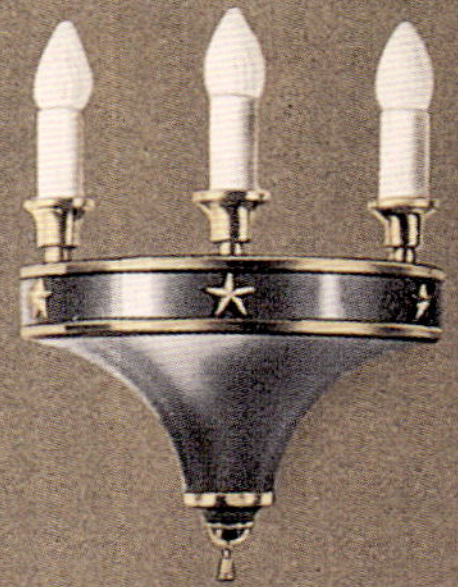

224

120

109

1724

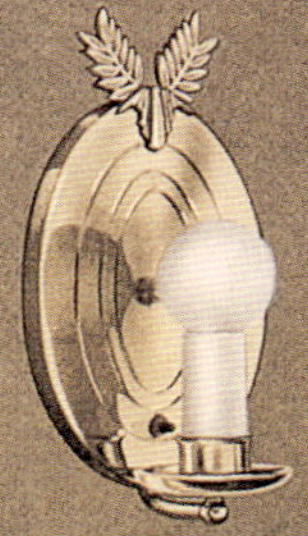

1726

1725

No. 101
Two-light bracket. Height 9½″. Spread 10″. Made for French hook attachment. Has switch. Shields not included. Finish: Colonial Brass.

No. 120
Five-light ceiling fixture. Over-all length 36″. Spread 22″. Shades not included. Finish: Colonial Brass.

No. 224
Three-light bracket with indirect light in center. Ht. 11″. Width 10″. Extends 4¾″. Has intermediate sockets and 2-way switch. French Hook Attachment. Finish: Colonial Brass and Black.

No. 109
Two-light bracket with etched glass chimneys. Height 9″. Spread 7″. Extends 4″. Has switch. French Hook Attch. Finish: Colonial Brass and Black.

No. 1726
One-light bracket. Back plate 8½″ x 6″. Height 11″. Extends 4″. Has switch. Finishes: Pewter and Gold or Colonial Brass.

No. 1724
Two-light bracket. Back plate 7″. Spread 9″. Keyless socket. Finish: Colonial Brass and Black with center ornament in Pewter.

No. 1725
Two-light bracket. Back plate 8½″ x 6″. Spread 8″. Extends 4″. Has switch. Finishes: Pewter and Gold or Colonial Brass.

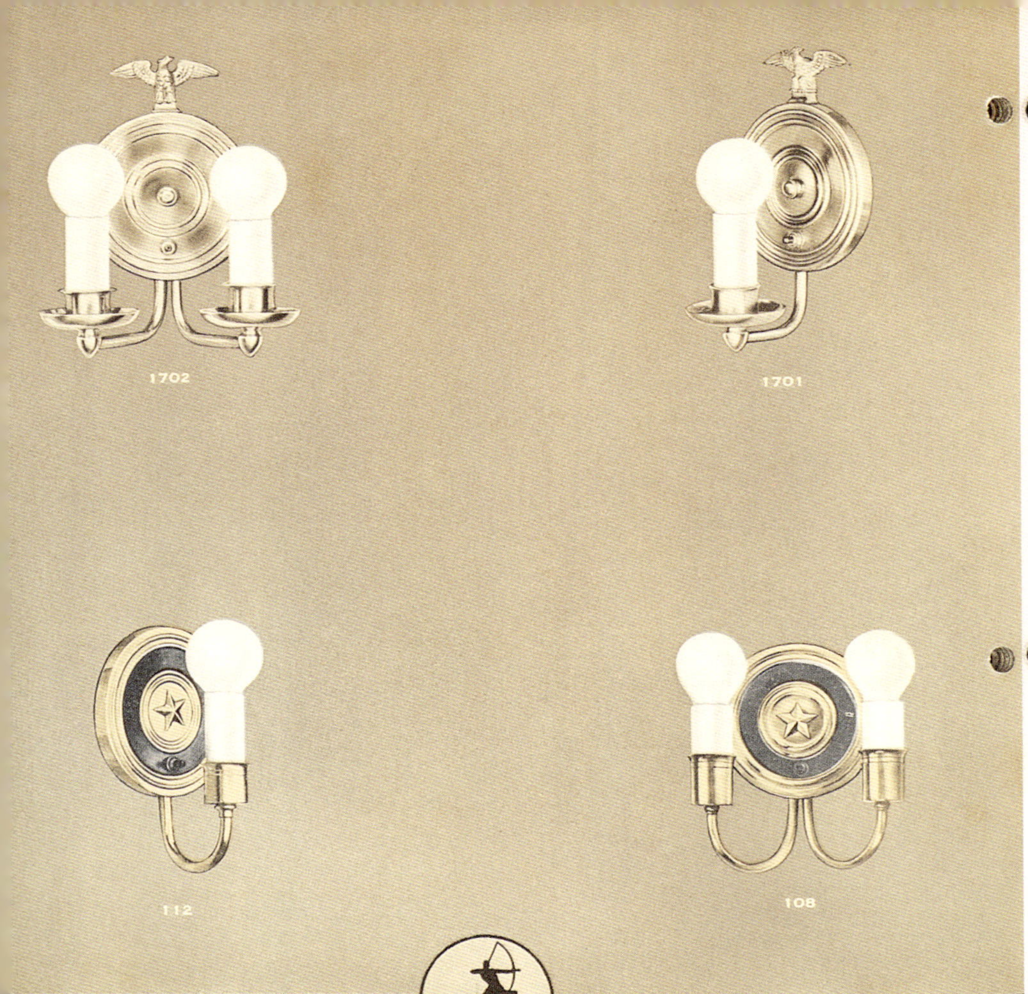

No. 1702
Two-light bracket. Back plate 5½″. Spread 8″. Has switch. Finish: English Bronze.

No. 1701
One-light bracket. Back plate 5½″. Extends 5″. Has switch. Finish: English Bronze.

No. 112
One-light bracket. Back plate 5″. Extends 3½″. Has switch. Finish: Colonial Brass and Black.

No. 108
Two-light bracket. Back plate 5″. Spread 7½″. Has switch. Finish: Colonial Brass and Black.

CHASE LIGHTING FIXTURES

In this Georgian dining room can be seen the No. 1714 Chase ceiling fixture and No. 1704 wall brackets. See page 30 for larger illustrations.

Suitable for Georgian Interiors

The Chase Fixtures in this group are also suitable for homes furnished in the style of Queen Anne, Chippendale, Adam, Hepplewhite, Sheraton or Colonial. They are shown on pages 30, 31 and 32.

The Georgian period expressed a dignified, leisurely order of life, which is reflected in this group of Chase Fixtures. In their creation we have favored the simpler Georgian designs because they are more fitting for the present day interiors.

We have made use of shells, urns, fretwork, flame finials, leaves and swag decoration, thus giving these Chase Fixtures a character and individuality all their own.

Made of Chase Brass and with beautiful, lasting finishes, your customers get quality and a combination of good workmanship and reasonable prices when you sell them Chase Lighting Fixtures.

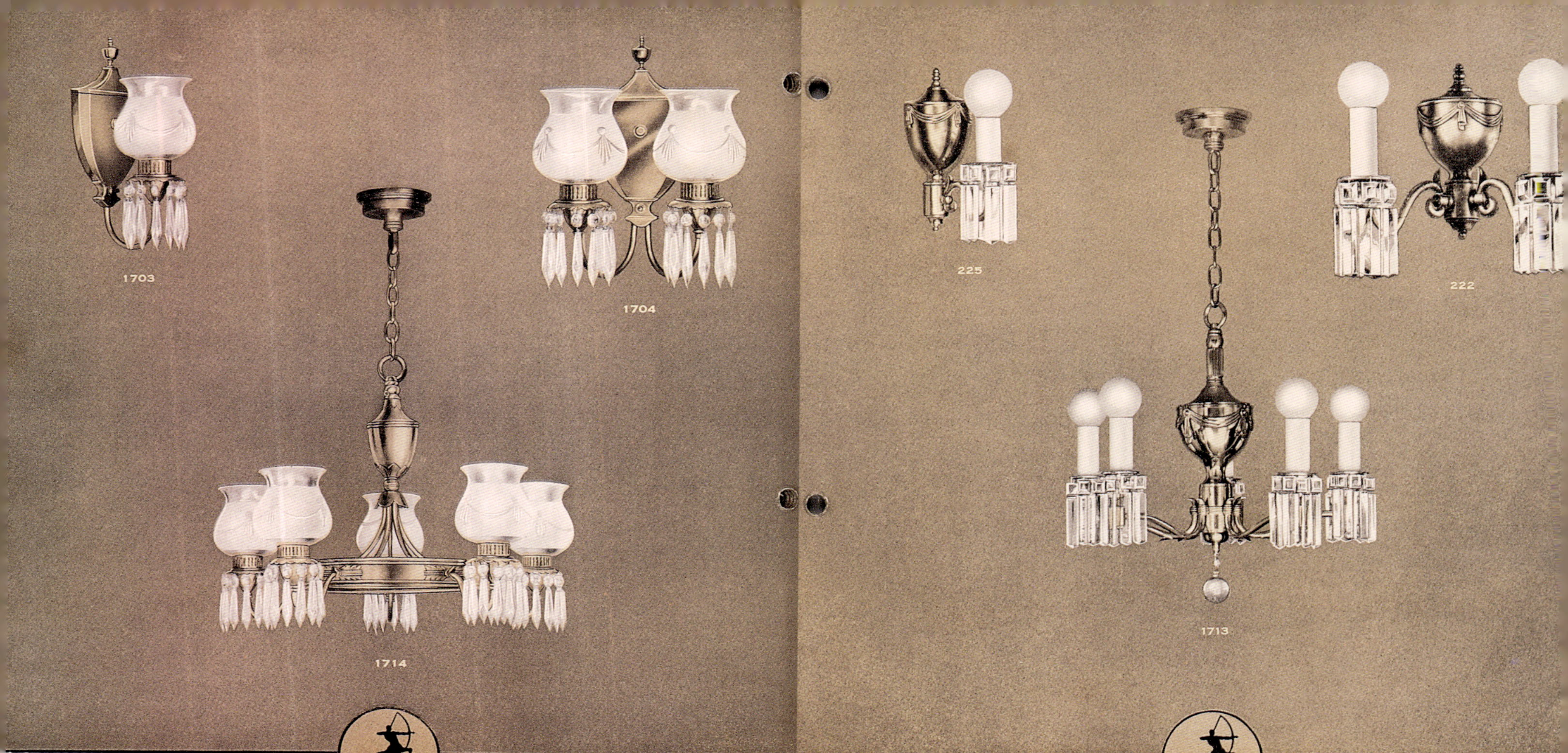

No. 1703
One-light bracket with cut glass chimneys and crystal prisms. Back plate 5″ x 9″. Extends 5″. Has switch. Finish: Colonial Brass.

No. 1704
Two-light bracket. Cut glass chimneys with crystal prisms. Back plate 5″ x 9″. Spread 8″. Has switch. Finish: Colonial Brass.

No. 1714
Five-light ceiling fixture with cut glass chimneys and crystal prisms. Over-all length 36″. Spread 20″. Finish: Colonial Brass.

No. 225
One-light bracket with crystal prisms. Back plate 8″ x 4″. Extends 5½″. Has switch. Made for French hook attachment. Finish: Colonial Brass.

No. 2
Two-light bracket with crystal prisms. Back pla 8″ x 4″. Spread 7″. Has switch. Made for Frenc hook attachment. Finish: Colonial Brass.

No. 1713
Five-light ceiling fixture with crystal prisms. Over-all length 36″. Spread 18″. Finish: Colonial Brass.

30

220

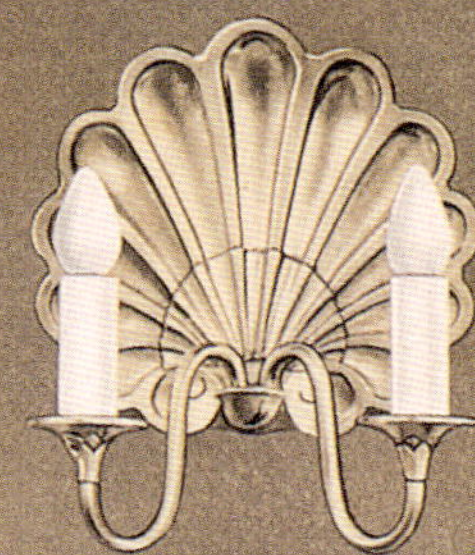

221

223

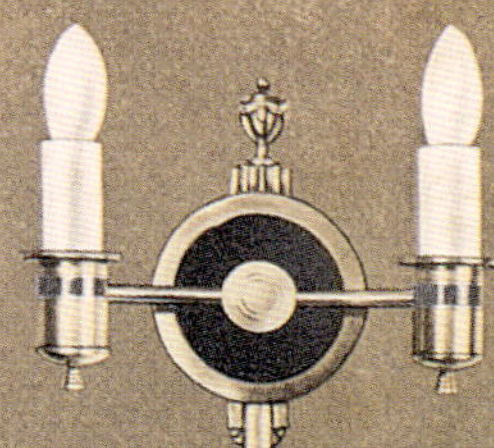

425

Vo. 220
'wo-light bracket with gunmetal mirror. Back plate 1″ x 7″. Spread 8″. Keyless socket. Finishes: :olonial Brass and Black or Brushed Pewter.

Vo. 223
)ne-light bracket. Back plate 9″ x 5″. Extends ·1½″. Has pull chain socket. Finish: Colonial Brass.

No. 221
Two-light bracket. Back plate 10″ x 10″. Spread 7″. Has switch. Finishes: Colonial Brass or Brushed Pewter.

No. 425
Two-light bracket. Back plate 9″ x 4½″. Spread 7¼″. Has switch. Finish: Black and Brass.

CHASE LIGHTING FIXTURES

This attractive Empire room is lighted with the No. 1600 Chase ceiling fixture and the No. 1651 wall brackets. Larger illustrations of these fixtures are on page 34.

Suitable for Empire Interiors

Because Federal and Empire periods were closely related in spirit and character, many fixtures may be used in either of these interiors.

Adding characteristic symbols of the time, such as shields, bundles of arrows and wreaths of laurel, Chase Fixtures in this group make possible a choice of either simple classic forms or the more colorful fixtures typical of this period.

For the person looking for lighting fixtures with the touch of Empire Symbols to go in rooms of this style, or for the many people who make their selections purely from eye appeal, this group offers a splendid selection of matching fixtures.

Like all other Chase Fixtures the basic metal of this group is either rustproof Brass or Copper — sturdily constructed and reasonably priced.

No. 1650

One-light bracket. Length 10″. Back plate 5″. Extends 5½″. Has switch. Finishes: Black and Gold or Brushed Pewter and Gold, with crystal trim.

No. 1600

Five-light ceiling fixture. Length 36″. Spread 18″. Shades not included. Finishes: Black and Gold or Brushed Pewter and Gold, with crystal trim.

No. 1651

Two-light bracket. Height over-all 10″. Back plate 5″. Spread 8½″. Has switch. Finishes: Black and Gold or Brushed Pewter and Gold, with crystal trim.

No. 441

Four-light ceiling fixture with metal shades to match. Over-all length 36″. Spread 16″. Finishes: either Empire White, Green or Red with Brass Trim.

No. 426

Two-light bracket with metal shades to match. Height 10″. Back plate 8″ x 5″. Spread 8″. Has switch, French Hook. Finishes: either Empire White, Empire Green or Empire Red with Brass Trim.

No. 42

Two-light bracket with metal shades to match. Bac plate 13″ x 4″. Spread 9″. Has switch, Frenc Hook. Finishes: either Empire White, Empire Gree or Empire Red with Brass Trim.

No. 44

Four-light ceiling fixture with metal shades match. Over-all length 36″. Spread 16″. Finishe either Empire White, Empire Green or Empire Re with Brass Trim.

o. 1664
ne-light bracket. Height 14″. Extends 5½″. Has witch. Shields not included. Finishes: Bone White nd Gold or Pewter and Gold.

No. 1665
Two-light bracket. Height 14″. Spread 8½″. Has switch. Shades not included. Finishes: Bone White and Gold or Pewter and Gold.

No. 1602
Five-light ceiling fixture. Overall length 36″. Spread 19″. Shades not included. Finishes: Bone White and Gold or Pewter and Gold.

No. 1662
One-light bracket with cut glass chimneys. Height 14″. Extends 5¼″. Has switch. Finishes: Bone White or Pewter and Gold.

No. 1663
Two-light bracket with cut glass chimneys. Height 14″. Spread 8½″. Has switch. Finishes: Bone White and Gold or Pewter and Gold.

No. 1661
Five-light ceiling fixture with cut glass chimneys. Over-all length 36″. Spread 19″. Finishes: Bone White and Gold, or Pewter and Gold.

CHASE LIGHTING FIXTURES

The Chase fixtures lighting this attractive dining room are No. 1658 ceiling and No. 1660 wall brackets. Larger illustrations of these are on the opposite page.

Suitable for
Neo Classic Interiors

The Neo Classic or Modern style, although new, is decidedly growing in use. In reality it is a successful blending of Ancient and Modern motifs.

In presenting our Neo Classic designs we offer ensembles of beautifully decorated and original looking wall brackets and ceiling fixtures that have a modern feeling and inspiration which makes them very striking. They are shown on the opposite page.

Unusual workmanship is apparent in every fixture, also the excellent quality of the materials, for we use nothing but the finest glass and only lasting Chase Brass as the basic material.

No. 1657
Five-light ceiling fixture with cut glass chimneys and crystal trim. Over-all length 36″. Spread 20″. Finishes: Bone White and Gold or Pewter and Gold.

No. 1659
One-light bracket with cut glass chimneys and crystal trim. Height 13″. Back plate 5¼″. Extends 5″. Has switch. Finishes: Bone White and Gold or Pewter and Gold.

No. 16
Two-light bracket with cut glass chimneys ar crystal trim. Height 13″. Back plate 5¼″. Sprea 8″. Has switch. Finishes: Bone White and Gol or Pewter and Gold.

No. 16
Five-light close-up ceiling fixture with cut gla chimneys and crystal trim. Over-all length 21 Spread 20″. Finishes: Bone White and Gold c Pewter and Gold.

CHASE LIGHTING FIXTURES

Lighting this charming English living room are the No. 721 wall brackets and No. 736 ceiling fixture. Larger illustrations of these fixtures are shown on page 42.

Suitable for
Early English Interiors

The simplicity of the designs in these fixtures makes them equally suitable for Norman Houses and many may also be used in Early American, Dutch Colonial, Spanish, and Italian type houses. They are shown on pages 41 and 42.

In this group, instead of creating wall brackets to definitely match the ceiling fixtures, we have followed the more desirable practice of creating brackets which, while related in design and finish, are sufficiently individual to permit the home owner to express his or her own ideas in the lighting decoration of a room or entire home.

Therefore, any wall bracket can be used successfully with the ceiling fixtures of this group, for in designing them we have purposely avoided the look of obviously matched sets of fixtures.

No. 715
Two-light bracket. Height 13½″. Spread 10″. Has switch. Finishes: Half Polished Iron, English Bronze.

No. 1708
Two-light bracket. Height 14″. Spread 10″. Has switch. Finish: Half Polished Iron.

No. 1705
Five-light ceiling fixture. Over-all length 36″. Spread 20″. Finishes: Half Polished Iron and English Bronze.

No. 713
Two-light bracket. Height 9½″. Width 9″. Has switch. Finishes: Half Polished Iron, English Bronze.

No. 736
Five-light ceiling fixture. Over-all length 36″. Spread 23″. Finish: Half Polished Iron.

No. 711
Two-light bracket. Height 13″. Spread 10½″. Has switch. Finishes: Half Polished Iron, English Bronze.

No. 721
Two-light bracket. Height 11″. Spread 7½″. Has switch. Finishes: Half Polished Iron, English Bronze.

No. 719
Two-light bracket. Height 12½″. Spread 9″. Made for French hook attachment. Has switch. Finishes: Half Polished Iron and English Bronze.

42

CHASE LIGHTING FIXTURES

The No. 1719 ceiling fixture and No. 526 wall brackets contribute to the beauty of this fine modern living room. Larger illustrations of these fixtures are shown on pages 44 and 45.

Suitable for Classic Modern Interiors

In presenting this group of Chase Classic Modern Lighting Fixtures, which are shown on pages 44, 45, 46 and 47, we answer the unprecedented need for modern looking and well designed fixtures. We have combined the best in modern design with modern scientific lighting.

The center ceiling fixture is usually the dominating source of light in most modern interiors. For such interiors we have created both close and hanging-type fixtures that are suitable for modern home

For supplementary lighting as well as good-lookin and nicely proportioned fixtures, the wall bracke are used successfully with any of the ceiling fi tures in this group.

Many of the Chase Classic Modern Fixtures mak use of a beautiful, lustrous, non-tarnishing chr mium finish and only the finest glassware is use

522

1718

541

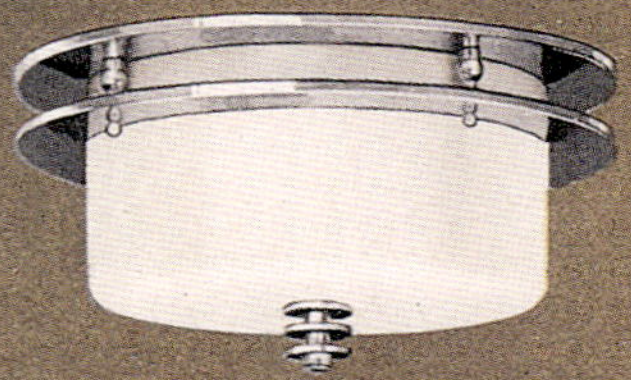

1719

1717

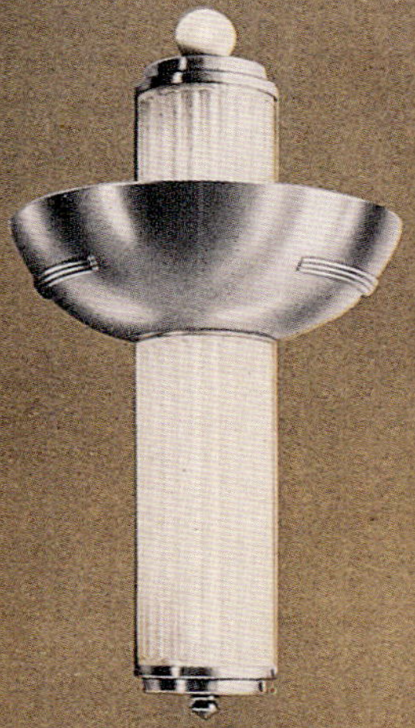

526

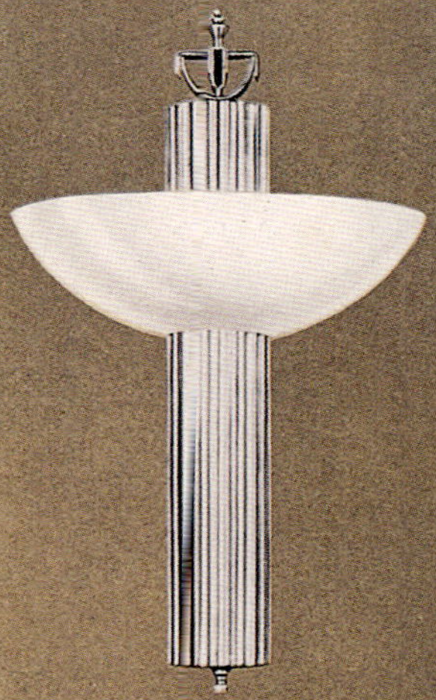

528

545

No. 522
One-light bracket. Height 23″. Over-all width 10″. Cylinder width 3¾″. Has switch. Uses tubular bulb. Finish: Satin Chromium.

No. 1719
Two-light ceiling fixture. Height 7″. Width 13″. Has 10″ Satin finish glass bowl. Finish: Brushed Pewter.

No. 541
Four-light ceiling fixture. Height 9¾″. Width 18″. Glass bowl has a satin finish and is 14″ in diameter. Finish: Satin Chromium.

No. 1718
Two-light ceiling fixture. Height 5½″. Spread 11″. Satin finished glass bowl with clear star decorations. Finishes: Brushed Pewter or Colonial Brass.

No. 1717
One-light bracket. Height 19″. Width 3¾″. Projection 2½″. Uses tubular bulb. Satin finished fluted glass column. Has switch. Finish: Satin Chromium.

No. 526
Two-light bracket. One bulb is in the fluted satin finished glass column and the other is in the indirect metal reflector. Lights can be used separately, or together. Uses both tubular and regular bulbs. Weight 17″. Width 10″. Cylinder width 3¾″. Has 3-way switch. Finish: Satin Chromium.

No. 545
One-light ceiling fixture. Over-all length 36″. Width 14″. Has central frosted glass cylinder and 6 semi-circular carved glass panels. Finish: Polished Chromium.

No. 528
One-light bracket. Height 16½″. Over-all width 10″. Back plate 2½″. Glass reflector is 10″ and extends 5¼″. Has switch. Finish: Satin Chromium.

523

1707

532

646

540

No. 523
One-light bracket. Height 11$\frac{1}{2}$″. Width 3$\frac{1}{4}$″. Has frosted glass cylinder and a satin finish carved glass leaf design. Pull chain socket. Finish: Satin Chromium.

No. 1707
Two-light ceiling fixture. Over-all length 36″. Has 14″ Satin finish glass bowl with ornamented silver design, also crystal trim. Finish: Brushed Pewter.

No. 532
Two-light bracket. Height 13″. Over-all width 3$\frac{1}{2}$″. Extends 4″. Satin finish glass cylinder. Has switch. Finish: Satin Chromium.

No. 646
One-light ceiling fixture. Over-all length 36″. Over-all width is 13″. It has a glass globe which is 10$\frac{5}{8}$″ in diameter. The glass globe has a satin finish with star decorations. Finish: Brushed Pewter.

No. 540
Six-light ceiling fixture. Has four lights in the frosted glass pockets and two lights in the center sphere. Length 36″. Width 16″. Has 3-way switch which controls lights separately. Finish: Polished Chromium.

46

MISCELLANEOUS WALL BRACKETS

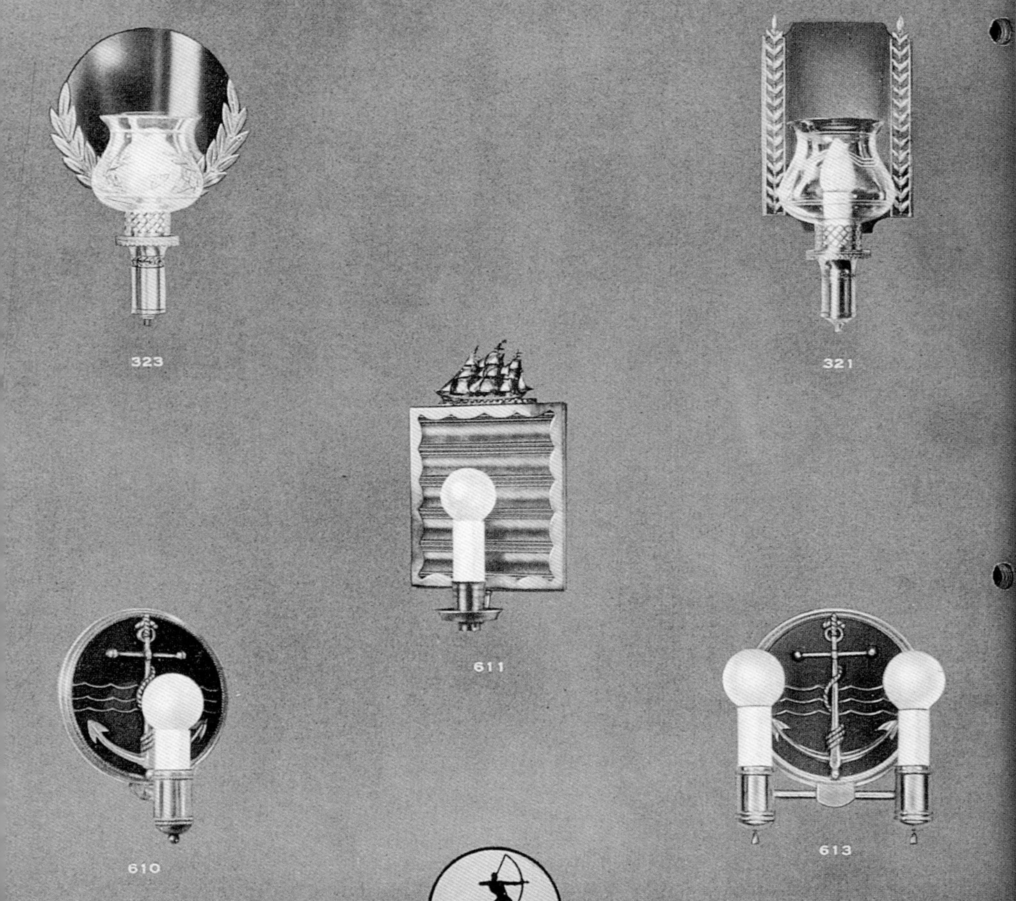

No. 323
One-light bracket. Height 11½″. Back plate 8″. Extends 5″. Has gunmetal mirror and clear etched glass chimney. Has switch. Finish: Colonial Brass.

No. 610
One-light bracket. Height 10″. Spread 7½″. Extends 3½″. Has switch. French hook attachment. Finish: Colonial Brass with Green Center.

No. 611
One-light bracket. Height 13″. Width 7″. Extends 4⅛″. Has switch. French hook attachment. Finish: Colonial Brass and Green Fresnal glass panel.

No. 321
One-light bracket with clear etched glass chimney and gunmetal mirror. Height 11½″. Width 6″. Back plate 8″ x 6″. Extends 4″. Has switch. Finish: Colonial Brass.

No. 613
Two-light bracket. Height 10″. Spread 7½″. Back plate 7½″. Has switch. French hook attachment. Finish: Colonial Brass and Green center.

HALL LANTERNS

No. 1656
Two-light hanging lantern. Over-all length 36″. Lantern is 6½″ square. Has clear glass panels with engraved design. Finish: Colonial Brass.

No. 422
One-light wall lantern. Height 13″. Width 6″. Extends 4½″. Fitted with clear glass panels. The two side panels are decorated with Silver etched Chinese figures. Finishes: Empire Red or Empire Black with Brass Trim, inside is finished in White.

No. 014
One-light wall lantern. Height 14″. Width 6⅜″. Extends 3½″. Fitted with light amber antique glass panels. Finish: Colonial Brass or Black.

No. 1720
Four-light hanging lantern. Over-all length 36″. Width of lantern 8″. Fitted with clear glass panels which have an engraved design. Finished in Colonial Brass.

HALL LANTERNS

No. 1723
Three-light hanging lantern with clear glass globe. Over-all length 36″. Width of lantern 10½″. Finish: Colonial Brass.

No. 106
One-light wall lantern with clear glass chimney and panels. Height 17″. Width 8½″. Extends 6½″. Finish: Colonial Brass and Black, inside finish, Red.

No. 107
One-light wall lantern with a clear glass globe. Height over-all 15″. Width 6″. Extends 6½″. Back plate 3¾″. Finish: Colonial Brass and Black.

No. 240
Three-light hanging lantern with clear glass cylinder. Over-all length 36″. Height of Lantern 21¼″. Width 9⅜″. Finish: Colonial Brass.

HALL LANTERNS

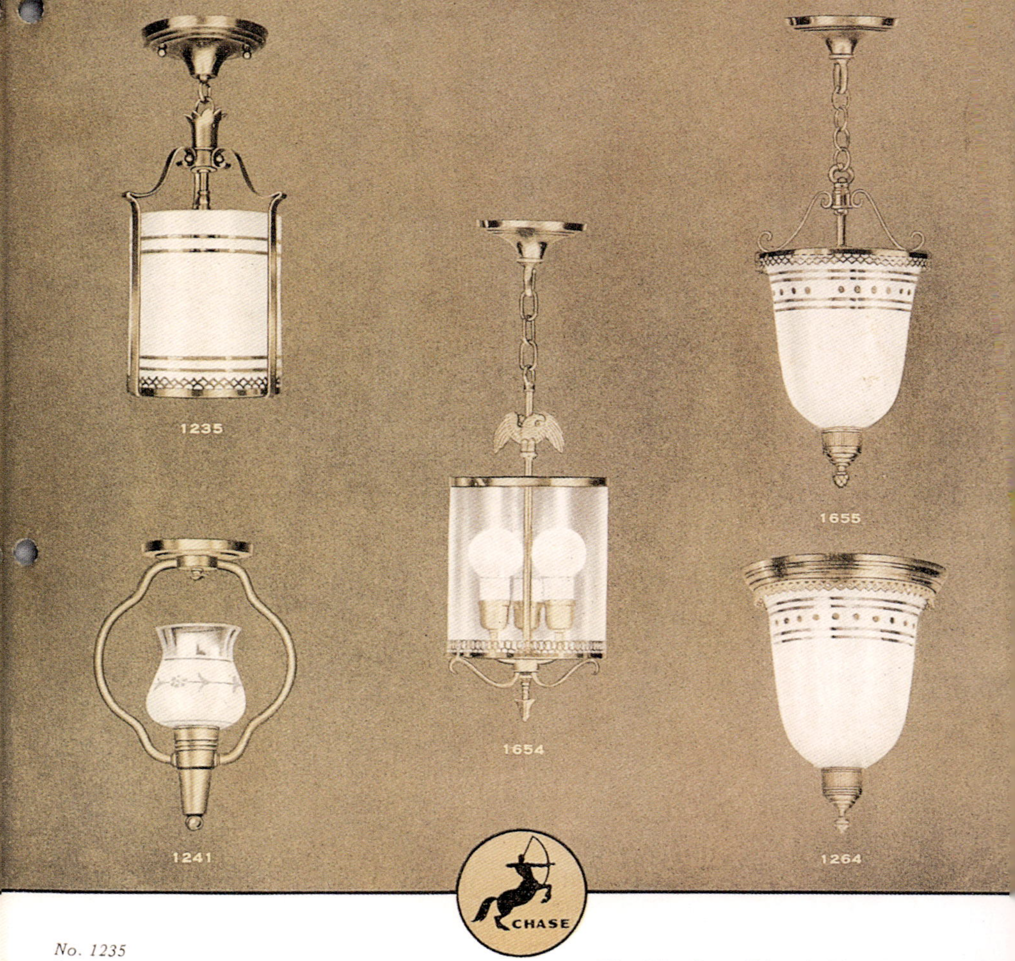

No. 1235
One-light hanging lantern with frosted glass cylinder and clear lines. Glass size 6″ x 7″. Over-all height 14¼″. Fin.: English Bronze or Colonial Brass.

No. 1241
One-light fixture with cut glass chimney. Over-all length 12⅛″. Width 8¼″. Finishes: Pewter and Gold, English Bronze, Colonial Brass.

No. 1654
Three-light hanging lantern. Clear glass cylinder size 7″ x 8″. Over-all length 36″. Finishes: Colonial Brass or Pewter and Gold.

No. 1655
One-light hanging lantern. Has a frosted globe with clear lines and ball design. Over-all length 36″. Height of lantern 14″. Finishes: Colonial Brass or English Bronze.

No. 1264
One-light close-up lantern. Has a frosted globe with clear lines and ball design. Over-all length 12″. Length of globe 8″. Finishes: English Bronze or Colonial Brass.

BEDROOM BRACKETS

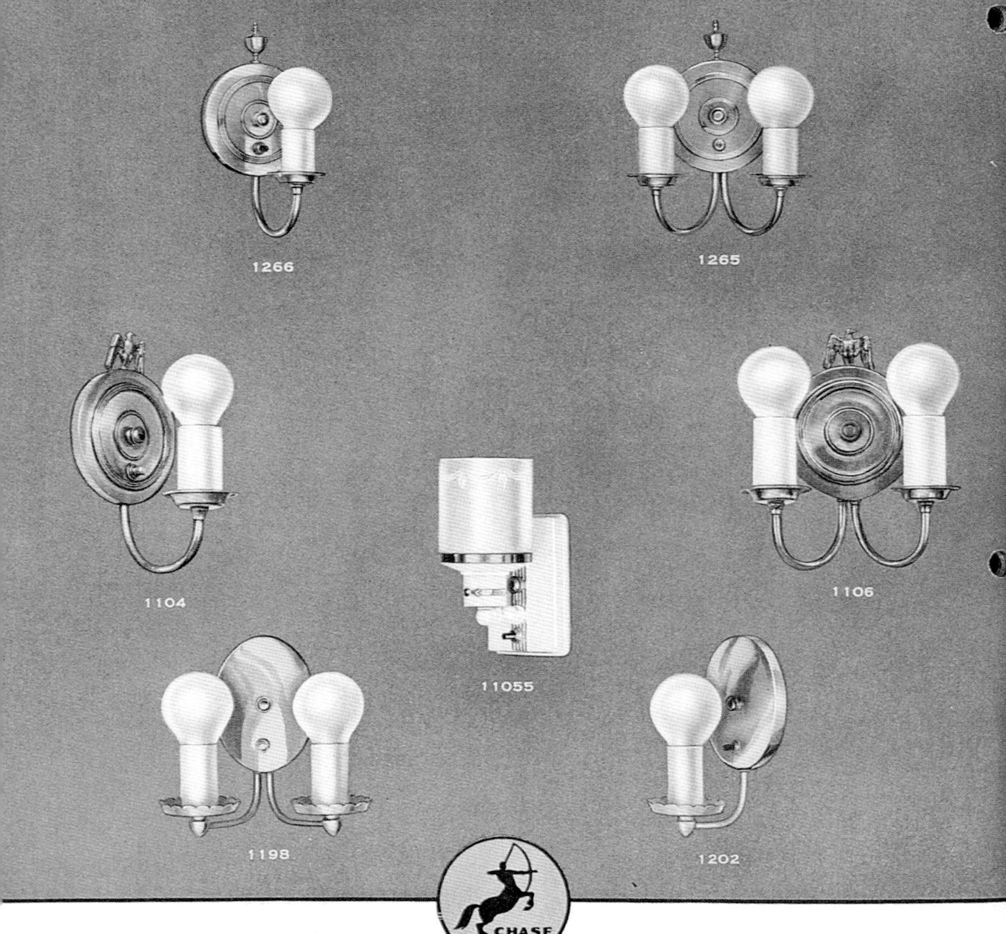

No. 1266
One-light bracket. Back plate 4½". Height 8". Extends 4¼". Has switch. Finishes: English Bronze, Colonial Brass, Ivory and Gold, Pewter and Gold.

No. 1104
One-light bracket. Back plate 4½". Extends 4¼". Has switch. Finishes: English Bronze, Colonial Brass, Ivory and Gold.

No. 1198
Two-light bracket. Back plate 5¼" x 3⅞". Spread 7½". Has switch. Finishes: Pewter and Gold, Ivory and Gold, English Bronze, Copper and Weathered Brass.

No. 1202
One light bracket. Back plate 5¼" x 3⅞". Extends 4¾". Has switch. Finishes: Pewter and Gold, Ivory and Gold, English Bronze, Copper and Weathered Brass.

No. 11055
One-light bracket with satin finish etched glass cylinder. Back plate 5" x 3¼". Extends 4". Has switch. Finish: Ivory and Gold.

No. 1265
Two-light bracket. Back plate 4½". Height 8". Spread 7½". Extends 3". Has switch. Finishes: English Bronze, Pewter and Gold, Ivory and Gold, Colonial Brass.

No. 1106
Two-light bracket. Back plate 4½". Height 8". Spread 7½". Extends 3". Has switch. Finishes: English Bronze, Colonial Brass, Ivory and Gold.

BEDROOM CEILING FIXTURES

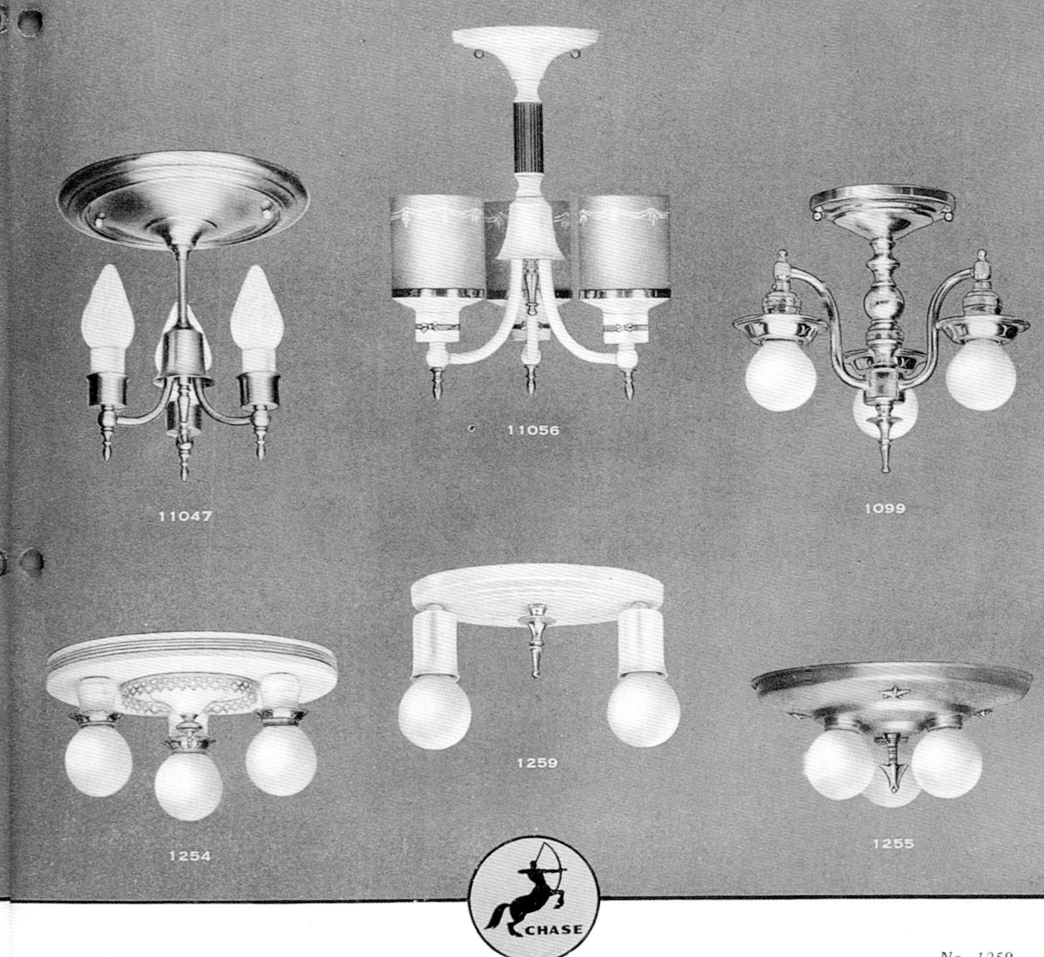

No. 11047
Three-light ceiling fixture. Over-all height 11". Diameter 9½". Finishes: English Bronze or Pewter and Gold.

No. 1254
Three-light ceiling fixture. Height 5". Diameter 10". Finishes: Ivory and Gold, Pewter and Gold.

No. 11056
Three-light ceiling fixture with satin finish etched glass cylinders. Over-all length 13". Width 10". Finish: Ivory and Gold.

No. 1259
Two-light ceiling fixture. Oval plate 8" x 6". Extends 4½". Finishes: Ivory and Gold, Pewter and Gold, English Bronze.

No. 1099
Three-light ceiling fixture. Over-all height 10". Width 10". Finishes: English Bronze, Colonial Bronze, Ivory and Gold.

No. 1255
Three-light ceiling fixture. Height 4". Diameter 9½". Finishes: Pewter and Gold, Ivory and Gold.

FOR KITCHENS, PANTRIES AND BREAKFAST NOOKS

BATHROOM BRACKETS

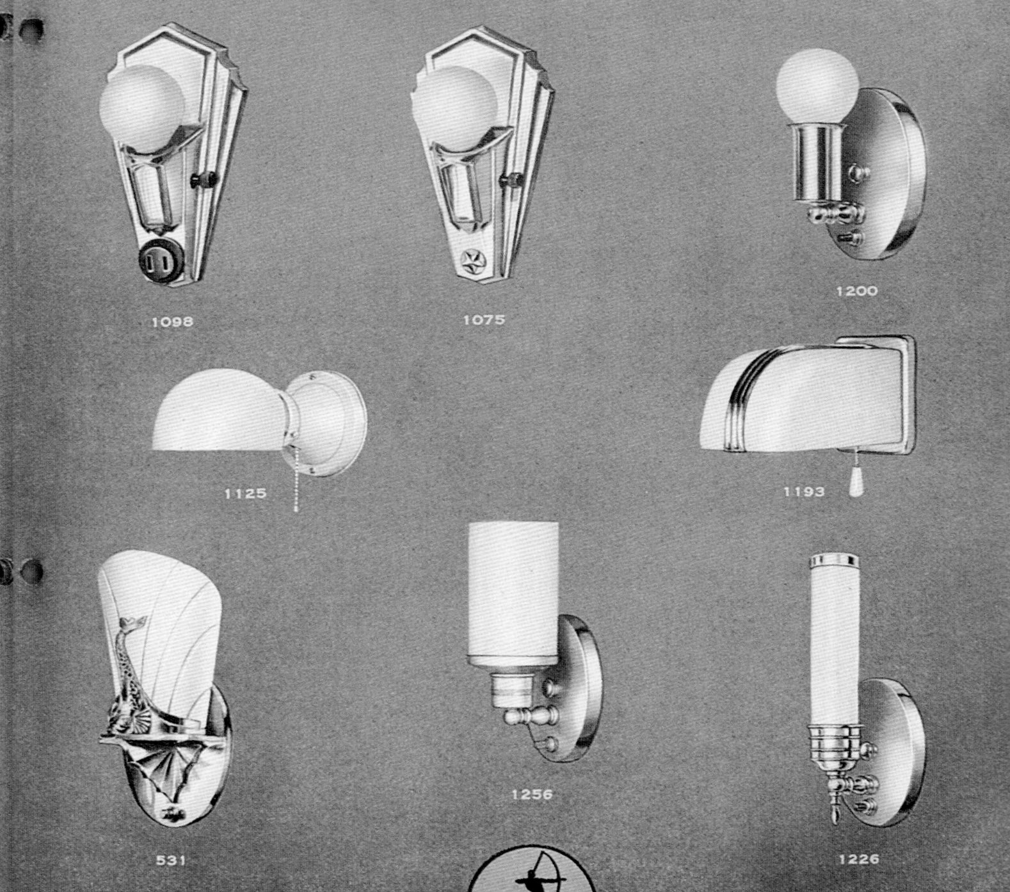

No. 1154
One-light chain pendant. Over-all height 36″. 4½″ canopy. 2¼″ holder. 6″ Opalescent glass reflector. Pull chain socket. Finishes: Polished Chromium, White Enamel. Order No. 1055 for key socket.

No. 1134
One-light bracket. Height 9½″. Back plate 4¾″. Extends 9¾″. Opalescent glass shade. Has key socket. Finishes: Polished Chromium or White Enamel.

No. 1258
One-light ceiling fixture with glass globe 9⅜″ dia. Over-all height 9½″. Holder 4″. Has keyless socket. Finishes: Polished Chromium, White Enamel. Order No. 1257 if pull chain is desired.

No. 1125
One-light bracket. Back 4½″. Extends 9″. Has an Opalescent glass reflector. Finishes: Polished Chromium, White Enamel.

No. 1246
Three-light ceiling fixture with an 11″ metal shade. Over-all length 36″. Finishes: Toned Pewter with Red shade or toned Pewter with Green shade.

No. 1232
Two-light ceiling fixture. Diameter 13″. Has 12″ Opal. glass bowl. Height 7″. Finishes: Satin Chromium, English Bronze, Toned Pewter. Order No. 1230 if a 10″ bowl is desired.

No. 1098
One-light bracket. Height 7½″. Width 4¼″. Extends 2¾″. Turn knob switch and convenience outlet. Finish: Polished Chromium. Order No. 1048 if keyless socket is desired.

No. 1125
One-light bracket. Back plate 4½″. Extends 9″. Has an Opal. glass reflector and 2¼″ holder. Finishes: Polished Chromium, White Enamel.

No. 531
One-light bracket with frosted etched glass reflector. Height 8¼″. Width 4¼″. Extends 4½″. Has switch. Finish: Polished Chromium.

No. 1075
One-light bracket. Height 7½″. Width 4¼″. Extends 2¾″. Turn knob socket. Finish: Polished Chromium. Order No. 1049 if keyless socket is desired. Order No. 1214 for pull chain socket.

No. 1256
One-light bracket with satin finish glass cylinder. Back plate 5¼″ x 3⅞″. Extends 4″. Has switch. Finish: Polished Chromium.

No. 1200
One-light bracket. Back plate 5¼″ x 3⅞″. Extends 3½″. Has switch. Finish: Polished Chromium.

No. 1193
One-light bracket with Opal. glass reflector. Back plate 4⅜″ x 3½″. Extends 7″. Takes a 60 watt bulb. Has pull chain socket. Finish: Polished Chromium. Order No. 1252 for keyless socket.

No. 1226
One-light bracket with Opal. glass cylinder size 1⅝″ x 7″. Back plate 5¼″ x 3⅞″. Extends 3¼″. Has switch. Finish: Polished Chromium. Order No. 1267 if keyless socket is desired.

BEAM LIGHTS

642

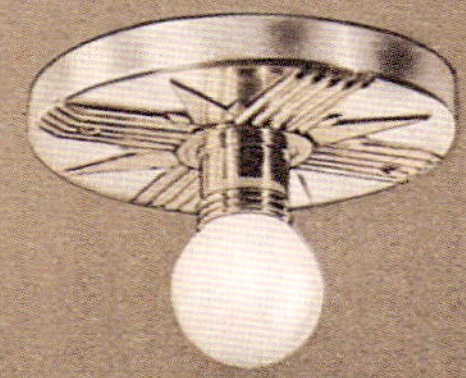
546

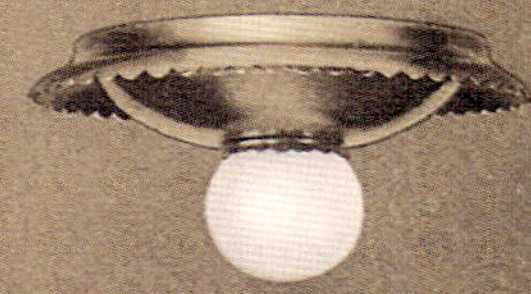
643

1566

343

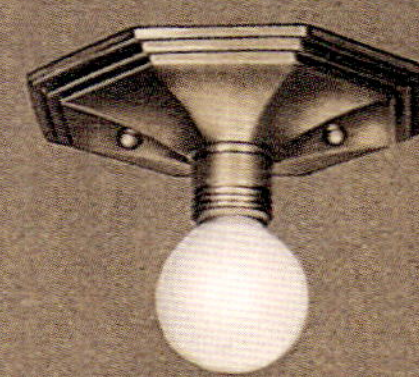
1199

1089

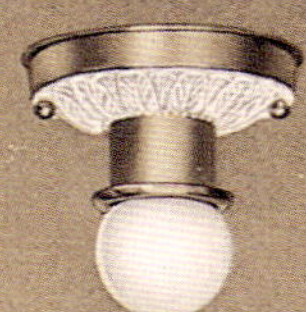
1565

1116

No. 642
One-light ceiling fixture. Height 4¾″. Width 8″. Finishes: Colonial Brass or Toned Pewter.

No. 1566
One-light ceiling fixture. Height 5½″. Width 5″. Finishes: Polished Chromium, Polished Gold, Toned Pewter, English Bronze.

No. 1089
One-light ceiling fixture. Height 6″. Width 5½″. Finishes: Polished Chromium, Ivory, Colonial Brass. Has pull chain socket Order No. 1088 if keyless socket is desired.

No. 546
One-light ceiling fixture. Height 5½″. Width 6½″. Finishes: Polished Chromium or Colonial Brass.

No. 343
One-light ceiling fixture. Height 5″. Width 6¾″. Finishes: Pewter and Gold or Black and Gold.

No. 1565
One-light ceiling fixture. Height 5½″. Width 5″. Finishes: Ivory and Gold or Toned Pewter.

No. 643
One-light ceiling fixture. Height 4¾″. Width 8″. Finishes: Colonial Brass or Toned Pewter.

No. 1199
One-light ceiling fixture. Height 5″. Diameter 6½″. Finishes: English Bronze, Polished Chromium or Pewter and Gold.

No. 1116
One-light ceiling fixture. Height 7½″. Width 4¼″. Finishes: Polished Chromium, White Enamel. Order No. 1133 if keyless socket is desired.

BRACKET LANTERNS

1711

1710

066

1709

No. 1711
One-light bracket lantern. Height of Lantern 13″. Width 6½″. Extends 9″. Has antique glass panels. Waterproof socket. Made of Copper. Finishes: Stained Copper or Black.

No. 066
One-light bracket lantern with antique glass panels. Height of Lantern 16¼″. Width 8½″. Extends 12″. Made of Chase Brass or Copper. Has waterproof socket. Finishes: Colonial Brass, Black, Stained Copper.

No. 1710
One-light bracket lantern with irregular antique glass globe. Height 14″. Extends 8″. Made of either Chase Brass or Copper. Finishes: Stained Copper or Black.

No. 1709
One-light bracket lantern with frosted glass cylinder. Height of lantern 14⅞″. Width 6½″. Extends 9½″. Made of either Chase Brass or Copper. Finishes: Stained Copper, Black, Colonial Brass.

BRACKET LANTERNS

1706

1722

1712

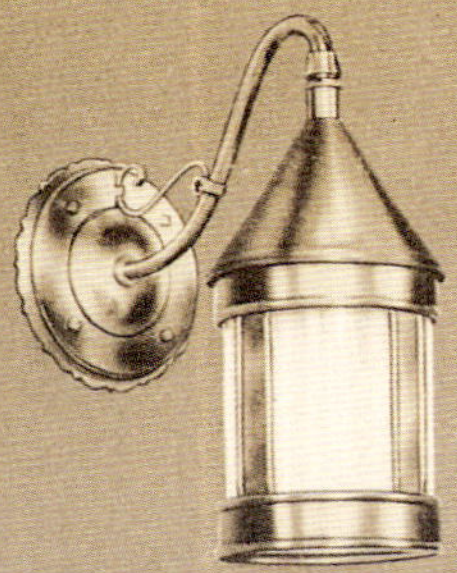

067

1215

No. 1706
One-light bracket lantern with a frosted glass cylinder. Diameter 5½″. Over-all height 14″. Extends 9″. Has waterproof socket. Made of Chase Copper. Finish: Half Polished Iron.

No. 067
One-light bracket lantern with frosted glass cylinder. Height of lantern 10⅝″. Width 7¼″. Extends 10¾″. Made of Chase Brass or Copper. Finishes: Stained Copper, Black, Colonial Brass.

No. 1722
One-light wall lantern. Height 14″. Width 6½″. Extends 3½″. Has antique glass panels and waterproof socket. Made of Chase Copper. Finish: Stained Copper, or Black.

No. 1712
One-light bracket lantern with a frosted glass cylinder. Height 13″. Diameter 5½″. Extends 8″. Has waterproof socket. Made of Chase Copper. Finish: Half Polished Iron.

No. 1215
One-light bracket lantern with frosted glass cylinder. Back plate 4¼″ square. Extends 6″. Height of lantern 9½″. Made of Copper. Has waterproof socket. Finishes: Stained Copper, Black.

58

HANGING LANTERNS

018

016

015

No. 018
One-light hanging lantern with a frosted glass cylinder. Over-all length 36″. Height of lantern 12″. Width 7¼″. Made of Chase Brass or Copper. Has waterproof socket. Finishes: Stained Copper, Black, Colonial Brass.

No. 016
One-light hanging lantern with antique glass panels. Over-all length 36″. Height of lantern 11½″. Width 6½″. Has waterproof sockets. Made of Chase Copper. Finishes: Stained Copper, Black.

No. 015
One-light hanging lantern with antique glass panels. Over-all length 36″. Height of lantern 14″. Width 8½″. Has waterproof socket. Made of Brass or Copper. Finishes: Colonial Brass, Black, Stained Copper.

5

HANGING LANTERNS

No. 1716
One-light hanging lantern with a frosted glass cylinder. Over-all length 36″. Height of lantern 11″. Width 5½″. Has waterproof socket. Made of Chase Copper. Finish: Half Polished Iron, Black.

No. 017
One-light hanging lantern with a frosted glass cylinder. Over-all length 36″. Height of lantern 14⅞″. Diameter 4⅝″. Has waterproof socket. Made of Chase Copper. Finishes: Stained Copper, Black, Colonial Brass.

No. 011
One-light hanging lantern with an antique bubble glass globe. Height of lantern 11¼″. Over-all length 36″. Width 6¼″. Has waterproof socket. Finishes: Colonial Brass, Black, Stained Copper.

No. 732
One-light hanging lantern with a frosted glass cylinder. Over-all length 36″. Height of lantern 14″. Diameter 5½″. Has waterproof socket. Made of Chase Copper. Finish: Half Polished Iron.

No. 1225
One-light hanging lantern with a frosted glass cylinder. Over-all length 12″. Height of Lantern 9¼″. Made of Chase Copper. Has waterproof socket. Finish: Stained Copper or Black.

SHADES AND SHIELDS

No. 8222-8225-8228
Parchment shade. Over-all height 4″. Top 3¼″. Bottom 4¼″. Has bulb clip holder. Color: Antique with bright gold decorations as shown above.

No. 8221-8224-8227
Parchment shade. Over-all height 3½″. Top 3″. Bottom 4″. Has bulb clip holder. Color: Antique with bright gold decorations as shown above.

No. 8220-8223-8226
Parchment shield. Over-all height 3¾″. Width 4″. Has candle clip holder. Color: Antique with bright gold decorations as shown above.

No. 8229
Silk shield. Over-all height 3¾″. Width 4″. Has candle clip holder. Color: White.

No. 8230
Silk shade. Over-all height 4″. Bottom 4¼″. Top 3¼″. Has bulb clip holder. Color: White.

61

Chapter 11
"Shutting Off The Lights: The End of Chase Lighting"

"It is hoped, and expected, that some of the Specialty (giftware) items will be ready for some of the larger stores throughout the country for the 1945 Christmas trade. That spells progress—sound progress—and the picture gets brighter every day." Chase News
September 22, 1945

The picture did get brighter, but unfortunately it did not include postwar resumption of activity by either the Chase Specialty or Lighting divisions. With defense contracts terminated by the end of World War II, Chase required new, and more financially viable outlets. These were outlets the production of lamps, fixtures, and metal giftware could not provide. Despite optimistic predictions, the Specialty and Lighting divisions did not resume postwar production.

A final Specialty stock list, prepared for Rodney Chase and dated September 8, 1942, indicates a considerable wealth of unsold lamp inventory still on hand. Included were over 2100 "AQUILLAS," 1300 "VICTORIAS," and (surprisingly, considering how infrequently they appear on the market), 1300 "SENTINELS." Today, collectors would snap them up; then, they were excess baggage.

From its prewar status as a manufacturer of finished product, the Chase Brass & Copper Co. moved toward its current status as a producer of raw material for other manufacturers. Today, Chase leads the industry in the production of brass rod, continuing to build on a company heritage that began in 1876.

While the Chase Lighting division may have flickered out, the glowing talent of the designers and artisans who powered it still burns bright. Their brilliant Lamps and Fixtures have lasted, as F.S. Chase hoped in 1934, "from generation to generation."[1]

"It won't be too long before the entire Factory plant is again humming with industry—with the production of those things we have all longed to see produced again, goods for a world at peace." Chase News
September 22, 1945

"Chase: Designed for Lighting—Brilliant in Style—and so exceptionally reasonable in price!" Chase Lighting Fixtures brochures, 1934

The golden age of Chase: the centaur gleams, on the back cover of the 1934 Chase Lighting Fixtures catalog. *Courtesy of John Myhre*

"Reconversion is a word that can actually be spelled in eight letters, and that word is 'headache'." After World War II, Chase faced the daunting prospect of reconverting from the production of wartime supplies to the production of lamps, lighting fixtures, and Specialty items. The prospect, never realized, was greeted with varying degrees of enthusiasm by Chase executives. They're shown glumly looking over bits of the Chase pre-war inventory, in this photo from the September 22, 1945 issue of *Chase News. Courtesy of State Archives, Connecticut State Library*

Gone, but not forgotten: Lurelle Guild's "COLONEL LIGHT," #27013, stands watch over a glittering array of Chase Specialty items. *Courtesy of John and Donna Thorpe*

Endnotes

Introduction

1. F.S. Chase, "Foreword," *1934 Lamps catalog*, New York: Chase Brass & Copper Co., Inc., 1934, p. 5.

Chapter 1

1. "If You Made 33,000 Brass Articles You'd Have 33,000 Troubles Too!," *Chase Diamond* 4, no. 16 (August 1922), p. 1.
2. F.S. Chase, "Foreword," *1934 Lamps catalog*, New York: Chase Brass & Copper Co., Inc., 1934, p. 4.

Chapter 2

1. Quoted in "Both Fish And Fowl," *Fortune* (February 1934), p. 90.
2. Ibid.

Chapter 3

1. Lurelle Guild, "The Designer Speaks," *1934 Lamps catalog*, New York: Chase Brass & Copper Co., Inc., 1934, p. 6.

Chapter 11

1. F.S. Chase, "Foreword," *1934 Lamps catalog*, New York: Chase Brass & Copper Co., Inc., 1934, p. 5.

Bibliography

Archival sources

Armstrong World Industries, Inc. Library, Lancaster, PA; Cleveland Public Library, Cleveland, OH; Connecticut State Historical Society, Hartford, CT; Connecticut State Library, Hartford, CT; Connecticut State Museum, Hartford, CT; Free Library of Philadelphia, Vine Street, Philadelphia, PA; Kennecott Library, Salt Lake City, UT; Library of Congress, Washington, D.C.; Mattatuck Museum, Waterbury, CT; National Portrait Gallery, Washington, D.C.; Omaha Public Library, Omaha, NE; Rochester Public Library, Rochester, NY; Silas Bronson Library, Waterbury, CT; Strong Museum Library, Rochester, NY; SUNY Library, Brockport, NY; SUNY Library, Buffalo, NY

Archives

Chase Brass & Copper Co., Inc., Montpelier, OH (includes annual reports, corporate and advertising brochures, *Chase Diamond, Chase News*), 1876–present.

Archival materials: Harry L. and Olga Laylon

Ashby, Justine Chase. *Document Of A Child*. New Hampshire: William L. Bauhan, 1980.

Badeau, E. C. "Industry's Metals Enter the Home." *Brass World* 26, no. 2 (February 1930): pp. 31-32.

"Both Fish And Fowl." *Fortune* (February 1934): pp. 40, 43, 88-98.

Chase Lamps & Lighting Fixtures catalogs. Waterbury, CT/New York: Chase Brass & Copper Co., Inc., 1934, 1937, 1938, 1940, 1941.

Chase Specialty Division catalogs. Waterbury, CT/New York: Chase Brass & Copper Co., Inc., 1930-1942.

"Chase Tower Opens." *The Gift And Art Shop* (June 1934): pp. 53-54.

Collins, Philip. *Smokerama*. San Francisco: Chronicle Books, 1992.

Correspondence, J. B. Kushlis, letter to Barbara Endter, September 12, 1988.

Correspondence, Harry Laylon, letter to Barbara Endter, March 30, 1991.

Correspondence, Harry Laylon, letter to Tetsumasa Suda, April 28, 1991.

Dufrêne, Maurice. *Authentic Art Deco Interiors: From the 1925 Paris Exhibition*. Woodbridge, Suffolk: Antique Collectors Club, 1989.

Encyclopédie des arts décoratifs et industriels modernes. Paris: Projets, 1925.

Endter, Barbara Ward. "Chase Brass & Copper Company—Specialties Showroom." *Chicago Art Deco Society Magazine* (Winter 1995): pp. 5, 24.

———. "Chasing the Centaur." *The Echoes Report* 4, no. 2 (Fall 1995): pp. 42-43.

———. "History of Chase Brass & Copper Co., Inc." 1998, unpublished.

Exposition des arts décoratifs et industriels modernes. Paris: Libraire Larousse, 1925.

"For Better Vision—Better Light." *Modern Plastics* (December 1937): pp. 17-21, 62.

Guild, Lurelle. *Designed for Living: The Blue Book of Interior Decoration.* Scranton, PA: Scranton Lace Company, 1936.

"Going On In The Trade." *The Gift And Art Shop/* (beginning July 1934) *The Gift And Art Buyer*, 1930-1942.

Gura, Judith B. "Modernism Milestone: The Story of the 1925 Paris Exposition." *Echoes* 7, no. 1 (Summer 1998): pp. 70-73, 97-98.

Home Owners' Catalogs. New York: F. W. Dodge Corporation, 1937.

Huxford, Sharon and Bob (eds.). *Schroeder's Antiques Price Guide*, 18th ed., Paducah, Kentucky: Schroeder Publishing, 2000, pp. 104-105.

Johnson, Donald-Brian, and Piña, Leslie. *Chase Complete: Deco Specialties of the Chase Brass & Copper Co*. Atglen, PA: Schiffer Publishing Ltd., 1999.

———. *The Chase Catalogs: 1934 & 1935*. Atglen, PA: Schiffer Publishing Ltd., 1998.

Kardon, Janet, ed. *Craft In The Machine Age: 1920-1945*. New York: Harry N. Abrams, Inc., 1995.

Kilbride, Richard J. *Art Deco Chrome: The Chase Era*. Stamford, CT: JO-D Books, 1988.

———. *Art Deco Chrome Book 2, A Collectors' Guide: Industrial Design In The Chase Era*. Stamford, CT: JO-D Books, 1992.

Koch, Gladys, and Robert and Rosa Thomas. *Chase Chrome*. Stamford, CT: Gladys Koch Antiques, 1978.

Laylon, Harry L. "The Chase Story," July 27, 1991, unpublished.

Lesieutre, Alain. *The Spirit and Splendour of Art Deco*. Paddington Press, 1974.
Linz, Jim. *Art Deco Chrome*. Atglen, PA: Schiffer Publishing Ltd., 1999.
Loring, John. "American Deco." *The Connoisseur* (January 1979): pp. 48-54.
Lougee, E. F. "From Old To New With Lurelle Guild." *Modern Plastics* (March 1935): pp. 14-15, 66-68.
Maloney, Cornelius F. "A Family Saga Woven Into City History." *The Waterbury Sunday Republican Magazine* (March 30, 1986): pp. 3-5.
———. "First Family of Brass Making." *The Waterbury Sunday Republican Magazine* (April 20, 1986): pp. 6-8.
———. "Days of Triumph and Tribulation." *The Waterbury Sunday Republican Magazine* (April 27, 1986): pp. 3-5.
———. "Early Chase Homes Were Centered In Town." *The Waterbury Sunday Republican Magazine* (May 11, 1986): pp. 3-5.
McFadden, R. S. "Designers' Ability Salvages Waste." *Design* (September 1933): pp. 20-22, 25.
"Merchandise Design in the Next 20 Years?" *The Gift And Art Buyer* (April 1937): pp. 56-59.

Periodicals (Chase advertisements and product announcements), 1930-1942

The American Home; Better Homes & Gardens; Copper And Brass Bulletin; Furniture Age; The Gift And Art Shop/(beginning July 1934) *The Gift And Art Buyer; House Beautiful; House & Garden; Ladies' Home Journal; Metal Industry; Modern Plastics; The Saturday Evening Post; Woman's Home Companion; Vogue*

Personal interviews, Olga Laylon, 1998
Pile, John F. *Dictionary of 20th-Century Design*. New York: Roundtable Press, 1990.
Post, Emily. *How To Give Buffet Suppers*. Waterbury, CT: Chase Brass & Copper Co., Inc., 1933.
Saving Your Eyes With Correct Lighting. Waterbury, CT: Chase Brass & Copper Co., Inc., 1936.
Sichel, Kimberly. "Walter Von Nessen: Early Post Modernist." *ID*, (May/June 1984): pp. 38-41.
Stewart, Karen J. *Chase Brass & Copper Company Collectors' Home Page*. (ChaseKrome@aol.com)
Stowell, Kenneth. "Here's What They Say About Fall Decoration." *House Beautiful* 78, no. 10 (October 1936): pp. 47-49, 102.
Striner, Richard. *Art Deco*. New York: Abbeville Press, 1994.
United States Patent Office Official Gazette, 1876-1942.
Van Hook, Barry L. *Art Deco Reflections Newsletter*. Mesa, AZ: The Chase Collectors Society, 1991—present.
———. "Chase: Art Deco Style For The Masses." *Chase Collectors Society Home Page* (http://www.public.asu.edu/icblv/chase.htm), 1997.
Visakay, Stephen. *Vintage Bar Ware*. Paducah, KY: Collector Books, 1997, pp. 64-71, entry on Chase Brass & Copper Co.
Watson, J. "American Way." *The Magazine of Art* 33 (November 1940): pp. 626-629.
Wright, Russel. "A Guide to Buying Modern." *Arts and Decoration* 42, (February 1935).

Chase Lighting Cross-Reference Index & Price Guide

The Chase Cross-Reference Index, compiled by Gary M. Piper, presents comprehensive identifying information about the Chase lighting inventory in a clear and easy-to-use format. Its purpose is three-fold:

1) to provide collectors, at a glance, with pertinent information about specific Chase items.
2) to serve as an index for locating photos and more detailed information about each object in this book.
3) to serve as a handy price guide!

The Cross-Reference Index has been divided into three categories: **LAMPS, BATTERY LIGHTS,** and **LIGHTING FIXTURES**. These are the category divisions utilized in this book, and are also the original inventory divisions of the Chase catalogs. For ease of reference, all "named" items are listed in alphabetical order. Fixtures added for the 1937 catalog were not given titles; these are listed in numerical order, by inventory number.

There are seven subcategory entries for each *Lamp* and *Battery Light* included in the Chase Cross-Reference Index, and six for each *Fixture*:

*__NUMBER__: the catalog inventory number assigned by Chase. If a subsequent number replaced an earlier one, this has been noted.

*__DESCRIPTION:__ the title given to each object by Chase. Additional identifying information is included, if necessary, to differentiate items that have the same generic catalog names, but are not the same (e.g., the two entries entitled "SENTINEL LAMP").

*__PAGE:__ the page number on which a photo of the item will be found. If a specific object appears in more than one photo, the page on which it is shown in the most detail has been included in the Index. Represented in this book are all Chase lamps, battery lights, and lighting fixtures shown in the Pre-1933 through 1942 Specialty catalogs, the 1934 Lamps catalog, and the 1934 and 1937 Fixtures catalogs. This represents the entire Chase lamp and battery light inventory, and all fixtures except basic variations to the standard line added after 1937.

*__CATALOG YEAR:__ the year(s) in which an item appeared in the Chase catalog, and the catalog page(s) on which it was shown. If no entries are given for a specific item, it is not depicted in any of the available Chase catalogs; however, period advertising has documented it as part of the Chase line. ("P33" indicates an item shown in the pages of a Chase catalog issued prior to 1933; only a portion of this catalog has been located, so it has not been possible to assign an exact year of issue.)

*__CHANGES:__ this category pertains to *Lamps* and *Battery Lights* only. Included are the year an item first appeared in a Chase catalog, available finishes, and any pertinent trim details. "38-C/wht, PC/wht," for example, indicates the lamp first appeared in the 1938 catalog, and was offered in *chrome with white trim parts,* as well as *polished copper with white trim parts*. If, in subsequent catalog years, the item was offered in additional variations, or if some of the design options previously offered were deleted, this has been noted, with the appropriate year in which the change occurred. (A list of abbreviations used in the *"Changes"* category follows.) For *Lighting Fixtures,* this information will be found in the Chapter 9 and Chapter 10 reprints of the 1934 and 1937 Fixtures brochure and catalog, and is thus not repeated in the Index.

*__BY:__ the designer of record for a specific item, as determined by patent application, period documentation, or Chase employee records. If no entry is given, the designer remains, at present, unknown. Such objects may be the work of designers listed elsewhere, or that of uncredited members of the Chase design department; however, verifying documentation has yet to be located. (A listing of designer name abbreviations follows).

*__PRICE:__ the suggested current price for an item on the collector's market, as outlined in the accompanying pricing guidelines.

About the Price Guide

Price research has been coordinated by John and Donna Thorpe of the Chase Collectors Society. In determining appropriate current prices on the secondary market, the Thorpes note:

There are "Chase lamps," and then there are *Chase Lamps!* Many fixtures, novelties, and smaller household lamps of the later Chase years were mass-produced for middle-income American homes, and are thus more readily available. However, the hand-assembled and exquisite line of 1934 lamps and fixtures designed by Lurelle Guild equal or surpass any high-end equivalent on today's market. Pricing will reflect this variance.

Whether or not a lamp "works" was not a factor in determining prices. Due to their age, *all* Chase lamps and fixtures should be re-wired before use. This will not detract from the item's value, or decrease its desirability. Re-wired with the correct silk-wrapped cord, a Chase lamp will actually increase in value, and become a safe addition to any home decor.

Ranges given in the Guide are for Chase lamps, battery lights, and fixtures in *"excellent"* condition. The term is defined as follows:

*No dents, cracks, or pitted chrome.

*Painted lamps must have their finish complete, with no flaking or chipping.

*Any original plastic trim must be complete, and free of chips.

*Original *metal* or *plastic* shades must still be attached to the lamp, and undamaged.

All other prices given are for lamps or fixtures *without* shades. Original Chase parchment or fabric shades turn up rarely on the secondary market, and those that do are often in poor repair. Substituting a vintage shade in a style similar to the original will not affect a lamp's value, but will in fact enhance its usability and appeal.

The following considerations may also impact value and should be noted:

*Items displaying flaws, which cause them to be graded less than excellent (as defined above), should be valued *significantly* less.

*If a lamp is available in more than one finish, chrome will usually command the highest price.

*Original paper or silk shades that do occasionally turn up in presentable condition will add a good 30 percent to the lamp values given.

*Lamps found in unused condition, in their original boxes, may bring a premium of perhaps 50 to 100 percent above suggested prices.

An asterisk ("*") denotes price ranges for items appearing less frequently in the marketplace. As such, a range has not yet become firmly established, and buyers may encounter a higher degree of price variance.

Some items have not been priced, but are instead captioned "ND" *("no data")*. These lamps made only brief appearances in the Chase line, and surface very infrequently today, even among seasoned Chase collectors. Their scarcity on the market makes it impossible to price them with any degree of accuracy; it would do the collector no service to "set" what would only be, at present, an artificial value. "No data" should not be taken to mean that these are objects of greater value than those priced, but simply that current reliable pricing information is unavailable.

A price guide is most effective when used as a reference tool, and a point at which to begin negotiations. Prices given here are a composite of actual current selling prices, and may vary according to locale and demand. Lower or higher prices will be dictated by the individual sales situation, and neither the authors nor the publisher can guarantee specific outcomes. We do, however, guarantee you'll find the quest for Chase lighting products illuminating. Our best wishes for your success!

Abbreviations Key

Metal Finishes
- **AmB:** Amber Bronze
- **AnB:** Antique Brass
- **AnC:** Antique Copper
- **AS:** Antique Silver
- **BN:** Black Nickel
- **BR:** Bronze
- **BrN:** Brushed Nickel
- **C:** Polished Chromium
- **EB:** English Bronze
- **EC:** English Copper
- **GTB:** Golden Triangle Brass
- **N:** Nickel
- **P:** Pewter
- **PB:** Polished Brass
- **PC:** Polished Copper
- **PN:** Polished Nickel
- **PS:** Polished Steel
- **SB:** Satin Brass
- **SC:** Satin Copper
- **SCh:** Satin Chromium
- **SGTB:** Satin Golden Triangle Brass
- **SN:** Satin Nickel
- **S:** Silver
- **SS:** Satin Silver

Trim Finishes/Colors
- **map:** maple
- **wal:** walnut
- **wd:** wood
- **blk:** black
- **blu:** blue
- **brn:** brown
- **grn:** green
- **org:** orange
- **tort:** tortoise
- **wht:** white
- **yel:** yellow

Periods/Styles
- **J:** Early English
- **C:** Early American/Colonial
- **F:** Federal
- **G:** Georgian
- **E:** Empire
- **M:** Classic Modern
- **A:** American Adaptations
- **NC:** Neo Classic
- **EG:** "Even-Glow" Fixtures
- **LAN:** Lanterns, no period
- **MISC:** Miscellaneous Fixtures

Miscellaneous
- **/:** "with" or "and"
- **a.:** added
- **d.:** deleted or discontinued
- **ND:** no data
- ***:** price range may vary
- **L:** Lamps catalog
- **LF:** Lighting Fixtures catalog

Designers
- **HD:** Helen Bishop Dennis
- **GG:** Ruth and William Gerth
- **LG:** Lurelle Guild
- **JK:** John E. King & Randal L. Hale
- **HL:** Harry Laylon
- **AM:** August Mitchell
- **RE:** Adolph Recker
- **HR:** Howard Reichenbach
- **VN:** Walter Von Nessen

CHASE LIGHTING CROSS-REFERENCE INDEX AND PRICE GUIDE

LAMPS

NUMBER	DESCRIPTION	PAGE	CATALOG YEAR												CHANGES	BY	PRICE
			P33	'33	'34	34L	'35	'36	'37	'38	'39	'40	'41	'42			
6323	ACADEMY	85												46	42-C, PB/wht, EB/brn		200-225
F550	ADAMS	104				25									34L-C/blk, Brass/blk	LG	450-475
F552	ADAMS (semi-indirect)	104				25									34L-C/blk, Brass/blk	LG	450-475
6196	ADAM STUDENT	85									69	63	54		39-PB, EB		125-150
C001	ADMIRAL	94				12									34L-Brass	LG	275-300
6166	ALDEN	61									74	68	58		39-PB / BR or WHT		60-70
6300	AMBASSADOR	65									64	60			39-Copper/wht or tort.		200-225
6306	ANCHOR	78										64			40-Brass		70-85
6326	AQUILLA	66												42	42-GTB/wht		75-100
M500	ARCADIA	90				50									34-C	LG	425-450
E302	ARGONNE	100				42									34L-Red/blk/brass	LG	250-275
F150	ARROW	105				24									34L-Brass/blk	LG	450-475
17102	ATHENA VANITY	70										69	58	48	40-SC, GTB		75-100
E351	AVIGNON	106				45									34L-Brass	LG	425-450
E352	AVIGNON (semi-indirect)	106				45									34L-Brass	LG	425-450
A11235	BALL (#01002, 1936 only)	60		34	33	56	30	39							33-C, PB/PC	GG	C-400-425
																	PB-300-325
6314	BARNEGAT	76											56	45	41-PB/red or grn		75-95
C005	BARNETT	94				13									34L-Brass/P	LG	250-275
6177	BEDFORD	63									63	59	51	41	39-AmB, S Coppertone		125-150
6195	BERKELEY	87									73	69	59		39-SB/bronze or wht		95-115
6143	BEVERLY	63									66	61			39-BR/wht/gold		100-125
25002	BINNACLE (wired)	75		19	35		29		42	47					33-PB /tube globe; 35-chg.to hr. glass globe; 37- chg. to tube globe	RE	35-45
															colored glass		←50-65
															1933 Chicago World's Fair		←100-120
6172	BOND	84									76	72			39-AmB		100-125
E304	BORDEAUX	99				39									34L-Red,grn,or wht /brass	LG	175-200
6179	BREWSTER	71									68	62	53	43	39-PB, EB		75-100
6167	BRISTOL	62									66	61			39-Wht, BR/gold		100-125
6142	BRUNSWICK	74									69	63			39-PB/map		75-95
6186	BURTON	63									66	61			39-BR/gold		100-125
6161	CARLTON	62									63	58			39-EB, Wht/gold		150-175
E309	CAROLINIAN	100				41									34L-Brass/wht	LG	350-375
E402	CARROLLTON	99				36									34L-Brass/wht	LG	425-450
A01008	CENTURY	89			32	57	31								34-Blk/C, Wht/C	LG	300-325*
E300	CHALFONTE	99				37									34L-Brass/blk	LG	450-475
6189	CHANCELLOR	85									76	72	57		39-EB, Coppertone/wht		100-125
E154	CHANTILLY	106				44									34L-Brass	LG	375-400
6192	CHATHAM	71									68	62	53	43	39-EB		85-100
G205	CHELTENHAM	98				32									34L-Brass	LG	275-300
E151	CHERBOURG	107				44									34L-Grn/Brass	LG	375-400
E157	CHERBOURG (semi-indirect)	107				44									34L-Grn/Brass	LG	375-400
6194	CHESTER	74									69	62	53		39-PB		65-80
G202	CHIPPENDALE	98				32									34L-Brass/red or grn	LG	350-375
A01004	CIRCLE	69			31	55	31	40	45	44	67	67	55	47	34-C, EB; 41-a. PB	LG	100-125
6198	CIRCLETTE	12									72	66	61	47	39-PN/blk, PB/wht		75-100*
6164	CLIFTON	70									74	68	58		39-SB/BR or wht		85-105
6191	CLIPPER	77									71	65	56	45	39-PB		110-135
27013	COLONEL	80			35		28	38	44	46					34-Red/yel/blk; 35-a. grn/wht, blu/wht, red/wht - all /blk	LG	250-275
27014	COLONEL'S LADY	80					29	38	44						35-Red/wht, grn/wht, blu/wht - all /blk; 37-d. red/wht	LG	250-275
F306	COLUMBIA	95				20									34L-Brass	LG	325-350
6151	COMET (METAL SHADE)	83									75	70			39-SB/wht	HR	95-115
6154	COMET	83									75	70			39-SB/wht or bronze	HR	100-120
6170	COMMANDER	67									62	58			39-Coppertone		250-275
6138	CONCORD	74									70	64			39-PB		65-80

NUMBER	DESCRIPTION	PAGE	P33	'33	'34	34L	'35	'36	'37	'38	'39	'40	'41	'42	CHANGES	B▾	PRICE
	LAMPS (continued)																
A27010	CONSOLE (GUILD)	89			33	57	30	39	45						34-C; 35-a. EB, SC; 36-d. C	LG	225-250
11240	CONSOLE (VON NESSEN)	26													P33-Brushed Chrome, Brushed Copper	VN	ND
17048	CONSTELLATION	81			31		30	40	44	46	67	67	55		34-C, PC, EB	VN	C-375-400
															PC, EB		←275-300
F132	CONSTITUTION	96				19									34L-Brass/blk	LG	325-350
F130	CONTINENTAL	96				23									34L-Brass/gray-grn	LG	300-325
6173	COUNCILOR	83									77	72	57		39-EB, Coppertone/wht		100-125
6303	CRESCENT	86									75	70	60		39-SB/wht, SN/blk; 41-a. SN/red		90-110
6156	CRESCENT (no reflector)	86									75	70	60	49	39-SB/wht, SN/blk; 41-a. SN/red		75-100
C004	DANFORTH	94				12									34L-Brass/S	LG	225-250
C040	DEDHAM	104				15									34L-Blk iron, PS/brass	LG	325-350
M350	DELPHIC	91				52									34L-C/wht	LG	500-525
M353	DELPHIC (semi-indirect)	91				52									34L-C/wht	LG	500-525
11243	DELTA	70	22												P33-SC, EB, SB		ND
A01003	DESK	82			30	54	30	40	45	44	77	72	57	46	34-C, EB; 41-a. PB		C-100-125
																	EB-75-100
6165	DISCUS	62									71	67			39-GTB/wht or bronze		75-95
M506	DORIC	102				48									34L-C/blu glass ball	LG	450-475*
E400	D'ORSAY (GUILD)	100				37									34L-Brass/blk	LG	450-475
6317	D'ORSAY (CANDLE)	68											51		41-PB, red		100-125
01010	DRUM (NOVELTY)	24					29	40	43						35-Red/blu, Wht/blk, Blu/red	HD	275-300
6324	DRUM - TABLE	79												47	42-C/red, PB/red		125-150*
6159	EDGEWOOD	88									74	68	58		39-EB/map, Wht/Blond map; 41-d. Wht		95-110
6157	EMPIRE	64									64				39-Br/gold, wht/gold		100-125
6149	ESSEX	66									67				39-wht/gold, BR/gold		ND
6325	FALMOUTH	72												44	42-PB		75-85
25007	FARMERS' LANTERN (wired)	30									46	42	28	23	39-PB/tin plate		45-60
6309	FARRAGUT	78										71	59	48	40-PB		85-100
6308	FARRAGUT (no reflector)	78										71	59	48	40-PB		75-90
M503	FLAME	90				50									34L-C	LG	425-450*
A01005	FLUTED BASE	89			30	55	31	39							34-C/blk	LG	375-400*
A601	FLYING CLOUD	102				54									34L-AnB/grn glass ball	LG	325-350*
C002	FLYING DOLPHIN	94				13									34L-Tin/Red, P/red	LG	225-250
6136	FORUM	65									66				39-wht/gold, BR/gold		ND
F140	GEORGETOWN	96				23									34L-Brass/wht/blk	LG	375-400
6144	GEORGIAN	64									65				39-PB/gold, wht/gold		ND
G206	GIRANDOLE	98				30									34L-Brass	LG	300-325
C006	GLOUCESTER	94				14									34L-Brass	LG	200-225
01001	GLOW	60	29	34	30		31	37	43	46	77	67	61		P33-PC/PB finial; 33-a. C; 34-a. C/blk; 35-d. C; 37-a. PC/wht	GG	PC-50-60
															C/blk & PC /wht		←100-125
G201	HAMMOND	97				29									34L-Brass	LG	325-350
6184	HAMPTON	61									69	64			39-PB, PC		75-95
M250	HELLENIC	91				52									34L-C/blk	LG	525-550
M252	HELLENIC (indirect)	91				52									34L-C/blk	LG	525-550
M502	IONIC	101				51									34L-C	LG	375-400
F135	IPSWICH (GUILD)	95				22									34L-Brass	LG	300-325
6313	IPSWICH (glass globe)	73											51	41	41-PB, SS		75-100
6312	JAMESTOWN	72											51	41	41-PB, SS		95-115
F134	JOHN PAUL JONES	34				18									34L-Brass/blk	LG	300-325
6160	KIDDIE	79									72	66			39-SB/blu, rose, red, or wht		65-85
6188	KINGSTON	74									70	64			39-Wht, red, or grn		65-85
E207	LADY GODEY	99				40									34L-Brass/ivory	LG	300-325
E450	LAFAYETTE	106				43									34L-Red, grn, or wht/brass	LG	400-425
E680	LAFAYETTE (semi-indirect)	106				43									34L-Red, grn, or wht/brass	LG	400-425
6168	LENOX	71									68	62	53	43	39-EB, PB		60-70
6322	LEXICON	87												49	42-EB, PB		95-120
6178	LEXINGTON	72									70	63	54	44	39-PB, SS		65-75
F136	LIBERTY	96				19									34L-Brass	LG	325-350

LAMPS (continued)

NUMBER	DESCRIPTION	PAGE	CATALOG YEAR												CHANGES	BY	PRICE
			P33	'33	'34	34L	'35	'36	'37	'38	'39	'40	'41	'42			
6321	LOMBARD	64												41	42-GTB, AmB/wht		125-150
M504	LUNA	102				51									34L-C	LG	425-450*
6185	MALDEN	68									64				39-Wht, red, or grn		ND
6181	MARLBORO	64									63	59			39-Wht/gold, BR/gold		125-150
F137	MARYLAND	95				21									34L-Brass	LG	375-400
25008	MASTHEAD LANTERN	24										44	30	23	40-PB/clear, red or grn globe	HL	125-150
6310	MASTHEAD (table)	77										65	56	45	40-PB/red or grn glass		125-150
E404	MAYHEW	99				38									34L-Brass	LG	275-300
17118	MELISSA	66												42	42-Wht/PB or C		110-120
G208	MELTON	97				29									34L-Brass	LG	275-300
6180	MILTON	74									72				39-PC, PB		ND
E303	MIRABEAU	98				42									34L-Red/blk/brass	LG	300-325
C003	MT. VERNON (GUILD)	94				14									34L-Brass	LG	250-275
6316	MT. VERNON HURRICANE	71											55	44	41-PB, SS		80-100
6147	NANTUCKET	77									71				39-PB		ND
E307	NAVARRE	98				38									34L-Brass	LG	275-300
6187	NEWPORT	76									73	71	59	48	39-PB/red & grn		75-95
6193	NEWTON	74									70	63			39-PB		65-85
G152	PADDINGTON	105				33									34L-Brass	LG	475-500
G251	PADDINGTON (semi-indirect)	105				33									34L-Brass	LG	475-500
6318	PARTHENON	29											52	43	41-Wht/PB, AmB		95-120
F131	PATRIOT	95				18									34L-Brass	LG	300-325
17110	PENELOPE	67											52	42	41-SS, PB		110-130
01015	PLANET	61								45	63	59			38-C/wht, PC/wht	VN	600-625
M505	PLATO	101				48									34L-C	LG	375-400
6183	PLYMOUTH	68									64	59			39-EB, PB		ND
6311	POTOMAC	72											54	44	41-PB, SS		95-115
6174	PRESTON	88									75	70			39-SB/blond or dark map		75-95
11144	PRISCILLA	111													P33-Brushed S, C, BR		60-75
6131	PRISCILLA (shaded)	71									68				39-Wht/gold, PC, PB		ND
G308	PRINCESS ANNE	97				28									34L-Brass, Brass/grn	LG	425-450
6302	PUTNAM	73									73	69	60	49	39-SB/wht or bronze		75-95
01011	QUILL	84						38	43	46	76	71			36-BR, PN/blk; 37-a. SB/ivory; 40-d. SB/ivory		90-105
01009	REEDED	65			32		28								34-PC, Wht		110-125*
6137	REGENT	29									65	60			39-Brass, Wht		95-115
F403	REPUBLIC	96				22									34L-Brass	LG	400-425
11242	RING	69	22												P33-SC, EB, SB		225-250*
E305	SAVOY	99				36									34L-Brass	LG	300-325
6304	SAYBROOK	12									75	70	60		39-SB/wht or BR		80-100
6035	SAYBROOK (no reflector)	12									75	70	60	49	39-SB/wht or BR		75-95
E600	SCARLET DRUM	100				40									34L-Brass/red	LG	275-300
16005	SCONCE LIGHT (wired)	110										43	29		40-PB, PB/PC		65-75
17112	SENTINEL	79											52	47	41-PB/red or blu		225-250
6171	SENTINEL (no figure)	66									62				39-Wht/coppertone, BR/coppertone		ND
6307	SETTLER'S HURRICANE	72										66	55	46	40-PB		50-60
6162	SHELTON	62										65	60		39-Wht, BR/gold		100-125
01006	SHIP AHOY	75			31										34-PB/red or grn		75-95*
11244	SIGMA	70	22												P33-SC, EB, SB	GG	ND
25005	SKIPPER'S LANTERN (wired)	112								45	46				38-PB		150-175
M200	SPARTA	101				49									34L-C	LG	350-375
6320	SUNBIRD	83											57	46	41-C, PB/blk		75-95
6176	SUTTON	83									67	61			39-SC/wht, rose, or grn		130-145
E301	SWAN	98				39									34L-Red, grn, or wht/brass	LG	200-225
01007	TANKARD	81			32										34-PC		ND
NS-597	"THE LAMP"	26													P33-SN/PB/PC	VN	ND
6182	TREMONT	65									62	58			39-Wht/gold, EB		125-150
E451	TRIANON	105				45									34L-Red, grn, or wht/brass	LG	275-300
M501	ULYSSES	101				49									34L-C	LG	375-400

NUMBER	DESCRIPTION	PAGE	P33	'33	'34	34L	'35	'36	'37	'38	'39	'40	'41	'42	CHANGES	BY	PRICE
	LAMPS (continued)																
G401	VICTOR HUGO	97				30									34L-Red, grn, or blk/brass	LG	400-425
E405	VICTORIA (GUILD)	100				41									34L-Wht/blk/brass	LG	375-400
6319	VICTORIA (glass globe)	67											52	42	41-PB, SS		110-130
F139	VICTORY	95				21									34L-Brass/blk	LG	375-400
F153	VIRGINIAN	104				25									34L-Brass/blk	LG	350-375
F155	VIRGINIAN (indirect)	104				25									34L-Brass/blk	LG	350-375
6153	WARWICK	87									73	69	59		39-BR, Wht/SB		95-115
F133	WASHINGTONIAN	95				20									34L-Brass/blk	LG	375-400
G203	WEDGWOOD	97				31									34L-Brass/grn/wht, AS/blu/wht	LG	400-425
6146	WESTBROOK	61									65	60			39-BR/gold, PN/blk		70-95
6190	WESTWOOD	87									74	68			39-BR/map, Wht/map		95-120
6305	WHEEL	77										65	56	45	40-PB/wal		95-120
6199	WILLIAMSTOWN	71									72	66	54		39-SGTB, SN		100-120
6301	WINDJAMMER	77									71	65			39-PB/ red or grn		75-95
G210	WINDSOR	97				31									34L-Brass/wht	LG	300-325
6155	WINTHROP	84									77	71			39-SB/wht or bronze		75-95
6175	WINTON	64									62	58			39-Coppertone/ wht or tort		350-375*
01014	WRITING PAPER	85								45	76				38-PC/map, EB/wal		100-125
A138	ZODIAC	103				56									34L-AnB/gray-blue	LG	300-325*
	BATTERY LIGHTS																
22003	AIRALITE	115		18	34		29	37	42	47	47	42			33-PN / "color" inlays red, blk, blu, grn; 40-d./ "color"inlays	AM	75-85
25001	BINNACLE	109		19	35		29	37	42	47	46				33-PB(tube globe); 35-chg. hr. glass globe; 37-chg. tube globe	AR	30-35
22001	"BOMB" FLASHLIGHT	115		18	34		28	37	43	47	47	42	30	23	33-PN	AM	45-65
11150	CANDLE LIGHT	114													P33-Ivory candle, base: blu,rose, orch,grn	AR	35-65
25006	FARMERS' LANTERN	111									46	42	28	23	39-PB/tin plate handle		35-50
9012	ILLUMINATED PENCIL	115										42	28	23	40-EB/wht, Red/wht, Wht red, Blk/PN	JK	250-275*
16002	LIGHTHOUSE	113					28								35-SB, SN		130-150*
11255	PILGRIM	110													P33-Ivory candle, base PB,PC,SN, or blu, rose, orch, grn		50-65
11256	SAF-CANDLE	113													P33-Ivory candle w/ Xmas red or Holly grn		ND
16004	SCONCE LIGHT	110										43	29		40-PB, PB/PC		40-50
25004	SKIPPER'S LANTERN	112								45	46				38-PB		80-100

CHASE LIGHTING CROSS-REFERENCE INDEX AND PRICE GUIDE

ALPHABETICAL FIXTURES

NUMBER	DESCRIPTION	PAGE	CATALOG YEAR					BY	PRICE
			34LF	37LF	38LF	40LF	41LF		
F123	ALBERMARLE	144	43					LG	475-500
M544	APOLLO	155	80					LG	325-350
M522	ATHENA	153	68	44	21	40		LG	575-600*
M546	AUGUSTA	155	80	56	24	48	42	LG	100-125*
M545	AURORA	154	76	45				LG	850-875*
F105	BALTIMORE	143	40					LG	175-200
E341	BASTILLE	151	62					LG	400-425
E440	BEAUVAIS	151	65	35	18			LG	375-400
E 442	BEAUVAIS (no shades)	151	65					LG	350-375
A1153	BENNINGTON	156	83					LG	100-125
A1151	BENNINGTON (no chimneys)	156	83	21	12	26		LG	75-100
A1103	BERKELEY (with glass bowl/pendant switch)	158	90					LG	25-50
A1177	BERKELEY (with pendant switch/no bowl)	158	90					LG	15-25
A1110	BERKELEY (with glass bowl/pull chain)	158	90					LG	25-50
A1178	BERKELEY (with pull chain/no bowl)	158	90					LG	15-25
A1111	BERKELEY (with glass bowl/keyless socket)	158	90					LG	25-50
A1174	BERKELEY (with keyless socket/no bowl)	158	90					LG	15-25
C015	BOSTON LANTERN (chain)	140	29	59	27	64	50	LG	125-150
C066	BOSTON LANTERN (wall bracket)	140	29	57	27	63	48	LG	125-150
A1109	BRIDGETOWN	157	90					LG	100-125
A1157	BRIDGETOWN (with bottom socket)	157	90					LG	100-125
G425	BRIGHTON	1,153	48	32				LG	125-150
G240	BROMPTON	147	50	50	27			LG	225-250
C031	BROOKFIELD	140	30	23	13			LG	175-200
C020	BULL'S EYE SCONCE	138	23	22				LG	125-150
A1114	BURLINGTON (with keyless socket)	158	91					LG	25-50
A1115	BURLINGTON (with pull chain)	158	91					LG	25-50
C643	CAPE COD	140	31	56	24	48	42	LG	50-75
F121	CHARLESTON	144	41					LG	225-250
G220	CHIPPENDALE (two lights)	147	48	32	19			LG	175-200
G226	CHIPPENDALE (one light)	147	48					LG	150-175
J717	CLARENDON	120	17					LG	150-175
A611	CLIPPER SHIP (one light)	126	82	48	15			LG	175-200
A612	CLIPPER SHIP (two lights)	126	82					LG	200-225
C030	COLEBROOK	140	31	22	13			LG	175-200
M528	COLONNADE	153	71	45	21			LG	450-475
F110	CONCORD (one light)	142	40					LG	50-75
F113	CONCORD (two lights)	142	40					LG	75-100
C021	CONNECTICUT SCONCE	138	25	23	13	26		LG	175-200
A1171	CORNWALL	41	88					LG	225-250
J731	CROMWELL	136	19					LG	225-250
M640	CYPRUS	155	79					LG	400-425
A1182	DARIEN	157	87					LG	50-75
C642	DEERFIELD	140	31	56	24	48	42	LG	50-75
M520	DIANA	153	73					LG	375-400*
M531	DOLPHIN	124	75	55	25	55		LG	200-225
A1099	DRAKE	157	89	18/53	23			LG	75-100
G644	DUNBAR	148	52					LG	300-325
E323	ELBA	37	57	48	17	22	18	LG	175-200
E343	ELYSEE	151	64	56	24	48		LG	75-100
A1148	ENFIELD	158	89					LG	100-125
A1147	ENFIELD (no chimneys)	158	89					LG	75-100
F424	FAIRFAX	143	38					LG	125-150
A1104	FAIRFIELD	41	84	18/52	15	29	32	LG	50-75

ALPHABETICAL FIXTURES (continued)

NUMBER	DESCRIPTION	PAGE	CATALOG YEAR					BY	PRICE
			34LF	37LF	38LF	40LF	41LF		
E342	FONTAINEBLEAU	151	61					LG	300-325
A1106	FRAMINGHAM	156	85	18/52	15	29	32	LG	75-100
G221	GEORGIAN SHELL (two lights)	146	47	32	19	25	27	LG	175-200
G227	GEORGIAN SHELL (one light)	146	47					LG	150-175
C022	GOODWILLIE SCONCE	138	22					LG	100-125
C026	GREEN MOUNTAIN SCONCE	139	24	22	13			LG	100-125
G243	GUILFORD	148	53					LG	400-425
J761	HADDON HALL (wall bracket)	136	18					LG	100-125
J732	HADDON HALL (chain hanger)	136	18	60	28			LG	100-125
C069	HADLEY LANTERN (wall bracket)	121	27					LG	125-150
C013	HADLEY LANTERN (chain hanger)	121	27					LG	125-150
F107	HAMILTON	144	42	50	26			LG	150-175
J711	HAMPTON	135	16	42	20			LG	125-150
C014	HARTFORD LANTERN	139	26	49	26	45		LG	125-150
J713	HATHAWAY	135	16	41	20			LG	125-150
G223	HEPPLEWHITE	146	47	32	19			LG	125-150
M529	IMPERATOR	153	69					LG	425-450*
E320	INDEPENDENCE	150	56					LG	175-200
C067	IPSWICH LANTERN (wall bracket)	121	28	58	29			LG	125-150
C017	IPSWICH LANTERN (chain hanger)	121	28	60	29			LG	125-150
F106	JAMESTOWN	122	42					LG	175-200
F101	JEFFERSON (two lights)	33	36	26	16			LG	100-125
F114	JEFFERSON (one light)	142	36					LG	75-100
M521	JUPITER	154	74					LG	75-100
A1116	KEENE (pull chain)	158	91	56	24			LG	5-10
A1133	KEENE (keyless socket)	158	91	56	24			LG	5-10
J719	LANCASTER	120	17	42	20			LG	150-175
E340	LEGIONNAIRE	151	64					LG	375-400
A1142	LENOX (no chimneys)	157	89	21	12	26		LG	225-250
A1145	LENOX (with chimneys)	157	89					LG	250-275
J765	LONDON TOWER (wall bracket)	136	18					LG	100-125
J735	LONDON TOWER (chain hanger)	136	18					LG	100-125
F103	MADISON	143	37					LG	175-200
A1154	MILFORD (with glass shade/pull chain)	158	90	54				LG	25-50
A1179	MILFORD (with pull chain/no glass shade)	158	90					LG	15-25
A1055	MILFORD (with glass shade/keyless socket)	158	90	54				LG	25-50
A1173	MILFORD (with keyless socket/no glass shade)	158	90					LG	15-25
M526	MINERVA	153	70	45	21	40	40	LG	450-475*
G242	MONMOUTH	148	53					LG	400-425
F100	MONROE	143	38					LG	150-175
F104	MONTICELLO	142	35					LG	200-225
E326	MURAT (two lights)	150	58					LG	75-100
E330	MURAT (one light)	150	58					LG	50-75
C011	NANTUCKET LANTERN (chain hanger)	140	29	60	28	64	50	LG	100-125
C060	NANTUCKET LANTERN (wall bracket)	140	29					LG	100-125
A1134	NASHUA	157	84	54	24	53		LG	15-25
A1175	NASHUA (no glass shade)	157	84					LG	5-10
A1075	NEWPORT (with turn knob socket)	157	86	55	25	55		LG	50-75
A1098	NEWPORT (with turn knob socket/outlet)	157	86	55	25	55		LG	50-75
A1048	NEWPORT (with keyless socket/outlet)	157	86	55	25	55		LG	50-75
A1049	NEWPORT (with keyless socket/no outlet)	157	86	55	25	55		LG	50-75
A11018	NORFOLK	158	88					LG	200-225
M532	OLYMPIA	124	75	46	22	40	40	LG	350-375*
E423	ORLEANS (two lights)	150	59	35	18			LG	150-175
E427	ORLEANS (one light)	150	59					LG	125-150
E431	ORLEANS (one light/no shade)	150	59					LG	100-125
E430	ORLEANS (two lights/no shades)	150	59					LG	130-150
M541	PARIS	155	78	44	21	41		LG	325-350*
G222	PEMBROKE (two lights)	146	46	31	19			LG	175-200

ALPHABETICAL FIXTURES (continued)

NUMBER	DESCRIPTION	PAGE	CATALOG YEAR					BY	PRICE
			34LF	37LF	38LF	40LF	41LF		
G225	PEMBROKE (one light)	146	46	31	19			LG	150-175
F324	PHYFE	143	37					LG	125-150
C023	PINE TREE SHILLING SCONCE	138	23	23	13	26		LG	75-100
M646	PLANETARIUM	38	79	47	21	41	40	LG	975-1000*
A610	PORT HOLE SCONCE (one light)	156	83	48	15	27		LG	75-100
A613	PORT HOLE SCONCE (two lights)	156	83	48				LG	125-150
C024	PORTSMOUTH SCONCE	138	24	22				LG	75-100
E322	RECAMIER	150	59					LG	175-200
E426	RICHELIEU (two lights)	123	58	35	18			LG	100-125
E429	RICHELIEU (two lights/no shades)	150	58					LG	75-100
E421	RICHELIEU (one light/with shade)	150	58					LG	50-75
E428	RICHELIEU (one light/no shade)	150	58					LG	25-50
A1183	RICHFIELD	157	87					LG	75-100
F120	RICHMOND	34	43	26	16			LG	400-425
J 721	RISING SUN	31	15	42	20			LG	175-200
M527	ROMA	154	72					LG	325-350*
C062	SALEM LANTERN (wall bracket)	121	27					LG	125-150
C012	SALEM LANTERN (chain hanger)	121	27					LG	125-150
F102	SALEM EAGLE	142	34					LG	100-125
A1089	SARATOGA (pull chain)	158	91	56	24	49		LG	25-50
A1088	SARATOGA (keyless socket)	158	91	56	24	49		LG	25-50
C068	SAYBROOK LANTERN (wall bracket)	139	26					LG	125-150
C018	SAYBROOK LANTERN (chain hanger)	139	26	59	29			LG	125-150
M533	SEA HORSE	154	74					LG	250-275*
G241	SHAFTESBURY	147	50					LG	225-250
A1143	SHELDON	157	87					LG	125-150
G420	SHERATON (two lights)	147	49					LG	150-175
G433	SHERATON (two lights/no shades)	147	49					LG	125-150
G432	SHERATON (one light/with shade)	147	49					LG	100-125
G434	SHERATON (one light/no shade)	147	49					LG	75-100
G224	SHERWOOD	147	49	26				LG	200-225
J736	SOMERSET	120	19	42	20			LG	225-250
A1125	SOUTHPORT	157	85	54/55	24			LG	15-25
A1176	SOUTHPORT (no glass shade)	157	85					LG	5-10
F108	STAR (two lights)	142	36	28				LG	75-100
F112	STAR (one light)	142	36	28				LG	50-75
E641	ST. CLOUD	151	65					LG	50-75
J715	SUSSEX	135	14	41	20			LG	125-150
M543	SYBIL	155	78					LG	200-225*
E321	TALLEYRAND	150	60	48	17	22	18	LG	175-200
E422	TEA TRADE	123	49	26				LG	150-175
M534	THESSALY	154	72					LG	325-350*
M525	THOR	154	73					LG	350-375*
A1101	TRENTON	158	88	18	15			LG	100-125
M523	TROY	153	70	46	22			LG	300-325*
E441	VENDOME	123	63	35	18			LG	375-400
E443	VENDOME (no shades)	151	63					LG	350-375
M530	VESTA	154	71					LG	175-200*
F325	VICTORY (one light)	142	39					LG	150-175
F328	VICTORY (two lights)	142	39					LG	175-200
F109	WHITE HOUSE	143	39	27	16			LG	150-175
C064	WILLIAMSBURG LANTERN (wall bracket)	140	28					LG	125-150
C016	WILLIAMSBURG LANTERN (chain hanger)	140	28	59	27	64		LG	125-150
G645	WINDSOR	148	52					LG	100-125
C025	WITCH LIGHT SCONCE	32	25	23	13	26		LG	175-200
A1150	WOODBURY	157	86	21	12			LG	50-75
A1152	WOODBURY (with chimney)	157	86					LG	75-95
G244	YORKTOWN	148	51					LG	475-500
M540	ZEUS	155	77	47	22			LG	850-875*

NUMERICAL FIXTURES

NUMBER	DESCRIPTION	PAGE	CATALOG YEAR					BY	PRICE
				37LF	38LF	40LF	41LF		
1193	(MISC) One-light bracket (7" ext.)	186		55	25	53	45		75-95
1198	(C) Two-light wall bracket (7 1/2" spread)	168/185		19/52	23	29	33		45-65
1199	(MISC) One-light ceiling beam (6 1/2" d.)	187		56	24	48	42		30-40
1200	(MISC) One-light bracket (3 7/8" w. x 5 1/4" l.)	186		55	25	55			45-60
1202	(C) One-light wall bracket (3 7/8" w. x 5 1/4" l.)	168/185		19/52	23	29	33		30-40
1214	(A) One-light bracket (pull chain version of A1075)	186		55	25	55			45-60
1215	(L) One-light bracket lantern (9 1/2" h.)	188		58	28	60	49		75-95
1217	(EG) Five-light ceiling fixture (22" spread)	164		10					150-175
1218	(EG) One-light ceiling fixture (9 1/2" w.)	164		10					50-75
1219	(EG) One-light bracket (6" ext.)	164		10	6	7	9		50-75
1220	(EG) Five-light ceiling fixture (20" spread)	164		11	6	11			150-175
1222	(EG) One-light bracket (7" ext.)	164		11	6	11			50-75
1223	(EG) Three-light ceiling fixture (18" spread)	164		11	6	11			100-125
1224	(EG) One-light wall bracket (6" ext.)	165		12	7				50-75
1225	(LAN) One-light hanging lantern (9 1/4" h.)	189		60	28	62	50		75-100
1226	(MISC) One-light bracket (7" cylinder)	186		55	25	55			45-60
1230	(MISC) Two-light ceiling fixture (10" bowl version of 1232)	186		54		52			30-50
1232	(MISC) Two-light ceiling fixture (13" d. x 7" h.)	186		54		52			30-50
1233	(C) Five-light ceiling fixture (26" spread)	167		16	11				150-200
1235	(LAN) One-light hanging lantern (14 1/4" overall h.)	184		51	26	44	37		60-85
1236	(C) Five-light ceiling fixture (20" spread)	168		19					125-150
1237	(EG) Five-light ceiling fixture (18 1/2" spread)	165		12					150-175
1238	(C) Five-light ceiling fixture (18" spread)	167		16					150-200
1239	(EG) One-light ceiling fixture (8 1/4" w. x 12 1/2" l.)	164		11	6	11			50-75
1240	(C) Five-light ceiling fixture (16 1/2" spread)	166		15	13	15			250-275
1241	(C) One-light ceiling fixture (8 1/4" w. x 12 1/8" l.)	167/184		17/51	10	20			50-75
1242	(C) Five-light ceiling fixture (16 1/2" spread)	167		17					150-200
1243	(C) One-light bracket (5" ext.)	167		17	10	20			50-75
1244	(C) Two-light wall bracket (9" spread)	167		17	10	20			75-100
1245	(C) Three-light ceiling fixture (16" spread)	168		19					100-125
1246	(MISC) Three-light ceiling fixture (36" overall l.)	186		54	24	31			100-125
1247	(C) One-light bracket (9" h.)	166		15	13	15			50-75
1248	(C) One-light bracket (6" ext.)	167		16	11				50-75
1249	(C) Two-light bracket (8" spread)	166		15	13	15			75-100
1250	(C) Three-light ceiling fixture (12" spread)	167		17	10	20			75-100
1251	(EG) Three-light ceiling fixture (14" spread)	165		12	7				75-100
1252	(MISC) One-light bracket (keyless socket version of 1193)	186		55	25	53	45		75-95
1254	(MISC) Three-light ceiling fixture (10" d. x 5" h.)	185		53	23	31	33		40-60
1255	(MISC) Three-light ceiling fixture (9 1/2" d. x 4" h.)	185		53	23	31	33		50-75
1256	(MISC) One-light bracket / satin glass cylinder (4" ext.)	186		55	25	55			30-45
1257	(MISC) One-light ceiling fixture (pull-chain version of 1258)	186		54	24	53			25-35
1258	(MISC) One-light ceiling fixture (9 3/8" d. x 9 1/2" h.)	186		54	24	53			25-35
1259	(MISC) Two-light ceiling fixture (6" d. x 8" h.)	185		53	23	30	33		50-75
1261	(C) Five-light ceiling fixure (19" spread)	169		20	12	25	27		225-250
1262	(C) Two-light bracket (7 1/2" spread)	169		20	12	25	27		75-100
1263	(C) One-light bracket (13" h.)	169		20	12	25	27		50-75
1264	(LAN) One-light close-up lantern (12" overall l.)	184		51	26				60-85
1265	(C) Two-light bracket (7 1/2" spread)	168/185		18/52	15	29	33		75-100
1266	(C) One-light bracket (8" h.)	168/185		18/52	15	29	33		50-75
1267	(MISC) One-light bracket (keyless socket version of 1226)	186		55	25	55			45-60
1530	(EG) One-light ceiling fixture (15 3/4" d.)	163		8					75-100
1531	(EG) One-light ceiling fixture (15 3/4" d.)	163		9					75-100
1558	(EG) One-light ceiling fixture (12" d.)	163		8	8	9			75-100
1559	(EG) One-light ceiling fixture (12" d.)	165		13	8	9	10		40-50
1560	(EG) One-light bracket (5 1/2" d.)	163		9	4	7	9		30-50
1561	(EG) One-light bracket (5 1/2" d.)	163		9					30-50
1562	(EG) Two-light bracket (13 1/4" spread)	163		9	4	7	9		50-60

NUMERICAL FIXTURES (continued)

NUMBER	DESCRIPTION	PAGE	CATALOG YEAR					BY	PRICE
				37LF	38LF	40LF	41LF		
1565	(MISC) One-light ceiling beam (5" w. x 5 1/2" h.)	187		56	24	49			10-15
1566	(MISC) One-light ceiling beam (5" d. x 5 1/2" h.)	187		56					20-35
1568	(EG) One-light ceiling fixture (12" d.)	163		8	8	9			75-100
1569	(EG) One-light ceiling fixture (12" d.)	165		13	8	8	10		40-50
1570	(EG) One-light ceiling fixture (12" d.)	165		13	8				40-50
1572	(EG) One-light ceiling fixture (16" d.)	163		8	4	8	10		75-100
1573	(EG) One-light ceiling fixture (16" d.)	163		9	4	8	10		75-100
1574	(EG) One-light ceiling fixture (8" d.)	162		7	8				25-40
1575	(EG) One-light ceiling fixture (16 1/2" d.)	162		7	5	6			175-200
1576	(EG) One-light bracket (14" l.)	162		7	5				100-125
1600	(E) Five-light ceiling fixture (18" spread)	176		34					300-325
1601	(F) Five-light ceiling fixture (18" spread)	171		25					350-375
1602	(F) Five-light ceiling fixture (19" spread)	177		36	18				325-350
1650	(E) One-light bracket (10" l.)	176		34					75-100
1651	(E) Two-light bracket (8 1/2" spread)	176		34					100-125
1652	(F) One-light bracket (10" h.)	171		25	16	23			50-75
1653	(F) Two-light bracket (9" spread)	171		25	16	23			75-100
1654	(LAN) Three-light hanging lantern (36" overall l.)	184		51	26				75-100
1655	(LAN) One-light hanging lantern (36" overall l.)	184		51	26				60-85
1656	(LAN) Two-light hanging lantern (36" overall l.)	183		49	26	44	39		225-250
1657	(NC) Five-light ceiling fixture (20" spread)	178		39	22	27			275-300
1658	(NC) Five-light close-up ceiling fixture (20" spread)	178		39	22				275-300
1659	(NC) One-light bracket (13" h.)	178		39	22	27			75-85
1660	(NC) Two-light bracket (8" spread)	178		39	22	27			100-125
1661	(E) Five-light ceiling fixture (19" spread)	177		37	17	45			325-350
1662	(E) One-light bracket (14" h.)	177		37	17	24			100-125
1663	(E) Two-light bracket (8 1/2" spread)	177		37	17	24			130-150
1664	(E) One-light bracket (14" h.)	177		36	18				100-125
1665	(E) Two-light bracket (8 1/2" spread)	177		36	18				130-150
1700	(C) One-light bracket (10 1/2" h.)	170		22	13	27	35		50-75
1701	(F) One-light bracket (5" ext.)	173		28	15	23			50-75
1702	(F) Two-light bracket (8" spread)	173		28	15	23			75-100
1703	(G) One-light bracket (5" w. x 9" h.)	174		30	19	21	17		75-100
1704	(G) Two-light bracket (5" ext.)	174		30	19	21	17		125-150
1705	(J) Five-light ceiling fixture (20" spread)	179		41	20				225-250
1706	(LAN) One-light bracket lantern (14" h.)	188		58	28				100-125
1707	(M) Two-light ceiling fixture (36" overall l.)	182		46	21				250-275
1708	(J) Two-light bracket (10" spread)	179		41	20				150-175
1709	(LAN) One-light bracket lantern (14 7/8" h.)	187		57	29				125-150
1710	(LAN) One-light bracket lantern (14" h.)	187		57	28	60	48		75-100
1711	(LAN) One-light bracket lantern (13" h.)	187		57	27				100-125
1712	(LAN) One-light bracket lantern (13" h.)	188		58					100-125
1713	(G) Five-light ceiling fixture (18" spread)	174		31	19				400-425
1714	(G) Five-light ceiling fixture (20" spread)	174		30	19	21	17		400-425
1716	(LAN) One-light hanging lantern (11" h.)	189		60					100-125
1717	(M) One-light bracket (3 3/4" d. x 19" h.)	181		44	21	40	40		325-350
1718	(M) Two-light ceiling fixture (11" spread)	181		44	21	41	40		400-425
1719	(M) Two-light ceiling fixture (13" d. x 7" h.)	181		44	21	41	40		325-350
1720	(LAN) Four-light hanging lantern (36" overall l.)	183		49	27	44	39		250-275
1722	(LAN) One-light wall lantern (14" h.)	188		58	29	61	48		125-150
1723	(LAN) Three-light hanging lantern (36" overall l.)	184		50	27				225-250
1724	(F) Two-light bracket (9" spread)	172		27	16				100-125
1725	(F) Two-light bracket (8" spread)	172		27	16	24			100-125
1726	(F) One-light bracket (11" h.)	172		27	16	24			75-100
11047	(MISC) Three-light ceiling fixture (9 1/2" d. x 11" h.)	185		53	23				75-100
11055	(MISC) One-light bracket (4" ext.)	185		52	23	30	32		75-100
11056	(MISC) Three-light ceiling fixture / satin glass cylinders (10" w. x 13" l.)	185		53	23	30	32		100-125

More Schiffer Titles

www.schifferbooks.com

The Chase Catalogs: 1934 & 1935. Leslie Piña & Donald-Brian Johnson. Price Guide by Barry L. Van Hook. Chrome and brass housewares created by Chase Brass & Copper Company during the 1930s are synonymous with Art Deco. Reprinted here are the company's 1934 and 1935 catalogs with objects designed by Lurelle Guild, Walter Von Nessen, Russel Wright and Harry Laylon. All are pictured with full descriptions, inventory information, and a current price guide.

Size: 8 1/2" x 11" Two complete facsimile catalogs 112 pp.
Price Guide Index
ISBN: 0-7643-0631-6 soft cover $24.95

Chase Complete: Deco Specialties of the Chase Brass & Copper Company. Donald-Brian Johnson & Leslie Piña. Gleaming chromium, brass, and copper housewares from the Chase Brass & Copper Co. stand today as icons of American Art Deco style. Here the entire Specialty line produced by Chase from 1930 to 1942 is presented with profiles of the industrial designers who made them. An essential reference for Deco collectors, this book features 650 full-color catalog and historical photos, vintage advertising, a complete cross-reference listing, and a price guide.

Size: 8 1/2″ x 11″ 552 color photos, 71 b/w photos 232pp.
Price Guide Index
ISBN: 0-7643-0843-2 hard cover $59.95

CHASE CHROMIUM BRASS & COPPER SPECIALTIES

CHROMIUM IS BEST OVER BRASS OR COPPER

CHASE CHROMIUM BRASS & COPPER SPECIALTIES

CHROMIUM IS BES BRASS OR COPPER

CHASE

CHASE CHROMIUM BRASS & COPPER SPECIALTIES

CHROMIUM IS BEST OVER BRASS OR COPPER

CHASE CHROMIUM BRASS & COPPER SPECIALTIES